NO RETREAT

NO RETREAT

The Secret War Between Britain's Anti-Fascists and the Far Right

Dave Hann and Steve Tilzey

MILO BOOKS

First published in November 2003 by Milo Books

ISBN 1 903854 22 9

Typeset in Plantin Light by Avon DataSet Ltd,
Bidford on Avon, Warwickshire, B50 4JH

Printed and bound in Great Britain by
Cox & Wyman Ltd, Reading, Berkshire

MILO BOOKS
10 Park Street
Lytham
Lancs FY8 5LU
info@milobooks.com

I went to Spain to kill as many fascists as possible; that's all the less to kill when they get here.

Fred Baxter,
Canadian International Brigade veteran

Dedications

In memory of my grandparents. It is only now that I can appreciate how much they shaped and influenced my life. Also dedicated to the memory of Joe Strummer, whose words and music eventually woke me out of my stupor.

I would also like to take this opportunity to thank the following people for their help, support and inspiration while I was writing this book. Toddy (Vinny the Chin), Mark T, Solo, Hefty, Carl, Big Match Brian and Dublin AFA (still flying the flag), Shep, Alex, Griff, Steve my co-author (pull your finger out mate!), Wigan Mike, the Bolts, Gary F and Porky (wherever he is). Also love to Seanin, Nick and Cath (the three amigos). Last but not least, my fondest regards to Louise, unpaid proof-reader, researcher, editor, coffee maker, lover and friend.

And with one or two notable exceptions, everyone who stood and fought the bastards to a standstill.

No Pasaran.

Dave

Dedicated to Ian 'Stig' Macintosh, Mickey Fenn and Phil Pyatt: socialists, trade unionists, anti-fascists and comrades. No longer with us but who will always be remembered.

I would also like to thank the following people in particular for their help and support while I was working on this book: Boylie and all the United and JMC crew, especially Jeff, Stu and Carly; MCM, Graeme, Alex, Rors, Rodney R and Danny, Debs, Glen *aka* Seba, Martin, Greeny, Cheesy Brian, and to Dave when I needed a kick up the arse to keep going.

Also to mam and dad.

And to all the comrades who were beside me on the streets during those mad days. Respect always.

Steve

Contents

If I Die on a Nazi Street . . .

THIS IS THE story of the long war against fascism that was waged on the streets of Britain's towns and cities between the years 1977 and 1997. This book focuses in particular on the battles fought in and around the Manchester area, because that's where the two authors happened to live, but similar stories could be written about many other parts of the country. It is a story that until now has remained largely untold, due to the unlawful and violent methods that were sometimes used to curb the activities of the fascist gangs. We believe it is important to tell it because social historians and political commentators alike would have you believe that the fascists can be defeated solely by the tactic of noisy but essentially passive demonstrations. As you will see, this is far from the case.

We tell how a group of militant street-fighters formed what were known as the "Squads" to confront the National Front in the late Seventies and early Eighties, and later how Anti-Fascist Action's "Stewards' Group" fought tooth and nail against the British National Party (BNP), Blood & Honour (Blood and Honour), and Combat 18 (C18) in the mid-Eighties and early Nineties. Both the Squads and the Stewards' Group were the type of organisations that the media loved to describe as shadowy or subversive, and of course it is true that militant anti-fascism occasionally requires its participants to operate outside the law in order to achieve its goals. The fear of arrest and infiltration meant that we had to operate in a semi-clandestine manner at times, but this was viewed as merely a sensible precaution which would allow us to carry on with the job in hand.

We believed that fascism is an ideology that thrives on inspiring fear in its opponents. We also believed that it has to be confronted on its own terms, and that fascist groups have to be challenged physically as well as politically. Fascism loses much of its appeal if it is seen to lose in the very areas where it claims to be the strongest, and that means on the streets, on the terraces, and in white working-class communities that have long been neglected by politicians of all persuasions. If you inflict a humiliating defeat on a fascist organisation in front of people they regard as their natural constituency then it not only demoralises them, and cuts the ground from under their feet, but also offers encouragement to any potential opposition.

The Squads and the Stewards' Group had a policy of "No Platform for Fascists", which meant exactly what it said on the box: no marches, no rallies, no paper sales, no leafleting, in fact no public events at all. If it was in our power to stop them then we would, by whatever means we had at our disposal. Now there are any number of so-called anti-fascist or anti-racist groups that would claim the "No Platform" slogan as their own, but whose first instincts would be to avoid any contact with the fascists. We used to joke that these people must carry their own crash barriers around with them, because whenever we saw them they were safely corralled into their pens like so many sheep. The essential difference between us and them, was that we were not in the business of complaining about the fascists, we were in the business of stopping them.

Many people have argued that we were as bad as the fascists ourselves, because we denied them the freedom of speech. We fully accept that freedom of speech is a fundamental human right, but one that shouldn't be abused. If you argue that you should be allowed the freedom of speech to promote policies that deny that very same right to people purely on the basis of skin colour or nationality, then actually no, we don't believe that you have a legitimate complaint when someone hits you over the head with your megaphone.

If this book seems to concentrate too much on the physical battles waged against fascist gangs, then that is because it is the area that was sadly neglected by many of those who would declare themselves to be anti-fascists. We recognise of course that there is more than one way to skin a cat, and wouldn't dream of suggesting that violent confrontation is the only way to defeat fascism, but it is an essential weapon in the anti-fascist armoury, a weapon that all too often anti-racists and anti-nazis refused to pick up. If it seems that sometimes all we were doing was slugging it out toe-to-toe with the fascists, then that would only be a half-truth, a half-truth given some credibility because all too often we had to fill in the gaps left by others, but a half-truth nonetheless.

The argument put across by the middle-class left was that we substituted political violence for political activity, but the truth is that we always tried to do both. We saw the use of violence as essentially tactical and episodic, a short-term answer to a long-term problem. We saw it as a stop-gap solution to blunt the cutting-edge of fascism and to curb their ambitions until such time as an effective political opposition to them could be put in place in whatever areas they were operating.

During two decades of anti-fascist work, we have been vilified and stereotyped as red fascists, renegades, bootboys, thugs and romantic adventurists, but during that time we have also produced millions of leaflets, organised countless gigs and benefit concerts, spoken at schools, community centres and colleges. We have also brought out newspapers, magazines and football fanzines, and put on exhibitions, carnivals, marches, public meetings and countless other events. We have produced our own videos, CDs, television programmes and web-pages. We have also spoken on TV and radio and been interviewed in newspapers and magazines at home and abroad. Hardly the CV of mindless hooligans.

If it was the case that we were simply hooligans or adventurers just looking for an excuse for a fight, then there were surely more rewarding arenas to perform in than the rough end of the political market. There were after all, precious few plaudits to be gained from our involvement with the far left or the anti-racist movement. An all too typical scenario would involve us launching a pre-emptive strike on a gang of fascists gathering to attack a left-wing march or meeting, and then being told that we were nothing more than a bunch of thugs by the people whose arses we had just saved.

Nevertheless, and despite the carping criticism, we still firmly believed in the correctness of what we were doing, and it was this belief that more than anything enabled us to face down sometimes overwhelming numbers. We weren't necessarily harder or tougher than the fascists, and we were hardly ever in a position of being numerically stronger, but we rarely lost a dust-up with a fascist gang despite being "always outnumbered, always out-gunned".

It goes without saying that the actual act of physically fighting fascists is not exactly a barrel of laughs, and it is clearly not for everyone. It can be dangerous and painful, and the risks of injury and imprisonment are obvious. The hours can be long and sometimes boring while you sit around in a pub or cafe for ages waiting for something to happen. There were plenty of times when nothing did happen, and you were more likely to spot Elvis walking down the street than a member of the BNP or NF. You can't earn a living fighting fascism either, unless you're some kind of liberal, state-sponsored outfit designed to make no discernible difference whatsoever to the status quo. So unless you were on the dole, you had to squeeze all this activity in between working eight hours a day as well.

So why would anyone subject themselves to all this possible pain and discomfort? Well the obvious answer is because we believed that fascism has to be stopped. It offers no solutions to society's problems, and instead panders to greed, selfishness, fear, intolerance and racism. Fascism feeds on the discontent and anger felt by whole sections of the working class driven to the margins of society by the policies of successive Labour and Tory governments. Instead of directing that anger against the politicians and bosses who have caused all the misery in the first place, fascism turns it in on itself by dividing people along racial lines. It is the politics of fear and envy, the politics of the schoolyard bully picking on the vulnerable and the isolated. Fascism works by finding the nearest and easiest identifiable targets and blaming them for society's ills. In the 1930s and '40s it was the Jews that bore the brunt, while the present day bogeymen are . . . well take your pick: blacks, Asians, Irish, gays, single mothers, Afghanis, Moslems, and asylum seekers of all creeds and colours.

Of course, not all racist attacks are carried out or even encouraged by card-carrying fascists, but where fascist groups are established there is a vicious spiralling of such attacks as the race-haters are given a veneer of legitimacy, respectability and political importance. However, it would be wrong to think of fascists as nothing more than gangs of organised racists, as some liberals would have you believe. Fascism is much more than that. Fascism has been described as a razor in the hands of the bosses, and history shows that the first instinct of fascist leaders and their followers is the protection of the ruling class and its interests. In the first instance, fascism turns the working class against itself by dividing people along racial lines, and as part of this process it also attacks the organisations that work to defend the interests of the poor. Right from the very beginning, fascism has viewed workers who organised themselves as their natural enemies, from Mosley's Blackshirts in the 1930s, who attacked striking workers and unemployed activists, right through to Combat 18, who publish hit-lists of trade unionists, left-wingers and community activists.

Let's make no mistake about this, the bloke pouring petrol through some Asian family's letterbox tonight is tomorrow's potential prison camp guard, torturer or secret police officer. Fascism starts out with small acts of dehumanising cruelty and ends up in places like Auschwitz or the Stadium in Chile, where Pinochet's torturers trained their guard dogs to rape women prisoners. Remember this when some liberal commentator tells you that the best way to deal with fascism is to ignore it, sweep it under the carpet and forget about it. History shows us what happens when you ignore fascism; it does not magically disappear but grows unseen like a malignant cancer, festering and spreading amongst the human debris cast adrift and ignored by society. Ignoring fascism, like ignoring a final demand, never makes it go away, it just leaves you with a bigger bill to pay at the end of the day.

However, history also shows us that fascism can be defeated when confronted forcefully. We took our inspiration from those who fought fascism at the Battle of Cable Street in the East End of London in 1936, from the 43 Group and the 62 Group who organised in squads to fight fascist gangs in the Forties, Fifties and Sixties, and from countless others who recognised that the best answer to fascist aggression is sometimes a tyre iron across the head. You don't have to take my word for it. How about this piece of advice from a certain Adolf Hitler:

> Only one thing could have stopped our movement – if in the days when we were small and weak, our opponents had understood our aims and intentions, and smashed

with the utmost determination the nucleus of our new movement.

In Manchester, this theory was taken and shaken like a rat by anti-fascists. We got ourselves organised and set about the task of smashing the movement he inspired with the utmost determination.

STEVE'S STORY

CHAPTER ONE

The Fightback Begins

Lewisham, 13 August 1977

On the morning of Saturday, 13 August 1977, I was sitting on the top deck of a number 99 bus heading into Manchester city centre. Traffic was light given the early hour and before I knew it I had arrived at the bus station beside Piccadilly Gardens. In my pocket was a ticket for the Charity Shield match between Manchester United and Liverpool at Wembley. I had picked up the cherished item only the day before from a mate who couldn't get time off work.

My problem was that I had lost a lot of money in a card school the night before and was short of readies. In any case, all the coaches were fully booked at that late stage, so I decided that my best bet was to try and "jib" down to London on the train. I had jibbed it before on a couple of occasions but lately it had been coming on top and the guards and ticket collectors had been warned to be especially vigilant on big match days.

Jumping off the bus, I headed up to Piccadilly Station, but as I crossed the top of Aytoun Street I noticed a half-full coach waiting outside the old dole office. A couple of lads were stood outside holding up a large Union Jack flag, and I immediately assumed that they were United. With the coach only being half-full, I decided to chance my luck and ask if they had any spare seats.

"Going to Wembley lads?"

"No mate, we're the National Front and we're going to London to march against the niggers," one of them replied.

Now although I never considered myself political, I suppose I had a few daft racist ideas, like many other white lads I knew at the time, and so I did not have any strong objections to travelling with them. I offered them a couple of quid for a seat, thinking I could do one to the match when the coach reached London. To my surprise and delight they let me on.

As I climbed on board, someone gave me a couple of NF leaflets, and I settled down next to this hard-looking bastard in a combat jacket. He had a scar on his chin and a Manchester City pin badge on his lapel. I stuffed the leaflets in my pockets unread. I had heard quite a bit about the NF on the news, but they seemed to be based mainly down in London, where they marched about a lot and there was always loads of trouble. It seemed quite exciting, I suppose, but as a nineteen-year-old lad, football was what interested me, and United were my life.

A couple of other lads came over and started chatting to me. They said the coach was just waiting on some lads to arrive from Rochdale before it set off for Lewisham, where they were going to meet up with other NF supporters for a march. They explained that they were expecting trouble from left-wingers and blacks, and said that it was likely to get quite violent. Now, as a United fan home and away in that period I wasn't exactly unused to that kind of thing, and had been involved in odd bits and pieces of trouble myself, although I never considered myself a hardcase. United's Red Army had rampaged across the country in an orgy of violence and destruction throughout the Seventies and to be honest, although I found this kind of large-scale violence exciting, I was not at all tempted by their offer to go on the march.

A couple of other NF guys arrived with a crate of beer and I decided to nip over to the paper shop on Piccadilly Plaza for a can of pop and a newspaper while we waited for some out-of-towners. I squeezed past the bloke who I took to be the organiser, a balding, middle-aged guy with thick-rimmed glasses who was collecting money from people. "Don't be long," he said as I got off the coach.

I was about halfway to the shop when I heard an almighty crash. I turned around quickly to see that the front window of the coach had been put through and that at least twenty blokes in balaclavas, crash helmets and scarves were attacking the vehicle and its occupants. I stopped dead in my tracks and watched as iron bars and wooden poles rained down on the NF supporters who had not managed to make it back on board. The others cowered inside as the side windows were smashed, and I'm sure someone was attempting to drag one of the NF guys through the broken windows.

At this point I decided to get off up to the train station and follow my original plan of jibbing it down to London. I didn't know what was going on and didn't want to know, I was just grateful that I was not on the coach when it had all gone off. I strode up Piccadilly Plaza thinking how lucky I had been, when suddenly I was grabbed by a big, bearded bloke who put me in a police-style arm lock. Another huge guy came up alongside me and whispered a few unpleasant comments in my ear about me being a little fascist bastard.

The first thing that went through my head was the thought that I was dead. These guys must have been involved in the attack on the coach, and had obviously connected me with the NF. I was warned not to struggle or to try to do a runner, and was taken to a little cafe around the back of Piccadilly, where we were met by six or seven other lads.

"Nice hit lads, and we've got a prisoner as well," said the bearded bloke as he unceremoniously shoved me into a chair at the back of the cafe. "This little prick was about to get back on the coach. He might have some information."

The other lads in the cafe crowded around me and started firing questions in my direction. Up until then I had been silent, possibly through shock or in case I said the wrong thing. However I quickly realised that I had some fast talking to do now, and started rifling through my pockets in search of the match ticket which I hoped would support my story. To my absolute horror however, the first thing I pulled out of my pockets was one of the NF leaflets I'd been given on the coach.

Things were not looking good and I started to panic. "Listen lads," I pleaded, "I don't know who you are, but I've done nothing wrong. I'm not with those NF guys, I just got on the coach so I could get to Wembley for the match." At last my fumbling fingers located the elusive ticket, and with a wave of relief I produced it for my sceptical audience. The tension eased slightly, although I sensed one or two of them might need a little bit more convincing. The guy with the beard seemed to accept my story, however, because he immediately put his hand out and apologised.

"But who are you lot?" I asked.

"We're anti-nazis," one of them answered, "and we fucking hate the NF."

One of the lads got me a coffee, and when he came back we started to chat away. Or rather he chatted while I sat and listened.

"These NF bastards have been getting away with hitting our people for too long," he said. "You can't just stand around shouting insults and waving banners at them when they're running around battering people. You have to speak to them in the only language they understand, and that's the fist, the boot and the iron bar. The NF believe in winning power through the use of political violence just like the Nazis did in Germany. We've got to oppose them by the same means. Those NF on the coach are on their way down to a big march in Lewisham, and we're going down there to give them another kicking."

I nodded my head in agreement. After what I had just seen, I could tell that they were deadly serious. It all seemed a bit strange to me and I had just started to make my excuses, saying that I needed to get off to the match, when a couple of lads came over from the other side of the cafe.

"Listen mate," one of them said. "We're United but we've jacked the game to go on this demo. If you want, we'll give you a lift down to London and drop you off near a tube station somewhere."

As I was weighing up their offer, a big guy in a donkey jacket walked into the cafe. "Right lads," he said. "Les has just parked up the coach. Everyone has got away from the hit okay but the place is crawling with cops. We need to get on board now and get on our way."

People started to walk out, and I sat there for a moment trying to decide what to do. Then I thought, what the hell, I would stick with them down to London and sneak away to Wembley at some point. After all, what harm could it do? As the coach pulled up outside the cafe I couldn't help glancing around nervously in case the NF had made their own plans to attack the anti-nazis' coach.

The coach was a twenty-nine-seater and the first thing I noticed was that it was being driven by one of the anti-nazis. I later found out that he had borrowed it from work. He pointed out to the lads all the best hiding places for their weapons, which included flares, iron bars, hammers and a custom-made cosh with nails sticking out of it. The driver unscrewed the coach's battery compartment and the weapons were hidden inside. Fucking hell, I thought, these guys really mean it.

We had a chance for a longer chat on the way down, and even though I had a few racist ideas, they put forward their arguments in a way I could understand. I started to take a liking to them, especially Mike, Les, Harold and Roy. Harold was a docker from Salford who was also a big United supporter. He was a funny bloke who kept us laughing for most of the journey with his caricatures of people he knew or worked with. On the way down we stopped at Hilton Park service station, but it was crawling with police, obviously because of the threat of trouble between United and Liverpool supporters. We were stopped and told that as the coach belonged to a Manchester-based firm, we would not be allowed to go into the services. The driver then told the police that we weren't football fans but a fishing club on its way to a competition. Amazingly it worked, and the police let us into the station. How we got away with that I'll never know, because we didn't exactly look the part of anglers, with not a welly boot or fishing rod in sight.

Back on the coach we passed a couple of dodgy-looking minibuses full of skinhead types. Some of the lads recognised them as Birmingham NF, and wanker signals were exchanged with equal feeling. At about 11.30 a.m. we drove past Brent Cross, where I had intended to get off and head up to Wembley, but I felt a twinge of conscience, and decided to stick around with my new-found friends for a while longer at least. They were meeting some mates in a pub in Kilburn, north London, before heading down to Lewisham. As we pulled up outside a big, tavern-style pub, a couple of lads gave us a wave and we piled off the coach.

As we walked over to the pub Les tapped me on the shoulder. "If you want to get off to the game now Steve, I won't be offended, but I would like to meet up with you again." He handed me a leaflet. "There's a meeting next week. You should come along to it."

I put the leaflet in my pocket. I was curious about all this business and I had already decided to stick around for a while longer and get off to the game later. "I think I'll hang around with you lot for a while Les," I replied. "I might even come down to Lewisham with you."

Some of the London lads had already heard about the hit on the NF coach and were eager for details. Most of the people around seemed like ordinary working-class lads, but there were a couple of studenty-looking types selling a paper called *Socialist Worker*. I bought one and shoved it in my back pocket. We jumped on the tube and headed off to New Cross, south London, where the NF were planning to assemble before they marched into Lewisham. There was already a massive police presence on the streets, and as we emerged from the station we were given a serious looking-over by several black lads who I was convinced thought we were NF. However a couple of black lads we had met at Kilburn appeared, and we headed off to the anti-nazi assembly point without incident.

Several hundred people had already gathered here to listen to speeches. After fifteen minutes, the police began to get agitated as reports filtered back of violence breaking out in the vicinity of New Cross. The police obviously wanted to break up the gathering and moved in to disperse the crowd. There was a lot of confusion and the police seemed to lose it. Quite a few people got hurt and a number of arrests were made. The police backed off, then made another charge, this time with horses, causing all sorts of injuries and mayhem. All this and not a single NF supporter in sight.

I stuck closely to the lads I had travelled down with, and along with the other anti-racists, I pushed and shoved against the police lines. I was not actually doing much more than that when I got whacked on the shoulder with a truncheon. I went down on my knees, the wind completely knocked out of me. A couple of the lads dragged me up and took me over to a shop doorway to get my breath back. The police were attempting to clear a path for the NF march but were struggling against huge numbers of counter-demonstrators, and had begun to lash out with their truncheons. Some of the demonstrators were also trying to break through police lines in an attempt to get to where the NF were assembling. I managed to get my breath back, and although my shoulder was still very painful, I wasn't at all put off, and threw myself back into the middle of the action.

The NF had gathered and under heavy police protection were readying themselves to march up Clifton Rise. Some people had managed to break through the police lines and as the march started the NF came under a hail of bricks and bottles. At the head of the march, I could see about twenty-five very heavy-looking guys. These, I later learned, were the NF's Honour Guard, essentially a hand-picked protection squad for the Front's leader, John Tyndall. A few yards behind them were the Colour Party, which consisted of about fifteen blokes carrying Union Jacks on metal-tipped flagpoles. The Colour Party marched in front of the main body of the NF supporters, which was surrounded by hundreds of policemen.

Several attempts were made to attack the march, which slowed its progress as the police struggled to clear a path through the counter-demonstrators. I threw a few bricks and stones at them, and also aimed a few kicks at one group who had broken away from the march to attack the anti-nazis. This lot were pummelled to the ground by fists and boots as superior numbers of counter-demonstrators piled into them. All along the route of the march the NF were getting serious problems as fighting and skirmishing broke out between the two sides. At one point the march was smashed completely in half as hundreds of anti-nazis broke through the ranks of police and engaged the Front in vicious hand-to-hand fighting.

On Lewisham Way, anti-racists and local people attacked the front of the march, and waded into the Honour Guard and Colour Party. The NF were now getting it from all sides. I looked at my watch: nearly 1.30 p.m. I really needed to leave now if I wanted to get to Wembley in time for the match, but I decided to stay put. Fuck the match, I thought. It's only the Charity Shield after all.

Then came the moment that was to shape the next twenty-odd years of my life. I suddenly heard this shouting from within the NF ranks. It was directed towards the group of lads

I was with, or to be more precise, towards me. It was the NF group from Manchester I had been sat on the coach with only a few hours before. Under a large "Manchester NF" banner were two individuals, one with a bandage on his head, the other with a plaster on his cheek, shouting and gesticulating towards me.

"You fucking bastard. You set us up. You're fucking dead," one shouted, and several very pissed-off fascists joined in the abuse. Fuck, I thought, and it all began to sink in. They think I set them up, and admittedly when you added it all up, it seemed to fit. Nevertheless, with a bit of bravado and my new mates behind me, I shouted back a few insults of my own. They were fucking angry though, and one of them got out a camera and took a photo of me, then dragged his finger pirate-style across his throat.

The Front did put up some resistance, and gave a good account of themselves at times, but they were completely outnumbered, and didn't have the weapons to hand that we did. Fighting was still going on in several areas, with a lot of the NF supporters now looking the worse for wear, but even with police protection the march was eventually stopped on Lewisham High Street. Fronters were running around in a blind panic, and the march just seemed to disintegrate as wave after wave of attacks hit them from all sides. Shortly afterwards the police put them on coaches and trains in a bid to stop all the violence. However, small-scale skirmishing continued. NF coaches were bricked as they left the area and the police again attacked the counter-demonstrators. Fighting went on under the clock tower for quite a while after the NF had left Lewisham, with the police now armed with riot shields. I found out later that this was the first time that they had been used in England.

I eventually managed to find some of the lads I'd come down with. They were all feeling pretty elated by the day's events.

"That was some fucking battle," one of them said. "I don't think the NF will want to come back here again."

"Yeah, but we've taken quite a few nickings," said another bloke. "We'll have to try and get them sorted before we leave London."

We agreed that it was probably best to get out of the area, and headed back up to Kilburn where our coach was parked up. We went for a drink while a couple of the lads tried to sort out what was happening with the guys who had been nicked. We knew for certain that a couple of people had been arrested early on, but there were others who hadn't been seen for several hours, and we were concerned that they had been lifted as well. At about 7 p.m. there was a loud cheer as a group of stragglers trailed into the pub, to be greeted like long-lost brothers.

We left London shortly afterwards, having been told by the police that those who had been arrested were being kept in until Monday morning. As it happens, they were released at about 9 p.m. that night and had to make their own way back to Manchester. The coach was full of excited conversation on the way home, and it seemed like everyone had a tale to tell. "Did you see that guy with the big plank of wood having it on his own with the NF," said one of the lads, "and the only one who had a poke back at him was some old fella. Well I saw him later and he said that the bloke he was hitting was one of his old teachers."

Another lad recounted how he had got pushed into the middle of the NF by the police following a bit of ruckus. "I was really hyped up," he said, "so I asked some Fronter beside me where he was from, and the bloke replied that he came from Hackney. I punched him in the face and said, 'Well here's a present from Manchester.' I had to leg it through the lines of police to get away, and spent the rest of the afternoon mingling with the crowds. I saw the bloke later as the Front were dispersing. I gave him a wave but I don't think he saw me."

It was a real buzz, and I felt as if I had been part of something really special. Not even being fingered as the guy who set up the ambush on the Manchester NF contingent could spoil my mood. In fact, at that particular moment, I was more concerned that my mam might have seen me on the telly.

When we stopped off at Sandbach Services, I bumped into a couple of United supporters I knew who were on their way home from the game. "It was really dire," said Alan, "a fucking awful scoreless draw." There was a brief pause as he looked at me. "But haven't you been to the game?"

"Well I had a ticket and I was in London," I replied mysteriously, "but you could say something else turned up."

When we got back from Manchester I took a couple of phone numbers from the lads on the coach and agreed to meet up for a drink the next weekend. At home in bed I started to relive the day's events and read the paper I had bought earlier. I liked what it said, and it had an impact on me. I could identify with the way it dealt with certain issues such as exposing the lies of mainstream politicians, and the unfair and unjust way working people were treated by the bosses and ruling classes. Although I had never considered myself at all politically minded, I think maybe the day's events had stirred up something inside me. I also liked the feeling of comradeship that I had experienced with the anti-nazi lads.

I had a job working on a stall in the Arndale Fish Market in those days, and it was in the fish market on Monday morning that events took a dramatic turn. I was setting out the stall for the day when a group of fifteen or twenty men walked through the main market and pointed over to me. I instantly recognised them as NF members, and then it dawned on me that I had told the guy with the scar and the City badge on the coach that I worked in town in the fish market. Bollocks, I'm in the shit, I thought, so I quickly gathered together some of the market lads, and the NF just walked past mouthing insults at me. "You commie scumbag," they said. "You and your red mates are fucking dead." They were no doubt a little put off by the sight of six or seven market lads all armed with very sharp filleting knives, and they didn't attempt to push the matter any further.

Nevertheless I was a bit worried, and at lunchtime I made a call to Les and told him what had happened. He immediately asked me what time I finished and promised me that a few lads would meet me after work in case the NF were waiting.

I was met by about fifteen guys, all tooled up, who walked me to my bus stop, and a couple got on with me just in case I was followed. It was very reassuring to have this kind of back-up, but also worrying because I now knew I was into something very serious.

The rest of the week passed off quietly until the following Saturday. A mob of NF came into the market when I was away from the stall and started throwing their weight around. Unfortunately for me the boss was around and he wasn't very happy when he found out why I was getting all this hassle. It ended in a barney and I walked out of the job. Bollocks to it all, I thought. The wages were shit anyway and stinking of fish all the time wasn't exactly doing wonders for my sex life either.

That night I went along to the meeting in Rusholme and met up with some of the lads from the coach. The meeting was really good. They talked about what had happened at Lewisham, and about what was being planned locally. A guy had come up from London and gave a talk about the history of fascism in Britain. He spoke about Oswald Mosley and the British Union of Fascists, and how they were stopped at the Battle of Cable Street. Afterwards we ended up in the Albert pub in Rusholme, a popular meeting place for the anti-nazis. I got really pissed and was somewhat embarrassed to discover that I had become something of a hero with this incredible story about how I came to be down in Lewisham.

I was somewhat less popular with the NF, for I later discovered that three Fronters had been unable to travel down to London because of the injuries they had sustained in the coach attack. The NF did manage to get a replacement coach down to London, although I sometimes wonder if some of them wished they hadn't, as Lewisham was not a happy place for a fascist that day, and quite a few of their comrades from across the country also ended up in the casualty ward. For me it was the beginning of a lifelong involvement in anti-fascism, and if I have to point the finger of blame at anyone for ruining my life then I'll point it squarely at Manchester United FC for winning the FA Cup four months previously.

The Squad
Once initiated into the politics of militant anti-fascism, I found that I craved more of the buzz that Lewisham had given me. The events of that day continued to make the news, and watching the film footage on TV gave me huge adrenalin surges. The papers over the next few days were full of stuff about the Battle of Lewisham. There were headlines like, "LONDON'S SHAME: 50 police hurt, 200 arrested". Another was "111 ARE HURT IN RIOT OF SHAME". The *Daily Mirror* ran the headline "WHY THE UNION JACK RAN RED WITH BLOOD". It went on to say that the flag had now become a symbol of hate.

The lads I had travelled down to London with were mostly members of the Socialist Workers' Party (SWP), and sometime in early September 1977, in an upstairs room at the Albert Inn in Rusholme, for 50p a week subs, I became a card-carrying member of the organisation. I felt as if I had a new vocation in life as a revolutionary! This was different from the "offs" I had been involved in with United during the Seventies. That was pretty mindless stuff, smashing up rail carriages, town centres and occasionally taking an end. I felt that this politics thing had a real purpose and logic, that there was a tangible enemy to hate, the NF, the bosses and the police. Although I still hated Leeds United.

From what I learned, the SWP had once been called the International Socialists, but had changed their name in the mid-Seventies. People said they were a Marxist/Leninist party, others that they were a Trotskyist party, but it meant nothing to me, because I had very little understanding or knowledge of politics, and it would be a while before I could say that I understood even the basics. The SWP were big on organising on the industrial front, supporting strikers and agitating in the trade union movement. They had a central committee that seemed to decide party policy on practically everything, and I became familiar with names like Tony Cliff, Duncan Hallas, Paul Holborrow and Alex Callinicos.

My first few SWP meetings were virtually always dominated by discussions on anti-fascism. Street activities such as the regular *Socialist Worker* paper sales were organised. Opposition to the NF and the more openly neo-nazi British Movement (BM) were also planned. In the late Seventies, NF marches and counter-demonstrations were commonplace, attracting widespread publicity and the inevitable violent street clashes.

The National Front had been launched on 7 February 1967 and grew off the back of Enoch Powell's infamous "Rivers of Blood" speech, the influx of Ugandan Asian immigrants into Britain, and the undercurrent of racism which infested the political climate of the time. Throughout the Seventies the NF had grown in size and had a membership rumoured at somewhere between 12,000 and 20,000, with a periphery many times larger. It was said that the NF had as many as 500 card-carrying members in Greater Manchester, although the active hardcore membership was a fraction of this.

One of the NF's leaders, Martin Webster, had proclaimed that they would kick their way into the headlines, and they were considered by some political commentators to be a radical new force in British politics. If you dug a little deeper, however, you soon noticed that although they peppered their politics with a smattering of lefty rhetoric, they remained at heart an inherently racist and reactionary outfit, whose middle-class leadership's obsession with Hitler was their one defining characteristic. The fact that the working-class membership of the NF were expected to carry out the mundane tasks and dirty work assigned to them by the party leadership further emphasised the comparison with Hitler and the Third Reich.

The NF were an anti-immigration party who believed in the forced repatriation of non-whites to their country of origin. They were also big on law and order. In other words they either wanted to "send 'em back", or "hang 'em and flog 'em".

The NF was a home for nazi sympathisers, old Mosleyites and disaffected Tories, but for a while in the Seventies they were a potent force on the streets, and were commanding significant electoral support in certain areas. People began to see them as a very serious threat, especially the immigrant communities who were often on the receiving end of their violent activities. Attacks on these communities increased whenever and wherever the NF had a presence, and in some areas such as Leicester and parts of London it was beginning to spiral out of control.

The local NF had been causing serious problems in Manchester. They held their own regular paper sale in the city centre outside what was then the Chelsea Girl store in Piccadilly, where they harassed and intimidated black and Asian passers-by. They were also taking liberties with their political opponents on the left, often attacking meetings, paper sales and other events.

Manchester NF had a hard-core of twenty-five to thirty lads, mostly in their early twenties. A lot of them were connected to Manchester City's Mayne Line Crew, who were one of the top football firms around at the time, with a pretty tasty reputation for getting stuck in. Strangely, the NF lads were often seen fighting side by side with City's large black following, but nothing was ever said about politics. This changed later, but at the time it never seemed to be an issue.

Meetings above the Albert continued, and I began helping sell the paper on Saturday mornings. However I was still following United all over the country and would find it difficult to commit to the more mundane activities such as paper sales. I have to admit that I found selling papers, leafleting and fly-posting a pain in the arse. I was also inundated with all sorts of left-wing pamphlets, magazines and books on Trotsky, Lenin and other communist leaders, and although I did have some sympathy for that stuff, what I really wanted to do was meet up with the lads again for some more of the same.

I need not have worried as things were about to alter in that direction. One evening my mam answered a knock at the front door.

"Stephen," she shouted. "There's someone at the door for you."

This sounded ominous. She never called me Stephen unless I was in some kind of trouble. As I approached the door I could see why she was a bit apprehensive. Two shady-looking characters were stood in the doorway making awkward conversation with her.

I instantly recognised JP and Coops, two of the lads who had been on the coach to Lewisham. JP was small, thin, bearded, and was in his late twenties. He was a college lecturer and was on the local SWP branch committee. An enormously charismatic guy, he had a wicked sense of humour and is still one of the funniest guys I have ever met. He was also, considering his small stature and background, one of the hardest bastards I have ever come across. This toughness, combined with an almost scientific cunning and a fierce passion and dedication to the anti-fascist cause made him a formidable opponent.

Coops was about the same age as me, but was square-jawed and built like a brick shit-house. Together, the pair of them looked like a couple of heavies chasing up an unpaid debt.

"Alright Steve," said JP. "We were just passing and wondered if you fancied coming out for a jar."

"Oh, er, okay," I said, wondering what the real reason was for this unexpected visit.

Grabbing my coat, I followed them sheepishly out of the house, smiling reassuringly towards my worried-looking mother. As we jumped in JP's car, he apologised for all the cloak and dagger stuff, and explained that I had been invited to an important meeting in Stockport which needed to be kept a bit hush-hush.

We arrived at a small pub near the town centre, and as I walked in I immediately noticed a couple of lads I had seen at an SWP meeting a week earlier. They hadn't actually gone into the meeting, but had turned up towards the end, and chatted to some of the lads downstairs after the meeting had finished. Harold and Rick were a lot older than the rest of us, perhaps in their late thirties. Nodding but saying nothing, they walked upstairs into a small meeting room. JP bought me and Coops a beer and we climbed up the stairs to find about ten lads already in the room, laughing and chatting. I spotted Les, who had driven the coach down to Lewisham, and he let on to me with a big beardy smile.

We waited a short while for a couple of late arrivals from Rochdale before JP began to speak. What he had to say over the next few minutes hit me hard and was met with hushed silence. This was our introduction to what became known as "The Squad".

"As most people here will probably know," he began, "the NF have been allowed to get away with murder in Manchester. They have attacked a number of anti-racist meetings in and around the city and several people have been badly injured.

They have also threatened to start attacking left-wing meetings and events, and have been holding their own events with impunity."

We sat listening intently as JP continued. "Yes, I know that on the really big events we can we can get a good turnout, but their leafleting sessions and paper sales are untouched. They've also been threatening SWP paper sellers every week in the town centre, and last week they attacked a paper sale in Withington, assaulting two female comrades. Well this is going to stop, because from today we're going on the offensive. And when I say today, I mean tonight, because after this meeting some of us are going to pay a little visit to one of our brave nazi heroes."

What JP advocated over the course of the next few hours was the setting up, formally, of an anti-fascist defence group. Its purpose would be to organise effective stewarding of left-wing events, but also to actively seek out and attack the NF whenever and wherever possible. It required, he stated, "an understanding and appreciation of the use of physical violence against our political opponents." JP's colloquialisms were to become a standing joke over the following years as he waxed lyrical about "having meaningful discussions with the enemy", i.e. kicking shit out of the NF. He was later nicknamed the "Ayatollah" and his motto was "vicious but fair". I would certainly agree about the viciousness but I don't know where the fairness came in.

"If you're not sure about any of this," continued JP, "you can walk out the meeting now, and no-one will think any the worse of you. If you stay, then you stay on the understanding that this is a job that has to be seen through to its conclusion no matter what the risks." No-one left the meeting, and alongside about twenty other lads in that small room in Stockport, I became a member of the Manchester Squad that night.

JP told us that similar groups were being set up in other parts of the country, especially in London, where the NF were regularly attacking SWP paper sales. The idea for an organised stewards' group to defend SWP activities came from a central committee member called John Deason. He organised the first groups in London after concerns were raised that the NF were trying to destroy the SWP's presence on the streets.

I had already seen evidence of this new approach to fighting the NF at Aytoun Street. It had involved a number of people who had not been previously organised, but who were determined to take the fight to the NF. The attack went off with almost military precision, and bolstered by its success the participants were eager for more. I learned later that the attack was in reprisal for a combined NF and Loyalist attack on a National Council for Civil Liberties (NCCL) meeting at University of Manchester Institute of Science and Technology (UMIST) students' union. The NCCL called the meeting to discuss civil liberties in the north of Ireland, which is why it was targeted by both the NF and Loyalists. It proved to be a pivotal moment in the fight between fascists and anti-fascists in Manchester.

Over thirty fascists and Loyalists had stormed into the meeting and attacked the audience and platform with bricks, bottles and chairs. Six people were badly injured in the ensuing fracas, with one man requiring nineteen stitches after a bottle was smashed in his face. Another man had his arm broken. The assailants were arrested by the police shortly after leaving the building, and among the items found in their possession was a large Ulster Volunteer Force banner. Many of those arrested were out-of-towners from places like Leeds and Birkenhead who had teamed up with local NF members to attack the meeting.

Despite reams of evidence and eye-witness accounts against those involved in the attack, Deputy Chief Constable James Anderton advised the Director of Public Prosecutions not to press charges. Eventually a successful private prosecution was brought by UMIST against four NF members, but the reluctance of the police to pursue the matter convinced many anti-fascists that the authorities were prepared to turn a blind eye towards NF aggression, and they decided to take matters into their own hands.

I had very little knowledge or understanding of Irish politics, in fact I was only just starting to get to grips with this whole anti-fascist thing, and this seemed to be on an altogether different level. Although of Irish descent, I had been appalled by the bombings carried out by the IRA over the years, particularly the Birmingham pub bombings in 1974 which killed twenty-one people. The fight against the far right forced your hand, however, because the NF often targeted the Irish community, attacking marches and meetings on a regular basis. In time, I would develop a greater understanding of Irish nationalism and a love of Irish culture, but for the moment I contented myself with being merely an anti-fascist.

One of those badly injured at UMIST was Graeme Atkinson from Stockport. Although not at the meeting in the pub that night, he was a key member of the Squad in its early days. He lives in Germany now, but he was originally from a mining family in the north-east of England. Other lads I remember being at the meeting were Paul B, Mike L, Harold, Roy Mc, Wilko and Ian "Stig" Macintosh. Paul was from Salford and was a hard lad who spent time in the merchant navy. He was the fittest bloke in the Squad, and didn't smoke or drink, but loved the women. His younger brother Brian got involved with the Squad a few years later, and you always felt good when they were out on an activity. Wilko was a builder from Heywood and a real character, stocky and solid. He was a handful, although like Paul he was not one you would trust with your sister. Roy was very much his own man, a top lad but a loose cannon at times. Mike L was a bit older than us but was a tough little bugger with a fearsome temper; he would never back down, even when it looked like it was coming on top. Stig worked on the roads for Salford Direct

Works. His mop of unruly red hair gave people the impression that he was a firebrand but he was actually quite a thoughtful and sensitive character.

The less said about Harold the better, because he would not appreciate being mentioned here. He was absolutely fearsome. He just did what he had to do and went home. He wasn't aloof or anything like that, it was just the way he was. I remember once when we were having a pop at the NF paper sellers in town, and Harold spotted this lone Fronter on his way to join his mates. Harold walked up alongside this guy and suddenly pole-axed him with a sea-fishing weight in a sock. He then walked off casually as if he was out shopping with his wife, leaving the NF guy out cold on the pavement. An ambulance eventually arrived to cart him off. He obviously didn't make the paper sale that day, and I doubt whether he had the enthusiasm ever again, because he has never been seen since that incident. Harold never mentioned it to us again, but it was legendary Harold, absolute folklore stuff.

Some of these guys were members of the Trades Council, or were SWP members who had joined the party after becoming involved in the rank and file union groups. These were groups of SWP-ers who organised themselves within their unions on bread and butter issues such as wage claims or actions against redundancy. Many ordinary union members were attracted to these groups and subsequently became involved in other SWP activities.

As the meeting ended, JP informed me, Wilko, Roy and Coops that we would be paying the Withington NF organiser a visit. The plan was to drag him outside the house and threaten him. We did not want to use any violence and we didn't want to go into his house because he had an Alsatian bitch, called "Eva" after Hitler's mistress Eva Braun. Rumour had it that he had trained it to attack black people with the phrase, "Get the niggers". I was chuffed that I had been chosen for the job but I have to admit that I was a bit apprehensive about coming across his right-wing growler.

We drove into Withington and parked up just around the corner from the Fronter's house. After knocking on his door a few times it became obvious that he wasn't in, and JP suggested paying a visit to another local Fronter who lived nearby. This bloke operated a secondhand goods business from his home, and had been fingered as one of the guys giving it the big one in Withington a few weeks earlier. I was relieved to hear that he didn't own a dog.

JP rapped loudly on the knocker, and we heard the sound of footsteps approaching the door.

"Who is it?" asked a man's voice.

"It's Mr Jones," replied JP. "I've come about the table and chairs."

The door opened a fraction and we pushed our way in. We all had scarves over our faces, and I think we scared the living daylights out of him. His wife was watching TV as we burst in, and after the initial shock she started screaming abuse at us. However, her husband told her to be quiet and she calmed down immediately.

JP walked up close to the Fronter and looked right in his eyes. "Listen," he said. "We were looking for that arsehole up the road, but he was out. This is a warning to you and your NF mates. Take it seriously. If you persist in attacking and threatening our people we will hit you so hard you'll be pissing in your jackboots every time you hear a knock at the door. Now in your case that can be bad for business, but we fucking mean it. If you want to be brave then we'll see you in Withington on Saturday. Tell your mates one o'clock will do us fine, but I'm advising you now to get out of this game." We turned around and walked out of the house, leaving him to mumble his excuses to his wife, who was already berating him for his lack of bravery.

"Right lads," said JP. "That's the first and last time we ever go to someone's home. If they still want it after tonight then we'll have a full team out on Saturday waiting for them."

The NF did a no-show at Withington the following Saturday, but we knew that it was only a matter of time before we put into action what we had discussed earlier that evening.

Nowhere to Hyde

During the course of the Stockport meeting, JP had mentioned that he had heard rumours that the NF were planning to organise a big march somewhere outside London, and that Manchester was one of the venues being considered. At the time no-one paid much attention to the rumours, but it was confirmed a few days later that they were indeed intending to march somewhere in Greater Manchester, possibly Stockport or even Manchester itself. I was annoyed that the NF thought that they could come to my town giving it the big one, but also buzzing with anticipation at the prospect of a re-run of Lewisham.

As soon as there was official confirmation of the exact location, JP said he would call a Squad meeting to discuss tactics on the day. I was attending SWP meetings as well during this period, and although there was a nod and a wink relationship between the two groups, and even though most of the Squad were actually members of the party, we did not officially exist. I'll explain later how this relationship came to an end. We never got any official confirmation of the exact location of the NF march, because James Anderton, who was by now the Chief Constable of Greater Manchester, banned all marches in the area for a limited period. Among those affected by the ban were the Salvation Army and the Boy Scouts.

Martin Webster was the man responsible for NF national events. He was their national activities organiser and was a pugnacious and overweight former member of the Young Conservatives. He had been in a couple of openly nazi parties before joining the NF, and had once told an interviewer that "we are busy forming a well-oiled nazi machine in this country." When the ban was announced, Webster declared that if necessary he would march along the route on his own to protest about the limitation of free speech. So on 8 October 1977, that's exactly what he did; well, unless you count the 2,000 police officers that accompanied him on his lonely walk through Hyde in east Manchester.

In the week before Webster's solo stroll, however, we began to hear rumours that a secret agreement had been reached between the police and the NF, which would allow the Front to march in Manchester despite the ban. One particular rumour started flying around that the NF were going to march in Stockport on the same day as Webster was due to walk through Hyde. The Socialist Workers' Party and other anti-racists made plans to mobilise their forces to counter-demonstrate in the town.

On the day itself, large numbers of anti-racists gathered in Stockport and Hyde to oppose the NF and Webster. The Squad were a bit dubious about the Stockport rumours, suspecting that they were police disinformation put out to wrong-foot any counter-demonstration, and so JP put spotters out on the motorway bridges to monitor the NF coaches as they came off the M6.

Forty members of the Squad were waiting in the Albert pub in Rusholme for definite news of the NF's plans. There were a few new faces in the crowd, black lads from Moss Side I had not seen before. They were tough-looking characters who looked like they could handle themselves. Mikey, Denzil and Big Bird were people you would definitely want as friends rather than enemies, and I felt that we could take on anyone with them on board.

As the morning wore on, I noticed JP talking to people in cars outside the pub, and it was obvious that they had been out scouting around and were reporting back to him. At one point he went into a huddle with Les, Harold and Rick, and shortly afterwards word went out that several coachloads of NF had been spotted pulling up in the Longsight area. Longsight is a racially mixed area with significant black, Asian and Irish communities, and the NF were obviously hoping to inflame racial tension by marching there. We were told to get ready to move off, and to meet up again at Longsight Market. This was a little way from where we were told the NF were gathering at Crowcroft Park.

We got up to the market in various cars and vans, and began to head towards Stockport Road via a couple of side streets. As we neared the main drag, I could hear a police helicopter overhead and the sound of drums beating in the distance. It was obvious that the march was already underway. We were hyped up now, and the pace quickened as we caught the first glimpse of Union Jacks and NF banners between the buildings. As we emerged onto the main road we were greeted by the sight of what must have been nearly a thousand NF supporters flanked by hundreds of cops marching up the road towards Belle Vue.

At this point, we had been joined by a number of local black and Asian kids who wanted to have a pop at the NF as well. There were also a couple of dozen assorted left-wingers and anti-racists who had somehow found their way to the area and were heckling the marchers. We raced down side streets, picking up whatever we could find for missiles to throw at the march, hurling several volleys of stones and coins at the NF before we were chased off by the police. This happened a couple of times before someone spotted a milk float, which was immediately ransacked. Armed with full bottles of milk we made another determined assault on the march and this time we got close enough to make sure that some of the missiles hit their targets.

Some of the NF tried to break out of the march to have a go back at us, but they were held back by the police, who called in reinforcements to clear us away from the scene once and for all. We felt that to avoid mass nickings we should take this opportunity to leave the area. The NF eventually made their way up Kirkmanshulme Lane and were allowed to have a short rally at Gorton Baths. While this was happening we evaded our police escort and doubled back to Matthew's Lane where the NF coaches were parked. We completely wrecked three coaches before we had to get off.

We hung about the area for several hours after the NF had dispersed, and as we were strolling back through Longsight Market, a minibus full of NF passed us going down Dickinson Road and got stuck in traffic. We picked up whatever we could find lying about and pelted it. The van pulled out of the line of traffic sharpish and shot through the lights on the wrong side of the road to get away.

The Squad took only a couple of nickings that day but all told there were twenty-eight arrests. Apart from the fascists who were nicked, I would say that James Anderton owes each and every one of those arrested a personal apology. If the Chief Constable hadn't done a secret deal with the NF that allowed them to march through an ethnically mixed area, and in the process deceived and hoodwinked the public and the anti-racist movement, then no-one would have needed to even bother getting out of bed that morning.

The Anti-Nazi League (ANL) was officially launched at a big press conference in London a month later, although of course we had been aware of the name, and the ideas behind the new organisation for some time. The ANL was a broad-based movement that united various shades of political opinion against the NF by the use of mass demonstrations and by exposing the nazi traditions of their leadership. The ANL was dominated by the Socialist Workers' Party, although Labour MPs, trade union leaders and a number of smaller left-wing groups and anti-racist/anti-fascist campaigns also got behind the campaign. The founding statement of the ANL was signed by celebrities like Brian Clough, Warren Mitchell and Keith Waterhouse, along with thousands of trade unionists, community activists and anti-racists. It attracted star sponsors from the worlds of music, sport and showbiz, and alongside Rock Against Racism it mobilised hundreds of thousands of people against the NF.

Rock Against Racism

The catalyst for Rock Against Racism (RAR) came from an Eric Clapton gig in Birmingham in 1976, during which the renowned blues guitarist allied himself with Enoch Powell's racially motivated Rivers of Blood speech. This, coupled with similar right-wing statements from David Bowie, prompted a number of people, including leading SWP members, to form RAR in a bid to counter what they perceived as a rightward shift in both music and politics. Three of RAR's founding members, Red Saunders, Dave Widgery and Peter Bruno, wrote an open letter to the music press:

> When we read about Eric Clapton's Birmingham concert when he urged support for Enoch Powell we nearly puked . . . Come on Eric . . . Own up. Half your music is black. You're rock music's biggest colonist . . . We want to organise a rank and file movement against the racist poison music. We urge support for Rock Against Racism. PS Who shot the Sheriff Eric? It sure as hell wasn't you!

RAR provided a platform for black and white artists to perform together and openly state their opposition to racism and fascism. The editorial in issue number one of the RAR magazine *Temporary Hoarding* proclaimed, "We want Rebel music, Street music. Music that breaks down people's fear of one another. Crisis music. Now music. Music that knows who the real enemy is. Rock against Racism. Love Music Hate Racism."

The emergence of punk rock at around this time undoubtedly helped the cause of RAR immensely. Punk had definite political undertones that were very much left-leaning. It was, in the early days at least, a libertarian and anti-authoritarian movement which attempted to forge links and draw parallels with reggae music and black culture. Little wonder then that punk allied itself to the cause of RAR and vice versa.

The success of RAR gigs around the country prompted the organisers to be more ambitious, and plans for a free carnival featuring several top punk and reggae bands were proposed. It was intended to be a huge affair with up to 20,000 expected to attend an open-air gig in London on 30 April 1978. In a deliberate challenge to the NF, the carnival was booked for Victoria Park in East London, an area regarded by the fascists as one of their traditional strongholds. It was also an area that had seen a recent upsurge in racist attacks, including the murder of a young Sikh boy, Altab Ali.

There was a push to get as many people as possible to the carnival from other parts of the country and Manchester was no exception. The few weeks before the carnival were spent in a frenzy of activity as we devoted every spare moment to promoting the carnival. During the evenings we covered the whole of Manchester in fly-posters, and during the day we went around schools, colleges and work-places handing out flyers and leaflets for the carnival. The uptake was phenomenal. In a short space of time we had filled twenty coaches, and we knew that even this was not going to be enough. In the end we had to book coaches from as far as sixty miles away to satisfy demand.

The carnival exceeded all expectations, with upwards of 80,000 punters enjoying a mix of punk and reggae from bands like the Clash, the Tom Robinson Band, Steel Pulse and X-Ray Spex. The massive turn-out sent a clear message that the recent upsurge in racism and fascism in the East End would no longer go unopposed.

Following the huge success of the London event, a number of other carnivals were organised around the country, including one in Manchester on July 15 of that year. Alexandra Park in Moss Side was booked for an open-air festival which featured Steel Pulse, the Buzzcocks and John Cooper Clarke, among others. The date and location were chosen deliberately and were significant because the NF had announced that they were standing in a by-election in Moss Side at that time. This was regarded as a highly provocative move given the multi-racial character of this tough inner-city area. Herbert Andrew, one of the NF's first twenty members and a stranger to Moss Side and its environs, was the candidate chosen to stand on their behalf.

In the run-up to the election, the Front announced that they actually intended to march through Moss Side itself. It sounded like a kamikaze mission to me, and the only rational explanation for such an inflammatory move was that they wanted to provoke rioting by black youths in the area and then capitalise on the subsequent media frenzy. The plan was quickly nipped in the bud by the authorities, and the march was banned. Not even James Anderton was foolish enough to allow the NF to ignite the powder keg that was Moss Side at the time. However, it appeared that some sort of deal had been cut which allowed them to hold a rally of sorts just on the edge of Moss Side.

JP had managed to get hold of some information which indicated when and where this rally was taking place. He was coy about where he had got the intelligence from, and would only say that "anti-fascism is more than just about cracking heads, Steve." Later on I would immerse myself in the world of intelligence gathering, but at the time I didn't press the matter further. We quickly started putting the word out, and on the day itself, roughly sixty Fronters found themselves cornered outside the Princess pub, opposite Hough End playing fields, by a mixture of Squad lads and locals. Although the police were in attendance, they failed to prevent serious fighting. Numbers were about even and it was a rum old battle, but as time wore on it became obvious that word had spread around Moss Side, and more and more locals turned up to join in the attack on the NF. The police were forced to escort them out of the area.

The Manchester Carnival was a fantastic success, with 35,000 enjoying an afternoon of free music and political speeches. There had been threats from the NF to disrupt the carnival and most of the Squad slept on the stage the night before the gig to ensure that no mischief took place. During the day I ended up stewarding the area at the front of the stage, and although there were a couple of drunken dickheads throwing bottles, the threatened disruption from the NF did not materialise.

My abiding memory of this time was a slogan painted on a wall near to where the new bridge in Hulme now stands. It stated: "KILL NF PIGS TO RAS." It was up for ages and I even had it printed on a T-shirt. It became a bit of a rallying call when we were out and about.

Carnival 2 in London was planned for Brockwell Park in Brixton on 24 September 1978, and featured the, by now, familiar mix of punk and reggae bands, including Sham 69, Aswad, Elvis Costello and the Attractions and Misty in Roots. As a spoiling tactic, the NF announced two weeks beforehand that they were going to march through the heart of the Bangladeshi community in Brick Lane on the same day. This was obviously an attempt to divide the anti-nazi forces on the day, and to cause headaches for the carnival organisers. There was some concern amongst the rank and file membership of the SWP that the NF should not be allowed to parade unopposed through the East End, but we were assured by the SWP leadership that everything was in hand.

> A common purpose and a united strategy will ensure
> that the Nazis do not succeed. Defend Brick Lane – the
> Carnival goes on.
>
> 　　　　　　(*Socialist Worker*, 23 September 1978)

I was already in London that weekend, stopping over with a
friend who lived in Tulse Hill, not far from Brixton. We
wandered over to the carnival, where I met up with some of
the ANL people from Manchester. The stewarding was being
handled by London ANL, so for me it was a day off to enjoy
the music and the sunshine. I was aware however of the
Front's announcement that they were going to march in Brick
Lane, but to be honest I thought it was a red herring and that
it wouldn't actually happen.

Within a short while, however, we started hearing rumours
that something was happening in the East End, but we were
assured from the stage that everything was being taken care of
and that there were plenty of people down at Brick Lane
helping the local community to defend the area. This was not
the case. Apparently Gerry Fitzpatrick, a leading SWP member
and ANL organiser, was contacted by activists in Brick Lane
and asked to announce from the platform that people were
urgently needed down in the East End. He refused and instead
told everyone that there were plenty of people down there and
the situation was under control. We found out later that there
were probably only a couple of hundred anti-fascists in the
area at this time and they were heavily outnumbered by NF. It
was a disgrace, because there were tens of thousands of
people at the carnival that day enjoying the free music and
listening to rabble-rousing speeches in the sunshine.

Fitzpatrick was not the only leading member of the ANL to
lie about the true situation in the East End that day. I also
recall Ernie Roberts, the ANL treasurer, assuring the audience
that there were 7,000 people defending Brick Lane and that
everything was okay.

Eventually, stories started filtering through the crowd that the East End was not adequately defended, and I noticed people all around me leaving the park for Brick Lane. The people I was with started to debate whether they should go down as well.

"Fuck the music," someone said. "We need to get down to the East End."

My mate from Tulse Hill agreed. "This is pathetic. We shouldn't be here having a party when the NF are goose-stepping up and down Brick Lane."

We managed to get on a tube, which was not easy because the police had obviously heard something was up and were trying to keep people away, but along with several hundred other anti-racists we pushed our way through. We headed eastwards on the tube with no clear plan in mind other than that we should try and help defend the Bangladeshi community in the area. As we emerged from the tube station, we were greeted by a massive police presence. It was obvious that other demonstrators had arrived before us and that there had already been running street battles with the police as they tried to stop people breaking through and linking up with the anti-racists and Bengali youth already in Brick Lane.

We spent the next few hours trying to outwit the police and get into the area where we knew the NF and anti-racists were, but it proved a frustrating experience because the police had things well boxed off. As the afternoon wore on, the futility of the situation became obvious and we decided our best bet was to leave before we all ended up getting nicked.

The following morning I learned that the NF had marched practically unopposed through the East End and had held a rally in Curtain Road, off Great Eastern Street. There had been a small, token anti-racist presence in the area to protest against their presence, but they were heavily out-numbered by the nazis and the police. Later that same evening, NF supporters rampaged through Brick Lane smashing the windows of Asian shops and homes and attacking passers-by.

I suppose I had my first inkling that we were not all on the same wavelength after Carnival 2. There was some criticism of the ANL leadership suggesting that they did not want a mass confrontation down at Brick Lane in case it scared off the star sponsors and MPs. Some suggested that this was not a mistake, nor an aberration, but the way forward in the eyes of the SWP/ANL leadership. Most of this criticism seemed to come from some of the smaller left-wing groups who never seemed to do anything other than criticise the SWP/ANL in any case, so I took that with a large pinch of salt. More worrying were the murmurs of discontent within the ranks of the ordinary party membership.

After the event, there was a bit of discussion in the Albert and elsewhere about what had happened, and the general consensus was that it had been a genuine mistake. I suppose I went along with this for the quiet life, and accepted that there had been a balls-up. After all, no-one could prove that people had been deliberately misled, and when Paul Holborrow, an SWP central committee member and ANL national organiser, declared shortly afterwards that "we collectively bungled it," I was prepared to believe him, and put the incident to the back of my mind.

The Lillywhites

After their "secret" march in Longsight, Manchester NF were getting quite cocky, and we were astonished to learn that they were putting together a football team, the Lillywhites, with the intention of joining an amateur Sunday Football League for the 1978-79 season. We didn't think they had a hope in hell of being admitted into a league, but after some shenanigans they were finally allowed to join the Tameside Sunday Morning League. Although the Lillywhites had been forced to declare that they were non-partisan in their attempts to get into the league, they were fooling no-one, and we vowed to disrupt their matches by any means necessary. One plan involved myself and a few mates forming our own team with the intention of getting into the same league as them. That plan was scuppered when the organisers at Tameside Sunday League smelt a rat. I suppose with a name like Red Dynamo, we weren't exactly hiding our light under a bushel. It had been a propaganda exercise from the off, but had it actually come to playing against the NF team, then I'm sure the match would have been abandoned before it started, because in those days, teams had to share dressing rooms.

With our official "fixtures" against the Lillywhites cancelled, we decided to arrange some pre-match hospitality for the NF team, and vowed to make their Sunday morning footballing experience as uncomfortable as possible. The Lillywhites were due to play their home games on the council pitches in Woodley near Stockport, and to their credit, workers for the Parks Department refused to open up the changing rooms for the NF team, forcing them to change elsewhere. It was about this time that we were beginning to pick up intelligence on the NF from various sources, and had started to put names to faces and find out the odd address. Plans were put in place to follow an NF-er, preferably a Lillywhite, from their home address to the place where they changed into their all-white kit. The idea was to attack them prior to the game when there was less likelihood of the Old Bill being around.

Large-scale demonstrations were also being planned against the Lillywhites, which would tie up police resources and allow the Squad to operate more freely. It had been argued strongly at Squad meetings that we couldn't afford to get tied up in pickets and protests ourselves, because that would have ended up with loads of us being nicked. The temptation to steam into the NF as they strolled past giving it the big one would have proved irresistible to some of our more hot-headed members. We had to be choosy and disciplined. We weren't a football mob, and we operated under totally different rules and circumstances.

Only on really big demonstrations, where we could operate under the cover of large numbers of people, or where we thought there were no police around, did we resemble a football mob. The element of surprise was a key tactic for the Squad. Small groups were at times more useful than big mobs, but it meant that you had to go in a lot harder and then make a speedy getaway.

We finally turned up trumps with the address of a Lillywhite team member a couple of weeks later, and one Sunday morning he was followed by a couple of Squad members to a pub called (ironically) the Boot and Clogger in Woodley. Further surveillance revealed that the NF team were actually getting changed in a box van in a car park at the rear of the pub.

The next time the Lillywhites attempted to get changed in the back of their van they were literally caught with their pants down. One Sunday morning (8 October 1978, according to newspaper reports), while the Fronters were enjoying a laugh and a joke inside their makeshift changing-rooms, about twenty Squad members suddenly appeared on the scene. We had been parked up around the corner, out of sight, waiting for Roy to give us the nod that the NF were inside getting changed. I saw him speak to JP, who shouted, "Come on, let's do it," before leading the charge around the back of the pub.

I was near the front of our mob, and as we rounded the corner I saw an old Luton box van with two or three NF-ers stood outside it. They immediately legged it, and were chased by a couple of Squad members. The rest of us tried to get at the five or six Fronters inside the van, and there was a bit of pushing and pulling with the shutters as the terrified NF tried to keep us out. JP shouted, "Fuck 'em. Push the fucker over," and we began rocking the van from side-to-side until it toppled over with the NF trapped inside, caught like rats in a trap. It made an almighty racket as it crashed over with a loud crunching sound that sent broken glass flying everywhere. We heard all sorts of squeals and yells from the van as the frightened Lillywhites fell onto each other, elbows and studs finding soft fleshy targets. There were cries of pain and anger as panicky Fronters trampled on their team-mates in the darkness. We added to their panic and confusion by banging on the sides of the van with bats and clubs. The windscreen and cab windows of the van were smashed, and one of the lads tried to set light to some petrol that was leaking out of the fuel tank. Fortunately for everyone involved, it failed to ignite.

After the hit, some of the Squad members got off home while the rest joined up with the 500-strong picket for the Lillywhites away match at Medlock Street playing fields in Droylsden. Fights broke out between Lillywhite supporters and demonstrators, and the NF showed their true colours by hitting a couple of women protesters. The NF team eventually lost the game 6–1.

Nearly all the Lillywhites' matches were played out against a backdrop of constant interruptions, as running battles broke out or spectators invaded the pitch to steal the ball or kick it into the nearby river. We tried all sorts of tactics to disrupt their fixtures. On one occasion we sprinkled broken glass and oil on the pitch the night before a match. This plan was rumbled when what might have been either a police patrol car or a carload of NF spotted us in the middle of the job. The car drove onto the park and caught us in its headlights and we had to run for cover, hiding in the long grass at the side of the pitch for what seemed like ages. The following morning the NF spent several hours cleaning up the mess. On another occasion we tried to steal the goalposts by sawing them into pieces, but this proved harder than we thought and the attempt was abandoned.

We also spoke to some of the opposition teams that the Lillywhites were due to play, and a few of them agreed to cancel their matches with the NF team, although some weren't interested, saying that you shouldn't mix politics with sport, and that sort of thing. Funny that, because by playing the NF team that's exactly what they were doing!

After about half a season of continuing protests, pickets and disruption, the council and the league decided that enough was enough, and the Lillywhites were basically forced to disband. We heard rumours that the league had been ordered by the FA to sort out the mess, due to the embarrassment being caused by our campaign.

The other thing that has to be said about the Lillywhites is that, as a football team, they were basically shit. They had a big fat bloke in goal, and were pretty unfit and generally lacking in any kind of skill. They only won a couple of games in their admittedly short existence, and were near the bottom of the league when they folded. What undoubtedly could not have helped is that, unusually for a team comprising right-wingers, no-one actually wanted to play out wide for them, due to the fact that protesters kept tripping them up or kicking them as they ran along the line. There were not many volunteers to collect the ball for throw-ins or goal-kicks either.

What started out as a potential propaganda coup for the NF instead became a good focus for the ANL to mobilise people. We considered the disbandment of the Lillywhites to be a defeat for the NF but we knew there was lots more that had to be done.

CHAPTER TWO

On The Offensive

The Battle for the City Centre

The Squad operated a three-tier structure. There was a hard-core inner circle of about fifteen lads and there was another grouping of about thirty that was brought in when the situation required larger numbers. A lot of things were done on a need to know basis, with precise details of what was about to happen sometimes only being given out to the lads in the outer circle minutes before the actual event. There was no disquiet, as some lads preferred to turn up just for the row. For bigger events we could pull in up to another 100 lads, with friends and family members joining up with lads from the black community in Moss Side. These links were developed through Rick, who was a community worker in the area and was well respected by the locals. It was all measuring up for very interesting times, as on paper at least we had begun to develop a very formidable outfit.

The NF paper sale in town became the next focus for our attentions. We viewed it as an affront to everything we stood for. *National Front News* was full of all the usual "all muggers are black", "sack Red teachers" and "Asians spread disease" bollocks that you would expect from the NF, and we basically decided that we weren't going to allow them to peddle their wares in the main shopping area of our city unopposed any longer.

We realised that if we attacked the paper sale head-on then

we would risk a lot of nickings, because there was always a big police presence nearby, and we therefore felt that the best time to hit them was prior to the paper sale. We assumed that they had a meeting place, because they always arrived in a big group, with some of them looking as though they'd had a few drinks beforehand. We decided to monitor the nearby pubs and as luck would have it we turned up trumps with the very first pub we watched. The Brunswick (now called Finnegan's Wake), just off Piccadilly, gradually filled with an assortment of fifteen or so NF types, who by the time they left for the paper sale at about one o'clock were well-oiled and boisterous. They marched up to the top of Market Street to be greeted by the Old Bill and began the usual ritual of flogging papers and insulting any non-white person who happened to be passing by.

Some of them wore Manchester City scarves, a couple wore full camouflage gear. They were an odd sight, but dangerous for all that. The usual faces were all present: Scotty, Sheepshagger, Mickey C, Carl H, Karl K, Ten Men, A.D. Jones and Viking, the hardcore of the NF in Manchester and mostly connected to City's firm. I have heard it said that Manchester had the biggest NF branch in the country outside London and it is true that on occasions they could pull out big numbers for one-off activities. A week-in, week-out paper sale is a different matter however, and it usually comprised just the hardcore and varying numbers of the less committed membership.

Scotty was an NF regular from Openshaw, a rundown inner-city area. He was one of City's top boys, and was among those who had given me grief in the fish market. He was a game lad, and we had more than a few run-ins with him over the years. Sheepshagger was so-called because of the long sheepskin coat he always wore. He was also a top boy at Maine Road, but with his long curly hair and beard he was often mistaken for a lefty. Mickey C was a bit of a headcase. He was never far away from the trouble we had in town with the NF, and was another one who was into the City hooligan scene. He got badly hurt following a fight with anti-fascists in the old Cyprus Tavern quite a while ago and was left scarred for life. Unbeknown to the anti-fascists, he happened to walk into the club with some City fans who were members of the left-wing organisation Militant. They ended up getting attacked as well, so belated apologies for that.

Ten Men more than matched his nickname. He must have weighed at least twenty-five stone but was more agile than you might suppose, especially when being chased by anti-fascists. A couple of Squad members, Greg and Paul B, once chased him into the Royal College of Music on Oxford Road and a tug of war ensued between the two anti-fascists and some security guards as the lads tried to drag him out onto the pavement for a kicking. Minus his shirt, Ten Men escaped into the building just as the police arrived. He was infamous for his attempt to run down some anti-fascists on Longsight Market on his motorbike. He was spotted by the police and was arrested and fined for that bit of dangerous driving.

Anthony David Jones was a podgy, bespectacled character who flitted in between the NF and the Tory party. He played in the NF drum corps and worked as an environmental health officer for the city council. There was a long campaign against him working in this role, and he was eventually demoted to pest control officer. He turned up at my flat one day to spray for cockroaches. This was in the mid-Eighties, when he was supposedly out of the Front, but I still didn't trust him. I moved shortly afterwards in order to escape the cockroaches and any possible repercussions. Viking got his nickname, I presume, for his long blond hair and blue eyes. He was from Beswick, another inner-city area that had seen better days, and was a United supporter, although I have never bumped into him at Old Trafford. I did spot him and some of his mates singing nazi songs in a bar in Rotterdam in 1991 when United were over for the Cup Winners' Cup final.

All of the above were on the paper sale that day, along with a handful of less well-known characters. After monitoring them for a while, we went back for another look at the Brunswick. As we scanned the area, JP turned to me and grinned.

"Look," he said, pointing towards a row of shops. "See the cafe and the amusement arcade?"

I nodded. The two shops were just along the road from the Brunswick, about thirty yards apart.

"When the NF leave the pub for their paper sale, they have to walk past both shops," he said. "If we put a team in the cafe and the arcade we could catch them in-between as they walk past."

With no more said, we headed off to meet the other lads at Hulme Labour Club. There JP outlined his thinking to the rest of them. He proposed splitting into two teams of around twelve, with one team in the arcade and the other in the cafe, plus a small stand-by team of six in the general area, at bus stops, shops and other inconspicuous places. Split-second timing was essential, with the team in the amusement arcade to steam in first from the front, and the group in the cafe to jump them from behind and capture any Fronters doing a runner. Anyone trying to escape across the road would be greeted by the stand-by team.

JP stressed that we had to be in quick and out fast, as we had to assume that there was a likelihood that plain-clothes Old Bill might be around. Escape would be made easier by the fact that the town centre would be busy with shoppers, and it should be relatively easy to lose yourself in the crowds. The date was set for two weeks' time when City were playing at home, as it was reckoned that the hard-core NF City elements were more likely to be there.

Over the next few days, escape routes were drawn up and weapon dumps located. A couple of us went into the cafe and the amusement arcade the following Saturday to check it out. One big problem was there would be a lot of hanging about and we didn't want to arouse suspicion. A solution was to put on City hats and scarves as if we were going to a game. It was also suggested that it might make getting away easier. Much as it might irk having to put on a City scarf, we reluctantly agreed. The amusement arcade was also quite small, so numbers were reduced in there and more people were positioned at bus stops and side streets.

Thursday night's Squad meeting at the community centre in Moss Side was incredible. There was a real sense of camaraderie and spirits were high. JP injected some humour into the meeting by wheeling out a flip-chart with a large scale map, and began to plot the battle-plan like a World War Two general, complete with baton. The teams were sorted out, with me being assigned to the amusement arcade with the responsibility of keeping in permanent eye contact with the spotter on the other side of London Road. His job was to watch out for the NF leaving the Brunswick and give the signal for the attack.

Not much to do but wait until Saturday. That night I found it hard to sleep. Friday was worse. I couldn't relax, tried to read – forget it. Saturday morning arrived and I got an early call from Coops. He was as wired as me. Coops was a Wythenshawe lad, who because of his job as a tool fitter became the Squad armourer. I got over to his house around 9 a.m. and just to keep ourselves occupied we spent the best part of an hour fashioning some metal pipes into weapons. Although everyone was required to supply their own weapons, it was always important to have a plentiful supply handy, and Coops's engineering skills were always appreciated.

At 11 a.m., JP arrived. He was wearing a wax jacket and looked as if he had just taken the dog out for a walk across the fields. He didn't seem in the slightest bit nervous. Many years later, some people who were around at the time but not necessarily involved in the Squad said that they thought he was a bit obsessive, cold or even callous. All I knew was that he was 100 per cent into what he was doing and inspired others with his commitment. If JP was there when something was going down, then you felt good. His knowledge and planning skills were spot-on, and the fact that he also got stuck in indicated to us that he was no general conducting a war from the rear.

We arrived at the rendezvous in Hulme and met up with the rest of the lads. The plan was to filter into town in small groups of two or three and sneak into the cafe and amusement arcade. Harold and Dave B, another Salford lad, were in town watching the pub. This was before mobile phones were invented, and we kept in contact with the lookouts through Roy Mc, who would relay information on his motorbike.

The NF team were already in the pub, and just after twelve o'clock the Squad were also in place. The cafe was doing a roaring trade in bacon sarnies, but those of us in the amusement arcade were finding it difficult to look inconspicuous, going through the motions of playing the fruit machines. Andy, one of the Stockport lads, was a bit of a gambler, and as he flitted from one machine to the other, we had to remind him why he was there.

We had not been in there long when we got the nod from the lookouts as the NF started to emerge from the Brunswick: four or five lads at first, then another half a dozen following a few feet behind. The Squad lads on the street started pulling up their scarves and pulling down their hats as we waited for the exact moment to steam into them. Those few moments while we waited for the signal to be given were incredible. A few nervous smiles, the odd nod, and then the signal to attack.

The plan had been to walk out of the arcade slowly rather than charge, but we were all hyped up, and were climbing over each other, knocking over cups of coffee, and bumping into other customers in our haste to get at the NF. A big roar went up as we charged into them. I was right at the front of our lot as we steamed in, hitting anyone who got in my way with a lead-filled chair leg. The element of surprise was on our side, and the Fronters were caught cold and flat-footed as we tore into them. Five or six of them were battered into the ground and stayed there. They were hit with all kinds of weapons, and a couple of them were begging for mercy as they attempted to shield themselves from the blows raining down on their heads. Not one of them fought back, or rather they were not given the chance to.

I chased one of them up a side street, hitting him across the back of his head with my chair leg. He went down, crying, "I'm not with them, I'm not with them. I'm just out for a drink."

"Fuck off nazi," I shouted as I hit him again, "I know who you are."

The two tossers who had recently been turning up at the paper sale in camouflage gear were among the first to go down, as a number of our lads seemed quite keen to have a pop at them. One of them was treated in hospital for stab wounds. We found out later that they were soldiers from Germany who were home on leave for a few weeks.

One Fronter was chased into the Grand Hotel foyer where he was kicked senseless. Another was knocked over by a car as he ran away. I heard afterwards that a few of the lads gave him a kicking as he was laid out in the road. NF newspapers and leaflets were scooped up from where they had been dropped by their terrified owners, and we began to make our getaway. All this had taken place in less than thirty seconds.

With the sound of sirens wailing in the distance, we dumped our weapons behind a hoarding and made our way back to the All Saints area. Coops was really high, reliving the attack, but JP was more downbeat. He had attempted to hit one Fronter with an iron bar concealed in a plastic bag but the bar had shot out mid-swing, leaving the carrier-bag fluttering harmlessly in the bloke's face.

JP dropped me and Coops back in Wythenshawe and we went for a drink in a local pub. I had a new job working for a fishmongers in Wythenshawe Civic Centre at the time, but they were all Tories and I hated it. The people I worked with were a real bunch of arse-lickers and grasses. I phoned in sick that morning so I could be in on the hit, but as luck would have it, I was spotted by one of their van drivers just as I was going into the pub. I knew he would stitch me up, but I couldn't be arsed even to think about it.

On Monday morning I was greeted by a stern-faced boss and knew immediately what was coming. Before he had chance to carry on with himself, however, I turned on my heels and started to walk out. I was stopped in my tracks when he shouted after me that the police had been in asking for me.

"What about?" I asked.

"Something to do with a fight in town," he replied, "and I gave them your address."

"Oh thanks mate," I replied as I slammed the door shut on my career in the fishmongers' trade.

I felt a bit sick after hearing that the police were on my case, and I went home to ponder the situation. Within half an hour there was a knock at the door and two CID officers identified themselves. After a few preliminaries they asked me to go down to the station for an interview.

It was basically a fishing expedition on their part. Everyone on the hit had been masked up and there was no real evidence or witness identification against anyone. The Fronters were still smarting from the attack on their coach before Lewisham, and had given my name to the police, adding that I worked in the Arndale Centre. My former boss had given the police my name, and details of my current employer, and the Old Bill had taken it from there. After an hour of questioning I was released without charge. As I left the station I was warned that from now on "we'll be watching you and your mates."

JP had also been picked up at work at about the same time as me and questioned about the attack. He had supposedly been identified while wearing a full-face crash helmet, and was unsurprisingly released without charge after he basically told the police that it was their job to prove that he had been there. When we met up later in the week, JP told us that from now on the Old Bill were likely to start taking an interest in us. They had not alluded to the existence of the Squad in so many words, but they definitely knew that there was a group of anti-fascist militants who were determined to take the fight to the NF.

The NF had suffered a number of casualties in the ambush, with five requiring hospital treatment. One of the squaddies was in Ancoats Hospital for several days having treatment for his wounds. It had been a successful hit, but no-one thought for a moment that the NF would disappear on the back of one good hiding. What we wanted to do was to make them wary, put them on the back foot, and maybe scare off some of the hangers-on. More importantly, we wanted to give anti-fascists the feeling that they could fight back and do something about the NF in Manchester.

It came as no surprise to us, therefore, when the following week the NF beefed up their paper sale with supporters from as far away as London. Even Martin Webster turned up to lend his support. We also knew that the NF were likely to look for revenge at some point soon, and we warned people to be on their guard. SWP paper sales were heavily protected for weeks afterwards. SWP meetings, especially in certain parts of North Manchester were well stewarded, and when the inevitable attack occurred we were ready for them.

A small SWP meeting in the Pack Horse pub on Deansgate was the target. About a dozen of us were stewarding the meeting. Half a dozen were drinking in the bar downstairs, a couple were out scouting, while I was upstairs in the actual meeting with three or four lads. All of a sudden I heard a shout, "They're here, they're here", and I looked out the window and saw a mob of twenty NF charging towards the pub. All the usual suspects were present: Scotty, Sheepshagger, Viking and the rest. There were also a couple of new faces that we hadn't seen before. I ran down the steps, and there was already a scrum in the doorway as the lads in the bar clashed with the first couple of Fronters brave enough to enter the pub. The landlord and a few locals were also involved as they struggled to break up the fight and stop the pub getting wrecked.

Because the fight was being fought in a bottleneck I couldn't get anywhere near it, but fortunately nor could most of the NF, who were watching the fight from outside. They definitely had superior numbers on this occasion but for some reason they did not press home the advantage, and started backing off. I don't know whether they thought that the landlord and his mates were on our side, or whether they were surprised by the ferocity of the anti-fascist defence, but either way they started to withdraw from the fight with nothing more accomplished than a couple of broken windows.

As the NF disappeared up Deansgate, one of the lads was dispatched to follow them. He reported back that they were sticking together as a mob and had plotted up in a bar in town. We thought that they might be planning more mischief and did a quick ring around for reinforcements. In the meantime, the landlord was doing his nut over the damage to his pub, and cancelled the meeting. The police turned up as well, but unlike the Front, we operated a policy of non-co-operation and ignored them.

There were a couple of reasons why we did not co-operate with the police. The first was obviously security. The less the police knew about what was going on the better as far as we were concerned. What we were involved in was illegal, and any conversation with the police, no matter how innocent seeming, could end up being used against you or your comrades. The second reason was one of political principle. We were, after all, members of an organisation that viewed the police and the state as the enemy, so why should we offer them any kind of assistance at all?

After the fuss had died down, we got people safely away from the meeting and then went searching for the NF in the town centre. We had an impressive mob following the ring-around, but unfortunately the NF had disappeared and the search proved fruitless.

The following week they tried again. The Troops Out Movement were holding a meeting in the town hall basement calling for the withdrawal of British troops from Northern Ireland, and there were rumours that the NF were planning a repeat of the UMIST attack. The tension heightened considerably when Troops Out members began receiving phone calls from the NF and Loyalists threatening to smash up the meeting.

We were prepared for them this time, and when a group of twenty-five Fronters were spotted on the other side of Albert Square, we rushed out of the meeting to confront them. Someone had put up a scaffolding outside one of the buildings on Princess Street, and a couple of the Fronters had grabbed some six-foot poles and were advancing across the square waving them at us. Bloody hell, I thought, this is a bit scary. Fortunately a couple of the lads had magnesium flares and fired them at the NF mob. They flew over the heads of the advancing Fronters and exploded with a loud bang and a shower of sparks against the walls and windows of the buildings behind them. This had a two-fold effect. It blunted the fascist advance almost immediately, and caused some of the less hardcore NF members to scarper off into the distance.

By now, big numbers of people had come out of the

meeting, and the Front were backing away from the Square shouting stuff like, "Hang IRA scum", and, "Murderers". I thought this was a bit out of order. It was only a meeting to discuss the withdrawal of British troops, not a pro-IRA rally or anything like that. The police turned up eventually, and true to form, the NF tried to grass up our lads for firing flares at them. The police grabbed a couple of people and started hassling them, but they had no evidence, and the NF were hardly impartial witnesses, so the matter was dropped after everyone denied everything.

The meeting resumed but the NF phoned in a bomb scare, and the building had to be evacuated. This has been a favourite fascist tactic over the years, which to my mind smacks of desperation. It means they are too weak, too cowardly and too lacking in confidence to successfully confront us, and have to resort to mischief-making.

JP disagreed. "We've got to hit them again, and hit them hard," he declared.

Stockport

As luck would have it, a couple of days after the attack on the Troops Out meeting we received information that the NF were going to hold a big meeting in a pub called the Bull's Head near Stockport Market. Martin Webster was due to speak and it was said that he was up in the Manchester area to urge the local branch to be more active, although there were also rumours that he was sexually involved with one of the younger male members of the branch.

We decided to attack the pub with smoke bombs and magnesium flares. These weapons were the speciality of the Manchester Squad, and if you ever see film footage of political demonstrations from the 1970s and flares and smoke bombs were going off, the chances are that a Mancunian Squad member was present somewhere.

Five of us met up in Wythenshawe to discuss what to do

about the NF meeting: myself, JP, Coops, Roy Mc and Wilko. JP was in favour of a small-scale attack.

"Listen lads," he said. "Virtually the entire NF leadership is coming up for this meeting. This is too good an opportunity to waste on a daft picket. A small team with the right gear can do them more damage than all the placard brigade put together."

Coops nodded. "You're right. If the SWP find out about it, they'll only call for a picket of the pub, and either the Old Bill will ban it or the NF will just move to another venue, and then we'll be back to square one."

We agreed, and after a bit more discussion we decided to hit the NF meeting with a small, hand-picked team of five, probably the five people sat in the room at that moment.

On the night itself I borrowed my dad's old Viva van and drove the five of us up to Stockport, parking in a quiet side-street near the pub. The four lads got out the back of the van, leaving the doors slightly ajar and me behind the steering wheel with the engine running in case we needed a quick getaway. We knew that the manager of the pub was sympathetic to the NF, as were the owner and bouncers of a nearby nightclub called the Blue Waterfall, so we didn't want to be out on the streets for too long in case things escalated out of control.

The lads went for a quick recce of the pub, making sure that the information we had received was correct, because the last thing we wanted to do was hurt innocent people. Our targets were the NF, and the NF alone. The curtains were drawn and the pub looked shut, but through a small gap they managed to see that the meeting was underway. A few minutes later they returned to the van.

Coops tapped me on the shoulder. "This is going to be easy," he whispered. "They've not even put stewards on the door."

JP was sat beside me in the front. "It's not doing the job that's going to be difficult, it's the getting away afterwards.

We should head towards Marple. They'll expect us to go towards Manchester so we should go in the opposite direction."

"Are we going to do it now?" I asked. "Cos there's a few people about and I'm worried about them clocking the van as we get away."

"No, we'll leave it for a bit," replied JP. "We'll come back at ten-thirty when it's quieter and do it then."

We drove out of the area and parked somewhere quiet for an hour or so, killing time and chatting until it got to about 10.30, when we returned to the same side-street. The lads went through the same procedure again, only this time they were carrying bricks, flares and smoke bombs.

I sat alone in the van for what seemed like ages, but was probably only a couple of minutes. My heart was pounding, and I think I was more nervous sat there in the van than I would have been actually doing the job.

Suddenly I heard the sound of running foot-steps and the lads piled into the back of the van shouting at me to get moving. "Drive. Drive," yelled Coops. "Put your fucking foot down."

Roy Mc was laughing his head off. "I'm having a big fat spliff when I get home," he grinned. "Did you hear the fucking windows go in?"

"Fucking hell," said JP with a wry smile. "They're not going to like that. Those flares went off a treat."

I put my foot down on the accelerator and sped off towards Marple as planned. I felt a bit left out and was dying to know the details of the hit. The lads told me that the plan had worked a treat. They had smashed the windows with the bricks, and then fired the flares and smoke bombs through the broken panes into the meeting. The whole job had only taken a few seconds and they had disappeared from the scene by the time the NF got their act together.

Job done, we made good our escape, and went home to our beds and our alibis. Local papers the next day had a couple of mentions of the hit, with quotes from the NF demanding that the police arrest those responsible. The landlord of the pub was quoted as saying that they would leave no stone unturned in their efforts to find the perpetrators. I believe JP was hauled in by the police again, but there was no evidence against him and he was released without charge.

Meanwhile, back in Manchester, we noticed that the NF paper sale was becoming more and more sporadic, with numbers falling as the hangers-on and fringe elements started drifting away. There was never a direct hit on the paper sale again, because we were wary of the police, who we knew were watching the situation closely. However there were a few incidents and skirmishes away from the area, including one where eight of us bumped into about fifteen of them beside Piccadilly Plaza. The Fronters immediately targeted two of the girls that were with us, Chrissy and Jill, who had plenty of bottle but were not exactly what you could call street-fighters. I was confronted by Neil Meade, an ex-Marine commando and bouncer at the Blue Waterfall, who put me on my arse. JP, Roy, Coops, Dougie and Wilko gave as good as they got, and by the time I got up again the NF were already running away. I think by now they had realised they weren't dealing with a bunch of students and hippies.

Sometimes we would turn up and take photos of the NF, which would infuriate them. At other times, a big group of ANL would completely surround their paper sales, making it difficult for them to actually sell any papers at all. It was a policy of harassment and it seemed to be working, as the paper sales became more and more infrequent, usually coinciding with a City home game so that they had more numbers. Eventually the paper sale stopped altogether as numbers declined to such a low level that it became unsafe and embarrassing for them to carry on.

It was around this time that the ANL and SWP first started to become critical of some of the methods used by the Squads, and we began to hear the word "squadist" being bandied about. We were openly criticised in branch meetings for some of the actions we initiated, but it was also clear that there were a lot of whispers and rumours flying about as well. The term squadist basically meant someone who was not interested in building a broader opposition to fascism, but who just wanted to organise in small teams to confront fascist gangs. My own feelings were that both types of activity were needed. I couldn't see why we shouldn't be allowed to get on with what we did best, while they got on with their jobs, but it was clear that the leadership and the party hacks were uneasy with the physical battles being fought and were pushing for the Squads to be disbanded completely.

What the SWP did not like was the stuff like the Bull's Head, where our actions denied them the opportunity to get loads of free publicity. I also think they were a bit worried that the Squad had taken on a life of its own, and that non-SWP people were involved. They were scared that the Squads were moving out of the SWP orbit, and that activities were being planned and executed without their permission. I have no doubt as well that they were extremely worried by the threats of retribution from fascists who had been injured and humiliated by our activities. I don't suppose it occurred to them that they had actually set up the Squads in the first place as a means of curtailing fascist violence and saving their own necks, but if it did then they kept very quiet about it.

We resented this criticism, especially because we felt we were winning the battle against the NF, who were being slowly driven out of town. As a result of our actions, attacks on left-wing and anti-racist activities had declined sharply as the NF were forced on the defensive. We had taken huge risks for the very people that were now turning against us, and as a result, myself and a few of the other lads started to feel a bit alienated from them. I felt that my real comrades were fellow

Squad members, not the politicos and party hacks of the SWP.

Heywood

Wilko was a top lad who had got involved with the SWP a couple of years earlier through the Right to Work campaign. The aims of the campaign were to provide a political platform for the growing number of unemployed people in the UK and to link their struggle with that of people in the organised workforce. It was highly successful and mobilised thousands of people to take part in propaganda stunts like the occupation of job centres and such like. The highlights were the annual Right to Work marches which crossed the country to protest against rising unemployment and the inaction of the TUC. Following his involvement in the campaign, Wilko joined the SWP, and immediately ran into trouble with local Fronters in his home town of Heywood. Unfortunately for the NF, Wilko was well known in the area, and some of his mates sorted out the problem for him.

Wilko joined the Squad a little while later, and shortly afterwards it came to his attention that NF were making a nuisance of themselves again, and were giving SWP paper-sellers in the town a load of mither. He asked us to lend a hand, and a load of us went up to take a look around. Wilko and his mates, who were a pretty scary bunch, wanted to take on the Front by doing a big hit on them similar to the Piccadilly paper sale job. The problem was that the NF in the area were being organised by a well-known criminal family, so we were aware that a big ambush could escalate the situation beyond our control. There was a real possibility of tit-for-tat reprisals, with the forces ranged against us including bikers, travellers and local villains. It was a tricky situation, and we were aware that locals like Wilko would suffer more than those of us who were coming up from Manchester.

Within a few days however, a truce was brokered, with the

NF more or less being told by the local villains that they had to back off from Heywood, but were okay to operate in Rochdale. Although we were itching to get at them, we were forced to accept the situation, and grudgingly went along with it. We did not view this as a defeat or as a sign that we were getting soft; after all, Heywood isn't Manchester, it's a few streets on a hill where whippets out-number people!

As it happened however, a few months after we had first been up there some members of this NF family had beaten up a mate of Wilko's son, and as it wasn't blatantly politically motivated we lent a hand in seeking revenge, without it necessarily affecting the "cease-fire". We drove up there, met Wilko, and had a little drive around town looking for these characters. We collared five or six of them coming out of a chippy, slightly younger than us, but old enough to be taught a lesson. They were bullies, and we didn't have any qualms about dishing it out to them. Those that didn't get on their toes quick enough were given a kicking, with one of them being humiliated by having a sausage stuffed into his mouth.

As we were outsiders there was there was little or no chance of being recognised and therefore no comebacks. Wilko was made up with the support of the Squad lads, and a few of his mates joined up with us over the next few months.

Winchester, 23 March 1979

Robert Relf first hit the headlines in 1974 when he put up a For Sale sign outside his house in Leamington Spa, Warwickshire, with the proviso "To a White Family Only" scrawled underneath. This earned him a couple of court appearances under the Race Relations Act and an eventual jail sentence for contempt of court when he refused to take the sign down. He went on hunger strike while inside, although there were rumours that he was secretly being given Complan by sympathetic prison officers.

Relf was released from prison by a friendly judge after a seven-week campaign and looked only slightly the worse for wear for his experiences. Throughout this period he was a bit of a *cause célèbre* for the NF and the British Movement, of which he was a member. The right-wing press also championed his cause and dubbed him a "race martyr", although sympathy among the media began to wane once his BM membership came to light. This sympathy was virtually extinguished when it was also discovered that he had once been a member of the Ku Klux Klan and was also a Hitler worshipper with a previous prison record for attacking an Asian shop.

In 1979, Relf found himself in prison again, and once more went on hunger strike. By now he was a member of the NF, and the Front were making huge political capital out of the situation. Relf was in Winchester Prison, and there had already been right-wing marches in the city on two consecutive weekends, with a third march and rally being planned for the following Saturday. There had been reports of trouble on the first two demonstrations, and because we had missed them we decided that we ought to make an effort to show our faces for the third one.

The first march had been organised by a group which called itself the Release Robert Relf Campaign. This appeared to be a coalition of various right-wing organisations and bodies who were claiming that Relf was just some poor oppressed white guy undone by an unfair system prejudiced in favour of black people and immigrants. The second march was a smaller affair called by the BM, who were still desperately trying to make some kind of mileage out of Relf's former membership of their organisation. The third march was being organised by the NF, who saw in Relf an opportunity to make the kind of political capital it needed to make an impression in the forthcoming General Election.

We took about twenty Squad members down to Winchester

the following Saturday, fifteen in a minibus and the rest in a
car. Winchester is a nightmare journey from Manchester and
we needed to get down there early so that we could make our
plans for the day and scout the town. This meant a really early
start for us, and it was still dark when I clambered on board
the minibus in Hulme with the rest of the lads.

Following United up and down the country meant I was
used to waking up early on Saturday mornings, but a few of
the other lads clearly enjoyed a lie-in on their weekends off
and were grumbling about the early start. Some of the older
SWP members who were in the Squad were not sympathetic.
They were veterans of dozens of trips around the country
supporting striking workers and had been heavily involved in
the Grunwick dispute in London in 1977. This had involved
numerous trips down to the Smoke to support workers who
had been sacked from their jobs in the photo-processing
factory. The strike was bitterly fought as the company tried to
bus in scab labour to replace the sacked workers. The dispute
turned violent on many occasions as the police fought running
battles with the pickets trying to stop the scabs getting through.

It was at Grunwick that people from Manchester met some
of the lads who went on to form the Squads in London. There
had been a couple of occasions when we had bumped into
them since then but the relationship was still very tenuous and
informal. Winchester changed all that.

We arrived quite early and parked up on the outskirts of
town near a park. As we made our way towards the city centre
it looked like we had successfully evaded any police surveillance, although we had heard that all police leave had been
cancelled and we knew that it was only a matter of time before
a group of twenty lads was tagged. It was pouring with rain,
and about twelve of us dived into a greasy spoon cafe while
we made our plans and sent out scouts. We were playing it
pretty much by ear, but what we wanted to do was track down
the NF hardcore early on and have a dig at them, before

joining up with the main counter-demo for another pop at the march itself.

The cafe was quite long and dog-legged at the bottom so that anyone sat at that end was out of sight of the street. We positioned ourselves here while an old Greek couple took our orders. We had just finished ordering when we heard a commotion, and shouts of, "You Paki bastard", and, "We'll fucking kill you". An Asian lad ran into the cafe pursued by four white lads clearly intent on giving him a right kicking.

Without waiting to ask questions, we piled into them. They were taken completely by surprise but managed to fend off the initial assault and had a right go back at us. We had numbers on our side, though, and in the end they took quite a bad kicking before they managed to scramble out of the cafe to safety. Craig from Stockport got a nasty cut from a flying dinner plate, which was probably friendly fire, but the fascists definitely came off worse.

"Those boys put up a good fight," said JP dusting himself down.

"I think they were BM Leader Guard," said Graeme. "They've probably turned up in Winchester for a bit of aggro and are hoping to pick off a few stragglers from the counter-demo."

By rights we should have cleared out of the cafe straight away, but hunger got the better of us, and we decided to quickly neck down our breakfasts before getting off. The owner was a bit put out but he had seen what had happened to the Asian lad and he let us stay and finish our scran.

I was just mopping up my plate with a slice of bread and butter when the back door of the cafe swung open and about fifteen lads walked in. We looked at them, they looked at us, and before I knew it we were having it again. Plates, teapots and cups flew through the air as the two sides clashed. I started grappling with some lad in a denim jacket, but before anyone could do any serious damage someone started shouting, "Whoa, stop." I looked up and one of our lads was pointing at an SWP badge on the lapel of one of the guys on the other side. "It's our own side," I said as we disengaged. The fighting stopped as the two sides eyed each other suspiciously.

"We're Manchester ANL," said Stig. "Who are you?"

"London ANL," replied one of their lads.

"I really don't think we should be fighting each other," said JP with a smile.

A couple of names were mentioned, and in next to no time it was like we had known each other for years. Amongst the London lads out that day was Malc, who was a postie at Cricklewood sorting office, Murph and Mickey O'Farrell who were both building workers. Another lad had the nick-name Moonface for some reason. He was a spot-on, funny lad who I really took a liking to. I had heard about Mickey O'Farrell before as he was a big United fan, famous for penning, "She wore a scarlet ribbon in the merry month of May", a terrace classic from the mid-Seventies, but I had never actually met him.

As we settled down to chat with our new-found comrades, the front door of the cafe was pushed open and in strode a load of Old Bill. We decided to all get up and walk out as if nothing had happened. They stood across the doorway and tried to stop us.

"No," shouted the lady behind the counter. "These boys have nothing to do with it. The trouble was caused by some skinheads who have just left." She threw us a wink as we left, and I smiled at her and winked back. Outside the cafe we organised a whip-round and passed it to the woman who had just saved us.

We had escaped a nicking. We knew it and the police knew it too, but there was nothing they could do about it. As they chattered animatedly into their radios, we walked into town with big grins on our faces. We were shadowed all the way by a couple of riot vans, which meant that any further fun and games at this stage was out of the question.

With this in mind we headed for the main anti-fascist demo outside the prison where 2,000 anti-racists and anti-fascists had gathered. The NF had not been allowed anywhere near the prison but had instead been marshalled out of town. I hoped the chants from the counter-demo would cause old Relfy to choke on his Complan.

Once the ANL protest had finished, we managed to swerve the Old Bill and hide in a pub until things quietened down a bit. Spotters were sent out to try to track down any stray groups of fascists, but we were running out of luck and time on that score. We had more or less given up hope of having another pop at the fascists when we got a report that some BM Leader Guard had been spotted drinking in a pub on the outskirts of town. We had a fair old mob out with us now, including the London lot, and an assortment of others, including a handful of local lads who had taken a dislike to the fascists.

We managed to get over there without attracting the attention of the Old Bill, and carefully approached the pub. Unfortunately a couple of boneheads drinking outside spotted us and ran inside. Seconds later, a dozen or so BM heavies ventured out but immediately retreated back into the pub and started making desperate attempts to barricade the doors. What a pathetic shower, I thought, as they started gesturing at us from the safety of the pub. If this was the so-called Leader Guard, then God knows how soft the rest of them are. Some of the pub windows were smashed but then we heard sirens wailing in the distance and we had to get off. It was a disappointing end to the day. I really expected better from the "elite" street-fighters of the BM.

As we made our way back to the rendezvous point, a vanload of Fronters started shouting abuse at us as they drove past. As often seems to be the way with these incidents, however, they got stuck in traffic a little further down the road, and the van was pounced upon with glee. Missiles and boots rained down on the bodywork and windows of the van as the Fronters cowered inside. The end result was a van that would need the services of a really good body shop to even remotely restore it to its original shape.

It had been a good day. We'd had a few pokes at the fascists, forced them to scurry about on the edges of town, and had for once taken no nickings. In addition we had made contact with a number of good anti-fascists. The cafe incident cemented our relationship with the London and Hatfield lads – who to this day are convinced they would have done us. We, of course, think differently.

I ought to mention Ian "Stig" Macintosh at this point. He was one of the original Squad lads from Salford who became very friendly with Mickey O'Farrell. Stig suffered from acute depression and ended up tragically taking his own life. He endured enormous personal conflicts which only a few people knew about, and which I won't detail here in respect to his family. Mickey and Roy Mc were closer to him than most, and they probably have a better idea than I do of the devils that were hounding him. Coupled with Stig's depression was a chronic drink problem that was causing a noticeable deterioration of his physical health, and his body was basically packing up. Stig was in a lot of pain, and his last few weeks were terribly sad. It was a crying shame to see him suffer, and I prefer to remember him with his mop of ginger hair and little chunky legs chasing fascists up the road.

At his funeral I remember Mickey saying that Stig had told him a few months before he died that he had been standing next to a workmate who was hit by a car and killed while they were digging up a road in Worsley. He said that drivers had just driven past and ignored them as he tried to flag them down. Stig felt that the minutes lost before an ambulance arrived may well have contributed to his friend's death.

Nobody seemed to give a damn, he thought. It was, felt Mickey, a factor in Stig's deteriorating depression. We all felt in some way that we had let Stig down. Maybe if we had spent more time with him, given him different advice, whatever.

I think Stig, throughout his short life, was really loved by many more people than he realised. We all miss him.

"Don't mourn. Organise," said Mickey at his funeral. It was a very moving day, and it brought us all closer together. It was a bond that for many years was very special, and a great sense of comradeship existed between us.

Leicester, 21 April 1979

In the build-up to the 1979 General Election, the NF announced that they were contesting 303 seats across the country. John Tyndall claimed that they were now "Britain's fastest growing political party", and it was predicted by some that the NF would beat the Liberals into third place. The NF were standing candidates in the Openshaw and Blackley constituencies in Manchester, as well as contesting seats in Bolton and Rochdale. The campaign in Manchester was very quiet, with both candidates keeping a low profile. No public meetings were organised in support of the two men and we started to get the feeling that they were running scared.

We leafleted and campaigned against the NF in the two seats without coming across them at all, and the general consensus was that these were just paper candidates put up for the election just to make up the numbers. There was a feeling in the Squad that it was all a bit of an anti-climax, and so when the NF announced that they were planning a national march through the centre of Leicester on April 21, a lot of the lads wanted to go down and try to stop them.

Leicester was considered something of a stronghold for the NF. They had a big, well-organised branch in the city, and had picked up close to 30,000 votes in the 1976 elections. Despite this, there was still considerable opposition to the march, and there were a lot of calls for it to be banned, given that it would be viewed as provocative in a town with a large Asian population. The Chief Constable of Leicester decided to let the march go ahead, however. He justified his decision by claiming that the NF had a democratic right to hold their march. What about the democratic rights of the many thousands of ordinary citizens of Leicester who didn't want their town centre polluted by race-haters?

The twenty-nine-seater coach we had used for Lewisham was again requisitioned, and we pulled out a good team for the trip, including quite a few new faces. On the way down to Leicester we stopped at a service station for a break. Half of our lot stayed on the coach, while the rest went for a scran in the self-service restaurant.

Fifteen of us walked into the restaurant and immediately saw a mob of twenty-five NF, including Sheepshagger, Scotty and a load of others from Manchester. Also present were a number of Manchester SWP-ers who had arrived on the official coaches and were mingling uneasily with the NF. As soon as we walked in, it went off. It was mayhem. Kitchen utensils and crockery were being launched over the heads of the horrified SWP hacks, who ducked for cover under the restaurant tables. It was just about to develop into a major battle when the police arrived and restored order.

We charged back onto our coach cock-a-hoop. "Where the fuck were you lot?" we mocked the lads who had stayed on the bus. "We've just had it with Scotty and his boys."

We had also taken the opportunity to help ourselves to some free scran during the melee. As we shared out our spoils with the lads on the coach, we laughed and joked about the looks of horror on the faces of the local SWP leaders as they witnessed this display of "gratuitous thuggery and opportunist looting".

After another hour or so, we approached the outskirts of Leicester. Every coach approaching the city that day was pulled over by the police, and everyone on board was searched for weapons, including all the women on the ordinary ANL/SWP coaches. Fortunately they missed our cache hidden inside the battery compartment.

When we got off the coach we were shunned by the majority of SWP-ers, who by now viewed us as nothing more than an unruly rabble of troublemakers. In contrast, the few local Asian kids who had turned up appeared to be relieved to see a crew who looked like they could handle themselves.

We met another half dozen lads who JP knew and started discussing what we should do. We didn't want to go on the main counter-demonstration against the march, judging that it was likely to be heavily policed, making any kind of protest ineffective. We all had maps, and JP and Coops looked at the route of the march for a likely spot to ambush the Front. A car park beside the route looked ideal. It was shielded from the road by some large advertising hoardings, and had a ready-made supply of rubble from some demolition work. We decided to split into two teams, with one throwing the smoke bombs and flares at the march from behind the hoardings, while the other would charge into the front of the march, taking advantage of the panic and confusion caused by the missile bombardment.

I was in the car park with the first group. As we waited for the march to approach, we collected bricks and bottles and stored them behind the hoardings. Anything that could be picked up and thrown was added to the arsenal. We heard reports that there had been numerous clashes all along the route and that the police were struggling to keep the demonstrators and counter-demonstrators apart. The strength of opposition to the march meant that the NF and their police escorts had to reconsider their route and they were forced to take a short-cut to their destination. Fortunately, this still meant that they had to pass our ambush.

Drums echoed up and down the street as the NF drum

corps and the vanguard neared our position. We heard
shouting and chanting from anti-nazi protesters heckling the
marchers, and the whirr of a police helicopter circling overhead
added to the highly charged atmosphere. We tried our best to
keep cool and wait for the right moment to strike. There was
always a temptation to jump the gun at moments like these as
the adrenalin surge suddenly kicks in.

Over the top of the hoardings we could now see the Union
Jacks of the NF's Colour Party right opposite us. We were
moments away from launching our attack. We waited for
what seemed like an eternity before JP finally gave us the nod,
and for the next thirty seconds or so a barrage of bricks,
bottles, rubble and smoke bombs sailed over the hoardings
and rained down onto the heads of the marchers. The top of
the flagpoles disappeared from view as the Colour Party
wavered and broke ranks.

This was the moment we had been waiting for. JP gave the
signal to break away from our positions and take advantage of
the confusion to steam into the march proper.

"Right," shouted JP. "Everyone get into them now."

We charged out of the car park and into a side street that
brought us into the path of the march, which at this point was
in disarray. The attack had spurred others into action and the
NF were getting it from all sides. We steamed into the front of
the march, attacking the Colour Party and the drum corps.

The second team was meant to join in the attack at this
point but had got caught up in some earlier disturbances
between marchers and protesters. This meant we were a bit
light on the ground and didn't make as much impact as we
had planned. The Front rallied as they realised how few in
number we were and for a moment things looked a bit tricky.

The police moved in and started making lots of arrests,
turning their dogs loose on us. JP was bitten on the leg but
managed to get away. It was coming well on top and we were
taking quite a few nickings. No-one said anything but we all

knew it was time to get out the area. It was watch your own back time and every man for himself. I tagged along with a couple of lads and followed the back of the march at a distance. There was still some sporadic fighting, but I'd had enough for the day. When we got back to our coach we discovered that seven Manchester lads had been nicked during the course of the day; there were apparently eighty-seven arrests in total.

While we waited around outside the police station for the lads to be released, a minibus and carload of Fronters turned up and attempted to attack our coach. I was on board at the time but quite a few of the lads were in a nearby pub or were off getting chips. Fortunately there were still enough of us about to fend off the attack and, after a bit of a row, we chased them off. Their car got stuck in traffic and the driver panicked and stalled the engine. I caught up with it and started booting in the lights and windows. Some of the other lads joined in, kicking in the bodywork. Someone tried to drag the driver out of the car, but he eventually managed to start the engine and drive off.

The nicked Squad lads were eventually released at about 11 p.m. They were facing charges like threatening behaviour, which no-one regarded as being at the serious end of the scale, and they did not seem particularly bothered about it. When they appeared in court a few months later, however, they were hit with fines of £250 or more. These were the biggest fines we had heard of in those days. It was a massive amount of money when it was all put together, but we made sure that none of the lads had to put their hands in their own pockets. Collections were made and benefit gigs were organised to help pay the fines and court costs.

Two days after the Leicester fracas, I was in the Albert having a drink with Coops, Jill and Chrissy when we heard on the news that someone had been killed by the police on an anti-NF demonstration in Southall, West London. A few people had gone down from Manchester and for a while we were concerned that it was one of ours that had died. I began to feel guilty that I hadn't gone down. Coops did too, but it had been on a weekday and we couldn't get the time off work.

"Shit," said Coops, "the murdering bastards have killed one of ours."

"Yeah," I replied. "They're just as bad as the fucking NF."

We later learned that the person killed was Blair Peach, an ANL member from East London. He had been struck over the head by an illegally armed member of the police's tactical response unit, the Special Patrol Group (SPG). The SPG had lost control of both themselves and the situation that day.

Southall was an area with a large and highly organised Asian population that had grown in both size and confidence over the years. Unlike Leicester, where the Asian elders had persuaded the youth to stay off the streets, the youth of Southall were likely to respond aggressively to any provocation from the NF. The Front knew this, and decided to hold an inflammatory meeting in Southall Town Hall, which one member forecast would be "like the battle of Khyber Pass". NF tactics at the time were designed to stir up trouble in Asian and Black areas, so that the race issue could be pushed to the fore in elections.

In the event, only about fifty NF turned up at Southall, faced by more than 3,000 protesters. The SPG were hyped up, charging into the crowd with dogs and horses, swinging truncheons and home-made weapons at people. There were an incredible 750 arrests, with 342 people eventually being charged. Five days after his death, on 28 April 1979, 10,000 people marched through Southall to mourn Blair Peach and protest at his killing. Despite widespread public protests, no public inquiry has ever been held and no member of the SPG has ever been brought to justice.

The NF fared badly at the 1979 General Election. They lost all of their deposits and received an average of just 1.25

per cent of the votes cast in the 303 constituencies in which they stood. This was partly due to Maggie Thatcher's anti-immigration speech shortly before the election, during which she declared that English people felt that they were being "rather swamped" by people of "an alien culture". The Tories also promised to repeal the Race Relations Act and placed a strong emphasis on law and order, which not only stole a lot of the NF's key policies but most of their votes as well.

Shirt of Red – Shirt of Blue

Following the collapse of their vote in the election, the NF split into a number of warring factions, and disappeared off the radar for a while. The big marches and rallies of the previous few years were put on hold as the fascists struggled to come to terms with the scale of their electoral defeat. The NF was in disarray, and went through a period of in-fighting which saw membership falling as it split and split again. The divisions were so fractious that at one stage there were four separate NF groups, each claiming legitimate status as the heirs of British fascism. The most important of these factions was led by the NF's ex-chairman, John Tyndall, and was to re-surface and gain prominence many years later as the British National Party (BNP). Martin Webster was hounded off the nazi scene altogether as more rumours surfaced about his homosexual affairs with young party members.

It has been argued that the self-destruction of the NF following the 1979 election came about solely because their abysmal electoral performance shattered the myth that they were a party on the up. It is true that the Tories had played the race card and stolen a lot of NF voters, but this alone couldn't account for the vicious in-fighting that followed. I firmly believe the physical and political pressure that the ANL put them under during this period had also taken its toll on morale. Virtually every NF march and meeting had been challenged in the run-up to the election, and many of them had been stopped. It was crystal clear that the NF were not winning control of the streets, and the realisation of that hurt them as much as their poor performance at the ballot box.

Unfortunately, the central committee of the Socialist Workers' Party decided that the Anti-Nazi League should also wind down its activities following the election, claiming that it had achieved its purpose because the NF were no longer a direct political threat. We began to notice that much less space in *Socialist Worker* was being devoted to the ANL, as the SWP decided that they were no longer interested in investing time and energy in what they saw as a defunct campaign.

They were forced into a re-think during 1980 when it became apparent that the fascist threat was far from finished. The NF may have fragmented, but its remnants were nastier, more vicious, and less inclined to wait patiently for an electoral break-through to achieve their aims. In addition, it was becoming clear that the British Movement (BM) was embarking on a campaign to recruit young working-class kids from the music scene and the football terraces. The BM was growing at an alarming rate during this period, despite being much more openly nazi than the Front.

The BM was a hard-line racist and nazi organisation which made no bones about its adherence to the political philosophy of Adolf Hitler. Its leader was the "Wirral Milkman", Michael McLaughlin. He had taken over the reins from Colin Jordan, who had been forced to resign after being arrested for stealing women's panties from a branch of Tesco. McLaughlin's father was a veteran of the International Brigades and a life-long socialist and Irish republican who was left broken-hearted by his son's political allegiances.

McLaughlin was a dour, uncharismatic leader. He was off-hand and pompous in his dealings with others, but he was also a meticulous and painstaking organiser. Under his guidance the BM geared its propaganda towards a young, white, working-class audience. It numbered about 2,000 members at this time, most of them unemployed skinheads looking for easy scapegoats and victims.

The ANL was revived nationally in November 1980 to deal with the growing threat of violence from the BM and the various NF splinter groups. We welcomed this apparent change of heart from the SWP leadership, and threw ourselves into the fray with renewed vigour, eager to drive the final nail into the fascist coffin in Manchester.

One of the strategies that we launched was a campaign around Old Trafford and Maine Road football grounds. The BM and NF were making themselves busy on the terraces at various grounds around the country, and we knew that we had to isolate any fascist presence at United and City before it was too late. Reds Against the Nazis leafleted Old Trafford on numerous occasions, with Pat Crerand, an ex-Celtic and United player, coming out on several occasions to help hand out leaflets. He also spoke at a couple of meetings we organised. Fascists have always had a hard time at United, and there was little opposition to the leafleting sessions.

Blues Against the Nazis (BAN) had a tougher time of it, and their arrival on the scene wasn't exactly greeted with universal approval. The City NF boys were well dug in at Maine Road, and had previously leafleted the ground themselves. The dozen or so BAN leafleters came under attack by the NF on the first occasion they turned up and were hard pushed to defend themselves. There were no Squad members in BAN, and in all honesty they were a bit lightweight for the job. I think we have to hold our hands up and admit that we made a serious mistake on this occasion. One of the women who was leafleting received a serious injury to her eye from an NF supporter's knuckle-dusted fist, and a couple of others received less serious injuries. The brave individual who assaulted the woman was forced to go on the run to Birmingham following this attack, and didn't dare to show his face in Manchester for well over a year. I hear that these days he is a committee member of a City supporters' club in the north of Manchester.

At the next home game, we beefed up our numbers a bit, taking about twenty over to Maine Road, including several Squad members. I always felt a bit of a fraud turning up at Maine Road to hand out leaflets, but BAN was short of numbers and there was no going back now that we had started down this particular path. The NF attacked the BAN leafleters again – only this time, after receiving a tip-off, members of City's black firm, the Kool Kats, steamed into the NF, chasing one leading member into City's souvenir shop and giving him a right kicking as the shop workers looked on horrified.

The Kool Kats had generally not bothered about the presence of NF lads on the terraces alongside them up until that point. "We're all City together," was the mantra used to justify the situation, but on this occasion a couple of the more sympathetic lads who were in contact with us decided that enough was enough. It was a pivotal moment in the situation at Maine Road.

The intervention of the Kool Kats signalled the death knell for the NF at Maine Road and their influence on the terraces went into almost terminal decline thereafter. They were still about on match days, and on occasions crawled out of the woodwork to make a nuisance of themselves, but their days of strutting around like they owned the place were over. These days, lads like Rodney and his mates are amongst the top boys at City, and they are well and truly behind the anti-fascist cause. It's nice to see that things have changed in that respect.

CHAPTER THREE

Locked Up, Kicked Out

The Rochdale Nine

It was becoming increasingly clear during this period that the fascists had given up the ghost in Manchester and had retreated into the sticks and satellite towns like Rochdale, Bolton, Stockport and Oldham. They made a few incursions into the city centre but were always looking over their shoulders.

During this quiet period I decided to try and sort out my personal life. A future as a fishmonger was not what I had in mind when I left school, so on the off-chance I wandered into Manchester Polytechnic one day in 1980 and got on a course. It was as simple as that. All of a sudden I was a student studying for a Diploma in Higher Education. I had never pictured myself as the student type but there I was on the first day of term walking up Oxford Road for my first lecture.

A couple of Squad members were students at the time and you would often bump into a few of the lads who were on the dole hanging around the Students' Union bar for the cheap beer. The first couple of months passed almost without incident, apart from one occasion when we steamed into a Dead Kennedys gig at the Students' Union to give some nazis a kicking after they were spotted throwing their weight around. We had previously warned the authorities at the Poly that there was a likelihood the gig would attract right-wing elements and had offered our services to help with security on the door.

The offer was regarded with some hostility and suspicion and was rejected out of hand. On the night, half a dozen of us hung around the area, monitoring the situation because some recent Dead Kennedys gigs had attracted the unwanted attention of right-wing skinheads.

Within a short while we clocked a number of dodgy types being allowed into the gig, and decided to take matters into our own hands. We walked straight past the Poly security and just steamed into a group of boneheads hanging around the bar. They were wearing BM insignia and were already starting to give it the big one.

It was all over very quickly; we gave them a right hiding. Afterwards we strolled out past the security, who stood there shaking their heads.

"Don't ever let them scumbags in here again," I told them, "or we'll do you as well next time. Got it?"

Later that same year, around December time, we heard that a student called Michelle Mole, from Littleborough, near Rochdale, was getting a load of grief from skinhead NF members up where she lived. She claimed that she had been receiving threatening phone calls and had been intimidated and jostled in the street, that sort of thing. Then one day we received an urgent message from her saying that she was in fear of her life and that she had been getting death threats posted through her letter-box. She also told of a number of threatening phone-calls claiming that the NF were going to come back that night and sort her out once and for all.

I managed to get hold of a van from the Poly, and did a ring around, trying to contact the rest of the Squad. We eventually rounded up nine lads who could make it at short notice. We hid a number of weapons in the van, because we didn't have a clue what kind of situation we were heading into, nor what numbers we might be facing.

On the evening itself, two or three Squad members didn't

show up on time. JP thought we looked a bit lightweight and asked me what I thought.

"Well there's a couple of lads in the Students' Union who might be a bit useful," I told him.

"I think we're going to need them," said JP. "See if you can get hold of them."

I went over to the Union bar and had a quick word with these lads. They were sound about it, and with no more said we were ready to go.

We had been given Michelle Mole's address, and we had nearly reached the estate where she lived when we saw a young skinhead coming from the direction of her house.

"Stop the van," JP shouted. "Let's have this little shithouse."

Mark, who was driving the van, pulled over, and three of us piled out, and bundled the skinhead into the back of the van for questioning.

"Think you're brave picking on women do you ?" I asked him.

"What's going on," he replied, shaking in his boots. "Let me go. Please let me go."

JP pointed to the NF badge on his jacket. "So what's this all about?" he asked.

"It's just a skinhead badge. It doesn't mean anything. I'm not NF honest."

We drove out of the area and questioned him some more, and although he admitted knowing some NF members, he claimed he wasn't really involved with them. He denied all knowledge of any campaign against this Michelle Mole, and because we had no real proof against him we were slowly coming around to the idea of letting him go. Just then a police patrol car pulled up in front of the van. Someone who spotted us pushing the skinhead inside had reported it to the Old Bill.

They questioned everyone for a while, and for some reason the skinhead went along with the story that everything was okay. I don't know if the police were completely convinced of our innocence, but they let us go on our way anyway, and as soon as we got around the corner we pushed the skinhead out of the van.

"Keep your mouth shut," Coops told him. "We've got your address and if you say anything we'll be back."

Apparently the skinhead then walked straight around the corner and flagged down a second patrol car, telling them that he had in fact been held against his will. The police then got a couple of vans and another patrol car sent to the area, and we were spotted, stopped and questioned again. This time they searched the van and found the bundle of weapons in the back, and the whole lot of us were arrested.

We were put in police vans and taken down to Rochdale police station. While waiting to be taken to our cells, I suddenly realised that I still had an iron bar in my coat. I took it out without anyone noticing and put it underneath a bench. Unfortunately it started rolling down a bit of a slope and ended up under JP's feet. He didn't want to be lumbered with it and kicked it back up the slope. It reached me and started rolling back down towards JP again. It had just reached a lad called Brian Braudley when the police noticed it rolling around, and he ended up taking the rap for it.

The police kept us in the cells overnight so that we could go up before a special magistrates court the following morning. It was pretty grim in the cells, but while we were banged up we had a chance to discuss the situation. A couple of the lads we had press-ganged from the Students' Union bar were really worried and I can't say I blame them, but people like Coops and JP were a bit more laid back and philosophical about the nickings.

"We had a good run," remarked JP, "but our luck was bound to run out eventually."

"We were getting too cocky," I agreed.

"Yeah," said Coops, "but as long as everyone sticks together we'll be all right."

Everyone agreed that the best thing was for us all to keep to the same script whatever happened. I think everyone felt better after the chat and we all eventually got our heads down. The next day we were taken to the court and charged with kidnap and possession of offensive weapons. Bail was granted on condition that we were not to come within three miles of Rochdale, nor to make any contact with the skinhead.

Harrogate

I knew I faced a lengthy prison sentence if convicted, and was tempted to take a back seat for a while, but fascist activity did not stop just because I was up on charges. Far from it.

There was an on-going campaign in Harrogate, Yorkshire, involving a lecturer called Andrew Brons, who just happened to be chairman of the National Front at the time. Students at the Harrogate College of Further Education understandably didn't want to be taught by a nazi, and started agitating to have him removed. We went over to Harrogate a number of times to assist them, and along with a number of other people, including a large group of Asian youth from Bradford, we scored some notable successes against the NF.

Les had recently been sacked from his job as a coach driver, and we no longer had the option of his twenty-nine-seater. Fortunately I now had some influence at the Students' Union, and managed to persuade the Poly to pay for a coach to take us over the Pennines for the first big demonstration, planned for 24 June 1981.

We filled the fifty-three-seater coach with a mixture of Squad lads and students and arrived in Harrogate at about midday. The plan was for a march through Harrogate which would focus attention on Brons, and force the authorities to kick him out. We heard that there had been some skirmishing with the NF earlier in the day when the march was assembling, and so we decided to get the Squad together and go for a mooch around.

The town was quiet and we had more or less decided to give up when someone ran over to say they'd seen some NF outside a pub near a kind of village green. We charged over there and spotted fifteen boneheads hanging around near a pub in the middle of a tourist area of quaint little craft shops and souvenir stalls. The NF were well outnumbered but were game for the row and there was a pitched battle on the village green as shoppers and tourists ran for cover. Flower beds were trampled underfoot and crushed by bodies being kicked all over them as running battles disrupted the peaceful lunchtime scene. Numbers were in our favour and it was a case of two or three onto one. Every time I went to hit a Fronter there were a couple of lads already on him, which was a bit frustrating. The police came screaming into the middle of the battle and started to make nickings. Roy Mc was one of the first arrested, and it was obvious that we had to make ourselves scarce. We got out the area as quickly as we could and rejoined the main demonstration. Another success on the day was achieved when a group of anti-racist skinheads snatched a "National Front Skins" banner from under the noses of the NF. It was set alight to loud cheers at the rally afterwards.

There were a couple of other times that summer when stuff went off in Harrogate, and Manchester lads were involved on more than one occasion. I was starting to get a bit more cautious by now and didn't travel as much with the court case looming, but I was happy to hear about the lads' adventures when they got home.

One story recounted with much hilarity concerned the fate of an unfortunate individual known as Steve Gaunt, who acted as Andrew Brons's minder. Following scuffles, he found himself handcuffed to a lamppost after being arrested. He was then attacked by anti-fascists. Years later Gaunt went off to fight for the Croatians during the Balkans war but returned to good old Blighty a few years later minus one of his legs.

In the Dock

The case against the nine of us arrested in Rochdale was due to be heard at the crown court in Manchester on 7 December 1981. We had all stuck together and intended to plead not guilty to both charges, but our case was weakened when Michelle Mole made a statement that dropped us right in it. After the court case, Ms Mole disappeared without trace and was never seen or heard of again. We were never able to prove it of course, but we had a strong suspicion that we had been set up by the police or Special Branch.

A few days before the trial date, our lawyers called a case conference where we were told that we could be facing up to five years inside if we were found guilty of the kidnap charge. We were then told that the prosecution were prepared to offer us a deal in which the kidnap charge would be dropped if we all pleaded guilty to the offensive weapons charge.

It was a difficult decision, but in reality we had no choice. There was a good chance that we could have beaten the kidnap rap but we could not escape the fact that the police had found an array of weapons in the van with our fingerprints all over them. After putting our heads together we agreed to the deal, hoping that our guilty pleas would be taken into account during sentencing.

On a bitterly cold day in early December, I arrived at Manchester Crown Court to await my fate. Outside the court, the father of the young skinhead was having a right go at the prosecution brief. He had just heard that the kidnap charge was going to be dropped and was absolutely livid. Fuck you, I thought, your son's a little racist scrote who was lucky he didn't get a right fucking hiding. My family arrived in court a little later. They were quite optimistic about the possible outcome of the case but I was prepared for jail, with six months being bandied about as the possible sentence.

We had been on bail for exactly a year and it was almost a

relief that the trial date had finally arrived. Due to an unfinished murder case, the barrister we had appointed to represent us was unable to attend on the day, although as we were now pleading guilty it was felt that this would not be such a big loss.

We were wrong. The barrister who stepped in to defend us was a right clown who couldn't have done a better job if he had been the prosecution brief. The day went badly for us, and I began to think that we would be lucky if we got only six months. We were given bail overnight for Judge Gerard to see the probation reports, and no doubt consider his sentencing. This was seen as a good sign by a few of the lads, but I knew that we were still going down, regardless of this apparent show of compassion.

That last night at home was hard and I wished that we had been weighed in earlier. I went to bed at about 2 a.m. but still couldn't sleep; in fact I was so nervous that I couldn't even face the fry-up that my mam made me in the morning. The last meal of a condemned man, and it ended up in the dog. There was plenty of small talk among the lads once we were back in court, but it could not diminish the all-pervading atmosphere of gloom. I wanted to be quiet and be left alone. I knew my family were over in the public gallery but I found it hard to look across at them.

Judge Gerard's summing up was all too predictable. He referred to us constantly as a violent, sinister, organised and dangerous "Trotskyist hit-squad", and concluded by saying that custodial sentences were inevitable. JP was fingered as the ringleader, and the judge made a point of telling the court that if there was any violence involved then I was likely to be at its inception.

Gerard began his sentencing. Mick B was the first to be weighed in. He was a Squad member from day one, who despite his quiet demeanour was a reliable and handy lad. He got twelve months, and I knew then that I was facing fifteen or eighteen months due to having a previous conviction for a minor offence at an anti-NF activity in Bolton.

I ended up with a fifteen-month sentence, although the scream from my mam in the gallery made me think for an instant that I had misheard the old git and he had actually given me fifteen years! JP was fingered as the ringleader and was also given fifteen months, along with another lad called Phil Pyatt. The rest got twelve months, except for a lad called Paul H who, because of his age, got only six months.

We were gutted at the length of the sentences but at that point you just have to accept the inevitable and get on with it. None of us had been inside before, and although we liked to think of ourselves as tough and streetwise, we were all a bit apprehensive about what lay ahead. We agreed that if we got any shit while we were inside then we should all stick together, a point that was driven home more forcefully after a prison officer in the holding cells started making veiled threats. "You boys think you're hard," he sneered, "but you're in for a nasty surprise when you get to Strangeways. A lot of people have heard about what you did, and they don't like it."

Prisoner M93794

The first part of our sentence was served in Strangeways, and the first face I saw as I was led through the door for processing was that of Brian Baldwin, who was not only local chairman of the Prison Officers' Association but was a member of the British Movement and was the northern organiser of the League of St George. He had also at various times been in the NF and BNP.

"Fucking hell," I whispered to JP. "This bloke's going to make our lives a nightmare."

"Don't worry about it," he answered, "we're his worst dreams come true as well."

"What do you mean?" I asked him.

"Well if we get any shit in here, we know where he lives, and the lads on the outside will pay him a visit," said JP quietly. "He knows that, and he knows we know that."

JP seemed confident enough, and if it was good enough for him it was good enough for me. Baldwin never spoke to us more than he absolutely had too, but he did look us in the eye and hold our gaze, as if to say, I'm still the top dog in here.

I was given a prison number, which I can still recall to this day – M93794 – and was sent to the clothing board for my uniform. I immediately rejected the first outfit they gave me and insisted on clothes that actually fitted me. I'm a tall lad but I would have needed to be the size of the Jolly Green Giant to fit that particular set of clothes.

A couple of dodgy screws did make an attempt to set up me and JP while we were in Strangeways. They started spreading rumours that we were nonces, and that we were into kidnapping little boys. A black lad called Danny told us that they had been putting it about that they would turn a blind eye if we got a hiding, and had bribed a con into having a go at us. Danny frightened off the con when he got word of the plan, and that was the end of that.

Eventually we were all allocated to different prisons around the North-West. Some of the lads went to HMP Wymott, near Leyland in Lancashire, while Phil Pyatt and I ended up in Haverigg in the Lake District. I was put in a cell with Kev Turner, a notorious nazi from the North-East. I couldn't believe it. The first person I had met in Strangeways was a BM organiser and now my cellmate was an NF organiser and singer in a nazi skinhead band called Skullhead. I was half-expecting to walk around the corner and bump into Rudolph Hess.

I think the screws were hoping it was going to kick off between me and Turner, but we were wise to their plans, and there was an uneasy truce for most of the duration of our little holiday together. Turner was smaller than I expected him to be and certainly not as tough looking as the photo I had seen of him in *Searchlight*. He had a tattoo of a Doc Marten boot on the side of his face that looked a bit like a sideburn, and made his face look lop-sided. He was reasonably intelligent, and there were times when I thought I was getting through to him when we occasionally talked about politics, but he had an image to uphold and he couldn't really be seen to be softening up.

Haverrig was a 'Category C' prison. It was a former RAF training camp, built in the 1930s or '40s, and had been used for German POWs in World War Two. It had lifers at the end of their sentences and guys in for driving while disqualified. Phil and I took the advice of other cons about keeping your head down, not to get involved in any wheeling and dealing and never to steal from a fellow con. With the vast majority of prisoners being burglars and thieves, pad thefts were a continual problem and I was robbed a few times by low-life scum. However the penalty for stealing from somebody's cell was summary and brutal, often resulting in broken limbs and even slashings. Bullying was a problem. Several prisoners used joeys to fetch and carry for them. Turner had a couple of them to run his errands. I felt sorry for them but I didn't interfere even when I saw some really bad cases of bullying.

One incident really sickened me. A young lad who was skivvying for Turner wanted out of the weaving shed, or monkey shop as it was nicknamed, because it was "doing his head in". The only way out was if you were unable to do the job physically. Turner offered to break his arm so that he could get a medical discharge. The lad was not too bright and agreed. So while Turner held his arm down, another con smashed it with a tubular steel bed-end. It broke so badly that the bone compounded. After that I thought Turner would never be any good and stopped trying to have any meaningful discussions with him.

Phil and I struck up friendships with a couple of cons, in particular Frankie, a tough little Glasgwegian in for armed robbery, and Dakes, an ex-squaddie from Ellesmere Port who shared our billet. I tried to make the best of our time inside. I went to the gym as much as possible and got on the prison football team. The physical training instructor was a sound guy and I think he had some sympathy with us. In a game against a local team (we played all our games at home) I came on as a sub when the score was poised at 1–1 and scored an absolute purler of a volley. The PI was ecstatic as the other team were the nick's biggest rivals and he took great pleasure in putting one over on them. You had to be careful though; you did not want to appear to be too friendly with the screws or you might be considered a grass.

My family were great. They wrote to me often, as did hundreds of other people, many of whom I didn't even know. Their letters were a continual source of encouragement. I also read a lot of books and I suppose I benefited educationally while inside, having plenty of spare time to read and study.

The only bit of trouble I had was with this squeaky-voiced so-called hardcase from Wigan. I worked in the canteen and one day he accused me of stitching him up at the servery while I was dishing out chips. With a screw looking over my shoulder to make sure you didn't give anyone too many it was a difficult job to do and nobody wanted to do it.

"Give us some more fucking chips, wanker," he mumbled, being careful not to let the screw hear his threat. I went to put a few more on his plate but the screw stopped me and I shrugged my shoulders.

"You fucking wanker," he added, "I'm going to do you."

Now he was one of these bodybuilder types and I must admit I was a little scared. Shit, I thought, all over a handful of chips. I wondered what to do. Frankie said I had to front him otherwise he would make my life a misery. It was not policy to go mob-handed or to use weapons when sorting out these types of issues, so he advised me to go to his cell and confront him. Frankie said that if I was getting too badly battered he would jump in and stop it, but added that he could not directly get involved as it would make me look like a shithouse who couldn't fight his own battles. This was not the advice I wanted to hear and I wished I had another route out of the problem, but I knew I would have to do it this way if only to save myself from accusations of cowardice.

I came off duty and met up with Frankie. He said he would wait in the corridor outside this guy's pad. As I went into the block I was shaking and I was also aware that there were other cons who suspected something was afoot. I walked over to this guy's pad and looked in. There he was, sat on his bed, taking his T-shirt off over his head. Fucking hell, I thought, what an opportunity, and launched myself at him in a frenzy. Somewhere along the way I also caught him in the bollocks with a boot and he yelped, then gasped, trying desperately to catch his breath.

"I've had enough," he squealed, and I shouted at him, "Well don't fucking give me grief over a few lousy chips, you twat."

I was a relieved man as I came out of the cell, and I'm sure people were shocked to see me emerge unscathed. "Nice one," Frankie said. "You won't get any more grief out of him."

The geezer ended up in the prison hospital, as my lucky shot in the nuts had really fucked him up. According to one of the hospital orderlies, one of his bollocks had swollen up like a grapefruit and the other one had shrunk to the size of a pea. I heard later that he was inside for robbing an old lady's house, and felt even better about doing him.

While all this was going on inside, a campaign was launched by people on the outside to raise money to help with travel costs for visits, family expenses and hardship caused by the loss of a breadwinner. The fund also made sure all the prisoners got a few little extras and luxuries. One of the lads inside dropped out of political activity and said he didn't want his name associated with the campaign, so although nine people had been convicted, it became known as the Rochdale 8 Defendants' Fund. Trade union branches, shop stewards' committees, numerous individuals and a variety of political groups and organisations made contributions and donations. Benefit gigs were held throughout the time we were inside, including one showcasing three of Manchester's top reggae bands. UB40 donated autographed LPs for a raffle.

Unfortunately, while all this sterling work was going on, moves were afoot by the SWP leadership to oust the trouble-some "squadists". Now that the threat from the fascists appeared to have receded and they no longer needed the Squads to protect their meetings and paper sales, we were viewed as a political embarrassment. The working-class character of the Squads did not sit easily with the overwhelm-ing middle-class membership of the party, and the cultural gap tended to exaggerate differences between the two groups. It did not take much, a few minor incidents, and all sorts of grievances came to the surface. Before long, the grapevine was reverberating with all sorts of wild and ridiculous allegations of "squadist" behaviour, including drunkenness, assault, even burglary.

I am not saying that we were always angels and it is probably fair to say that there were a couple of minor incidents of unruly behaviour that did not help our cause, but invariably they were blown out of proportion by the time they had gone through the rumour mill. One incident at the SWP's annual Easter camp at Skegness perhaps sums up the mood at the time. During the event there was a fight between a Squad member and a roadie of one of the bands playing there. It was a stupid incident and, as it happens, not exclusively the fault of one side or the other. The reaction of some party members at the camp was one of near hysteria, with everyone who was

deemed to be a "squadist" being held responsible, even those
who were nowhere near the incident. The political climate at
the time meant that three people were expelled despite the
fact that only one of them was actually "guilty" of anything.
There was a climate that the squadists were fair game for any
accusation, no matter ludicrous, because we were viewed as
being politically expendable. It was a witch-hunt, with
everyone pointing accusing fingers at the us.

It was clear that the party hierarchy of Tony Cliff and
Duncan Hallas and the rest of the central committee wanted
us out of the SWP, and were busy engineering the conditions
that would enable them to accomplish this. John Deason, who
had set up the Squads in the first place, was allotted a central
role in undermining the "squadists". It was a clever choice,
because Deason was well liked and popular, and I personally
believe that there was some arm-twisting going on behind the
scenes. Most of the branch organisers immediately fell into
line behind the central committee, and accepted the party line
on "squadism" without question. Party hacks travelled from
branch to branch spreading the word, and the majority of the
SWP membership blindly accepted it.

The Rochdale incident was the final straw for the SWP.
They were embarrassed by the whole thing and disowned us.
Never mind that we had gone out there to help this person
fight off an attack by NF skinheads. Never mind that we had
been jailed by the State for our efforts, and never mind the
fact that the SWP were supposedly committed to overthrowing
the very same system that had locked us up. It was more a
case of "how do I explain this in the staff common room
tomorrow?" and "prison is probably the best place for them."

The SWP Central Committee even set into motion their
"control commission", which was basically a kangaroo court
set up and run by themselves to deal with the "squadist
problem". It was a farce. The control commission was basically
used to rubber-stamp central committee decisions and make

everything appear kosher and above board. Various individuals were summoned to appear before the commission and forced to go through the humiliating rigmarole of defending themselves against some ridiculous accusation or other. It was nothing more than McCarthyism under another name.

I received my expulsion letter from the SWP while I was still in prison. I had not even been given the option of defending myself before the control commission, although I don't suppose it would have made any difference. I had had an SWP "Red Fist" tattooed on my arm the day before receiving my letter, which pissed me off no end. JP was expelled at the same time, alongside several other members of the Rochdale 8. A lot of Squad members on the outside also received expulsion orders during this period and a lot more resigned in protest. No doubt the SWP and the Left as a whole believed that they had seen the last of us and the comfortable middle-class game of left-wing politics could now carry on as before without all these ruffians stirring things up.

They were in for a shock, because while we were inside serving the remainder of our sentence, we started to hear about a new organisation called Red Action. None of us on the inside knew what the score was with this new group, but we grasped that it was formed by a number of people who had either left or been expelled from the SWP and who wanted to carry on the fight against the fascists. The emergence of Red Action coincided with the winding up of the ANL, which came to a faltering and inglorious halt sometime during 1982. For many of us it was the end of an era, but also the beginning of a new and exciting period in our lives.

Red Action was formally launched at a meeting in London in January 1982, although it had been discussed and formulated for some months prior to that. Apart from the working-class character of its membership, its emphasis on internal democracy and a willingness to physically confront the fascists, there was very little to differentiate Red Action politically from the SWP. This was understandable in the early stages of the organisation I suppose, because for practically everyone involved, the SWP had been the sole provider of their political experiences.

I was released from prison in October 1982, after serving ten months and one day. I was the last of the Rochdale 8 to be released, as I had lost a day for a trivial breach of prison rules. People on the outside organised a big party for me which was DJ'd by Mick Hucknall, later of Simply Red fame. I was obviously pleased to be out and really enjoyed my first few days of freedom. Prison was bad but not as bad as I had expected. I suppose it was a positive life experience, and one that has made me a stronger person, although I do regret the upset that it caused my family.

I immediately joined Red Action. They were already at the forefront of the fight against fascism, and were welcomed with open arms by many of those previously involved with the Squads. It was our own organisation and we set our own agenda. Those that weren't with us were not necessarily against us, but to all intents and purposes were irrelevant. We felt we could now concentrate on the job in hand without the worry of being stabbed in the back. We didn't have the resources of the SWP, nor the political know-how, but we had loads of commitment and enthusiasm. Red Action had members in Manchester, London and Hertfordshire, as well as a smattering of individuals around the country. The geographic spread of its membership matched almost exactly the areas where SWP members had been expelled for squadism.

A couple of the lads who had been jailed didn't handle it to well, and basically dropped out of political activity, although they were replaced by a number of new lads who had come on board. We still had a strong and militant set-up in Manchester, which was a legacy of all the good work we had done previously in fighting the NF. Denis, Greg, Mikey and Dessie were all hard lads, but had politics as well, and through them we began to cement relationships with a lot of black lads from Moss Side and Hulme.

JP however, eventually decided to call it a day. He was initially enthused by the setting up of Red Action, but became disillusioned by the lack of impetus and progress made by the Socialist Federation, an umbrella group of left-wing organisations of which Red Action was a member. The purpose of the Federation was to create unity among some of the smaller left-wing groups on issues like anti-fascism, but it eventually succumbed to ego and in-fighting. JP's domestic life had been screwed up by prison as well. He was one of the few married men in the Squad, and was under pressure from his wife to keep his nose clean. He had also lost his job as a lecturer and was no longer able to teach, although he did get some sort of "advice worker" type job shortly afterwards in Liverpool. After that finished he moved up to Scotland in 1985 and as far as I know is still up there.

Coops also dropped out of the scene, and over time most of the other Rochdale 8 lads went their separate ways too. It was sad to see them go, but the influx of new faces more than made up for those who had left. I got my place back at the Poly, and was now studying a politics and history degree. I had lost none of my enthusiasm for anti-fascist politics, and was gaining a better understanding of wider political issues. Within a couple of years I was elected vice-president/external affairs of the Students' Union, and on the night of my election victory I met Linda, who was later to become the mother of my son. One spooky consequence of my election win was that I now had regular use of the same van that we had been nicked in a couple of years previously. That was a strange feeling.

The early Eighties were busy years and there were so many things going on that they all tend to blur into one. In particular, we always seemed to be travelling down to London for some demonstration or other. One event that sticks in my mind is when about fifteen of us, a mixture of Manchester and London lads, were guarding a load of equipment in Hyde Park prior to a march. The particular cause that was being promoted that day is lost in the fog of memory, but it was a pleasant day and no-one really anticipated any mither from the fascists. That was until someone spotted a team of about seventy lads gathering 100 yards away from where we were stood.

We knew immediately that they were not friendly and a couple of lads started breaking up the placards that had been dropped off earlier to try to make weapons out of the flimsy bits of wood they were attached to. The mob on the other side of the park started walking towards us, and then broke into a run. People were shouting, "Stand", and, "Don't run", and we formed a kind of semi-circle around the equipment in preparation for the onslaught. This was one of the few times that I was really scared. I thought we were going to get killed, or at least very seriously injured.

The mob advancing towards us were British Movement. I recognised a few faces from *Searchlight*, including "Mad" Matty Morgan, a member of the Leader Guard, who was heading straight in my direction. I think the BM were a bit freaked by the fact that we did not run away and you could sense that a lot of them were a bit dubious about things, thinking that it must be a trap or something. Just by standing our ground, we had sown a seed of doubt in their minds.

That did not stop Matty Morgan and a handful of others, who steamed into us. I hit Morgan over the head with a piece of wood as the two sides clashed, and there was a brief battle. We came out of this quite well, because most of the BM didn't get involved. The majority of them were backing away as police and anti-fascist reinforcements arrived on the scene. As the BM retreated they left behind one of their number who was lying injured on the ground. Several anti-fascists wandered over to give him a kicking as he lay there but I didn't have the heart for it. I was just relieved that I had survived unscathed.

Stockport, November 1985

Stockport's close proximity to Manchester meant that we often engaged in anti-fascist activity in the town over the years. In the early days it had a reputation as a bit of a NF stronghold, probably an overstatement but it did seem that they had a base there and on more than one occasion we had some pretty scary set-tos with their paper sellers, who were attempting to establish a regular Saturday morning sale in the town centre. This was shortly after the Piccadilly hit and the NF were probably still smarting from the hiding they got and were making a bit of a show. However the paper sale didn't last long, which may have been due also to the fact that most of their members were more interested in staying in the pubs getting pissed. The calibre of some of the local NF left something to be desired and it was evident that amongst them were low-life criminal elements who could hardly be described as shining examples of the master race.

The NF drank in a couple of pubs in the town whose landlords were known to be sympathetic. In particular there was the Bull's Head, where they held regular branch meetings, and of course there was the infamous Blue Waterfall nightclub, whose owner was an NF supporter and who made considerable financial donations to them. Its bouncers were NF and it was no secret that an unofficial race bar existed at these places, which made us even more determined to fuck them off. We were helped considerably in this regard when we were handed a detailed local membership list by a spurned ex-girlfriend of one of the NF organisers. He was also a bit of a Stockport County hooligan. Doubly sad.

We made life extremely difficult for them in Stockport and were slowly grinding them down. So it came as some surprise when they announced that they intended to hold a national rally in the town. We honestly thought they were taking the piss. There did not seem to be any reason why they should choose Stockport above anywhere else. The local NF for all we knew consisted of one sad wanker in Cheadle (now a BNP member who recently stood for them in the local elections). They may have had a few from Manchester still, but the old Blue Waterfall lot had long since disappeared and the NF were pretty much a spent force in the town. I mean what did they do? No paper sales, in fact no public profile whatsoever, so we knew that the march would basically be about bringing a bunch of out-of-towners from their strongholds in London and Leeds into Stockport for a row.

We knew the SWP would organise a picket of the meeting as usual, but we were preparing our own reception for the NF which would involve more than standing behind lines of police chanting slogans. As well as all the new faces that had come in over the past couple of years, we had recently made links with some young black kids involved with City's Young Guv'nors football gang. Carl S had actually approached me wanting information about the NF rally, and we hit it off even though I was United. A few of the SWP lads – Dundee Dave, Corrigano and Killy Phil – had also decided to swerve the picket and join up with our lot. They were all Scottish lads who had been around during the early Squad days and had been supportive and friendly during the expulsions over the Rochdale 8 incident. However, they had remained loyal to the SWP despite having some reservations over our treatment.

Most of the former Squad lads who were still active in Manchester were now in Anti-Fascist Action (AFA), which had been launched at a meeting in the Conway Hall in London on 28 July 1985. This was an umbrella group for people who still saw the need to fight fascism, but who didn't agree with all of Red Action's other politics. The founding statement of AFA declared, "We see the need to oppose racism and fascism physically on the streets and ideologically."

On the day, we had a big turnout. I was campaigns officer at the Poly at that time and there were some very handy lads about, especially Nads and his pals from the Karate Society, who had turned up hoping to put some of their martial arts skills into practice (I had seen them train so I knew how dangerous they were). We had no real plan in mind, but as we had the numbers, our strategy was to avoid getting boxed in by the Old Bill, keep out of sight as much as possible but be near enough to move if any NF were sighted.

The SWP contingent had already allowed themselves and their placards to get hemmed in at the Town Hall by the Old Bill. This swallowed up valuable police resources and at least allowed us a bit more freedom to move about. I had very little time for the SWP following the expulsions but I had to admit that there were fringe benefits to be gained from what we called the "yah boo brigade".

With spotters doing all the pubs and the usual places, we felt it was just a matter of time before the NF showed up. As was normal practice on events like this, people were also assigned to watch out for coaches and minibuses coming in off the motorway. We also monitored the railway station for any sign of them arriving by train, as it was quite central and an obvious place to use as a rendezvous point.

I ended up at the station at various times during the morning and I must admit that as I walked up and down the platform I felt a bit like a POW from the film *The Great Escape*. I was thinking of the scene where they had escaped from the camp and were waiting around in their various guises trying hard not to let on to their fellow escapees. All that was missing was a Gestapo agent in a long black leather coat, Luger in hand, shouting, "Papers, papers."

Our spotters hadn't seen any fash in the town centre pubs nor any sign of them in vehicles. However a spotter at the station had seen a couple of dodge-pots hanging around. They weren't boneheads but they appeared to be carrying bags containing bundles of newspapers. I went over to the station for a closer look as I was pretty good at recognising faces. I immediately recognised one of them as Leeds NF.

"We're on," I said to Alan, who had spotted them first. "Stick close to this lot, and try to start a conversation with them, but be careful they don't suss you."

"Okay Steve," he said, as he walked off casually towards the two Fronters.

I found the rest of the lads in a pub and passed the word to a couple of other lads that two NF had been identified and that we should expect the station to be used as a rendezvous. Dundee Dave added that he had seen a couple of cars that he suspected might contain Fronters drive by the station approach. They had parked up near the town hall, which was only a matter of yards from the station. A couple of AFA lads were sent up in vans for a nosey and the rest, about thirty all told, wandered up there on foot. As we approached the town hall, I suddenly saw a group of fifteen or more NF-ers walk past the SWP picket and head directly towards us.

"Fuck me," I said, "where did that lot come from?"

"Who cares?" shouted Greg, "Let's just have 'em."

The Fronters clocked us straight away, and before we had a chance to get into them, they were already on their toes. They were chased down the station approach, running for their lives, with a police dog-handler in tow. Once inside the railway station, they started to barricade themselves in the glass-fronted ticket office, with only the Dibble and his dog left outside to fend off the anti-fascist mob. We were intent on getting at the Front supporters, and although there was only one man and his dog guarding the fascists he was doing a good job keeping us at bay. Several of the lads were bitten, and the dog was going berserk as his handler struggled to keep control. I had to laugh when I saw the Front pretending that they wanted to break out of the ticket office to have a go back at us. They were shitting themselves, but were kidding on that it was the dog-handler that was actually holding them back.

Some of the lads found some bricks in a nearby skip and started throwing them at the ticket office, but they bounced back off the toughened safety glass, as did a couple of smoke bombs hurled at the station. Through the clouds of billowing red smoke, I noticed that there was another door into the ticket office from inside the station, and shouted for some of the lads to follow me. About half a dozen of us skirted around the back of the station and attempted to kick in the glass door behind them. The Fronters were terrified; they were now getting it from both sides. I could make out a couple of NF big hitters from London. Eddie Whicker, who is well game, was in there and if anyone was going to be a handful it was Eddie. He was a hard bastard and would go down fighting. We didn't know it at the time but Eddie was carrying an axe under his coat, for which he was later nicked.

Meanwhile, the dog-handler had come under a hail of missiles, and when his dog was hit over the head with a brick he decided to call it a day. Now that the Dibble was out the way the lads tried to break into the ticket office, but the station manager had locked and bolted all the doors. We were tearing our hair out in frustration. They were literally inches away from our clutches, and now they realised they were safe, they started giving it the big one even more. I was really pissed off. I knew that we could not afford to hang around much longer because I could hear the sound of police sirens approaching.

"Come on. It's time to go," someone shouted. "The Dibble are on their way."

We had just started to move off when I recognised the NF's Stockport organiser among the crowds of onlookers. He was walking towards us with the two fellas we had spotted earlier with bags full of papers. They were trying to sneak past us, pretending to be ordinary rail passengers, but it was their body language and lack of interest in the events going on all around them that gave them away as much as anything.

As they tried to sneak past us I tipped the lads the wink. "Here we are boys. It's Tricky Dicky."

We pounced on them before they had a chance to get away. Someone hit Dicky with a brick and he went down like a sack of spuds. The others fared little better as they too were battered to the ground.

As soon as the job was finished we got off quickly, running down the station approach towards the A6. The police had arrived in force and everyone was on their toes, but as we were making our getaway we bumped into four NF supporters sat in a spanking new Saab which was stuck at a set of traffic lights. They were not sure if we were friend or foe. Dundee Dave soon put them in the picture by jumping on the bonnet and kicking in the windscreen. Corrigano weighed into the car, kicking in its headlights while the rest of us attempted to roll it over. A flare and a smoke bomb were fired into the car, and at this point the driver put his foot down and sped off, clouds of red smoke streaming from its windows. It looked for all the world like a poor man's version of the Red Arrows.

Unfortunately a couple of lads were nicked as they fled from the incident, and the rest of us decided to make ourselves scarce. Some went up and joined the picket at the town hall, and I wandered off into the town centre for a while until the heat died down. About eighty members of the Front were eventually allowed to hold a short rally in a car park at the back of the town hall. We decided that we'd had a good day and retired to the Albert for the "post-match analysis".

There were a number of small-scale skirmishes between AFA and the NF in and around Manchester during the mid-Eighties but these became less and less frequent as the fascists finally deserted the city completely. There were still bits and pieces going on, especially in places like Rochdale and Oldham, and we knew we could not afford to be complacent because they could be up to their old tricks again in next to no time. We had to remain vigilant, and with this in mind AFA set up an anti-fascist hotline inviting people to phone in with details of racist attacks and fascist activity in Manchester, so that we could more accurately monitor the situation in the city.

AFA was also involved in defending Viraj Mendis, a Sri Lankan refugee who sought refuge in a church in Hulme after receiving a deportation order. The fash made a couple of threatening noises in his direction, but on the whole this was a quiet period, and despite all our efforts people started to drift away from anti-fascist activity. By the end of the Eighties there were no more than a handful of people keeping the flame alive.

CHAPTER FOUR

Secret Squirrels

Bugging the NF

One of the most important requirements in winning any war is good intelligence. Because we were outnumbered in terms of street-fighters both locally and on a national scale, anti-fascists had to operate in a similar way to a resistance movement working behind enemy lines. By that I mean we worked in a covert and secretive way, choosing when to hit and when to lie low. Intelligence in these circumstances was not an added bonus, it was essential, as the attack on the NF paper sale in Piccadilly had proved.

Our first few nuggets of information came in the late Seventies, ironically enough from within the offices of Manchester City FC. As I mentioned before, some of the NF's top lads were linked to City's firm, and via a contact in the club's official membership office we managed to obtain quite a few names and addresses of the City NF boys.

Another large chunk of information dropped into our laps sometime in 1980, when a drunken NF member started blabbing everything he knew to an incognito female Squad contact in the Clarence pub in Rusholme after a City home game. During the course of the conversation he blurted out the venue of the NF's regular branch meetings, the branch organiser's home address, as well as several phone numbers, among various other gems of information.

Wilko introduced us to a mate called Mick, who was a bit

of a gadget man. He was into CB radios and was always messing about with electronic equipment and whatever technological gizmo was on the market in those days. Mick had made up some matchbox-sized listening devices powered by a small camera battery, which he thought we might find useful. We tested one of these devices and it worked up to a range of a quarter of a mile. We now knew, thanks to the blabbermouth in the Clarence, that the NF had regular meetings in a pub on Deansgate, and so we made plans to put the bug in their meeting room and eavesdrop on them.

The NF met every second Sunday of the month in an upstairs room in the Pack Horse pub, at the Knott Mill end of Deansgate. The Pack Horse was also used on occasions by the SWP and other left-wing groups, and I'm sure the NF thought they were being ever-so-clever and sneaky using the same pub as their political opponents. Although the bug was very effective, it could not guarantee more than twenty-four hours continuous reception. This meant that we had to book the room above the Pack Horse for Sunday lunchtime, to ensure that the bug had enough power to monitor the NF meeting in the evening.

We booked the room under a moody name, got eight or nine lads to turn up so that it looked like a bona-fide meeting, and planted the device behind a curtain pelmet. We tested the bug again, and it worked a treat. Later, in the evening, a two-man surveillance team sat in a car watching the NF arriving at the pub. One was taking photos, the other had control of the radio, making sure it stayed tuned to the same frequency as the bug. A stand-by team of four lads were within easy reach in case there were any problems.

The NF turned up at 7.30 p.m. and we managed to get off a load of photos as they arrived. The bug was on ordinary FM wavelength, and we listened to the meeting on the car radio, recording it as we went along. After the meeting, we played the tape back to the rest of the lads, laughing our bollocks off as we listened to the Front meeting. We couldn't believe we had pulled off such a top blag and that our first venture into the field of covert activity had been such an unqualified success. What was even funnier was when I got a mention at the meeting, referred to as Fish-Face, a nickname that the NF used from my days in the fish market. I was Public Enemy Number One in their eyes, and from what they were saying I needed a fucking good kicking. I still have the tape of that meeting at home, and if they ever read this book they will know how we managed to seriously "annoy" them for the best part of that summer.

I began to develop more of an interest in intelligence gathering after this, and because a couple of the older anti-fascists in Manchester had links with *Searchlight* magazine I started to become more and more involved with them and the *Searchlight* team. *Searchlight* started life as an information network for anti-fascist activists in the mid-Sixties and began to publish a monthly magazine in the early Seventies. It exposed the nazi backgrounds of some of the key players on the far-right scene in the Seventies and Eighties and also investigated the gun-running activities of some fascist groups and their links with para-military organisations like the Ulster Volunteer Force. *Searchlight* commanded a lot of respect from anti-fascists and anti-racists at the time, and I felt very drawn to it.

Searchlight's main role in those days was to monitor the various fascist groups and provide the "anti" movement with intelligence and information which could be used to damage them. This might be achieved through exposure in the media or by passing the information on to groups and individuals best placed to use it. *Searchlight* has a network of intelligence gatherers both inside and outside the fascist movement that provides vital information on the fascists and their activities.

My initial involvement was in organising meetings for *Searchlight* speakers in Manchester. I then got involved in various networking projects, and became responsible for selling the magazine in Manchester. I became a member of the *Searchlight* team in the mid-Eighties and travelled extensively with colleagues to Scandinavia, Germany and a number of ex-Communist bloc countries, establishing contacts with various anti-fascist organisations. Although I no longer have a lot to do with the organisation, I still have good friends at *Searchlight* and admire much of the work they do.

The Bin Men

It is common knowledge these days that vast amounts of useful and potentially damaging information can be obtained by trawling through people's rubbish. Journalists have long used this method to pick up juicy scraps of information on showbiz stars and the like, and we weren't averse to using whatever methods we could to gain the upper hand on the fascists. We did the bins of a number of fascist organisers over the years, and the amount of information we gleaned was incredible. They never seemed to take even the most basic of security precautions and would often dump whole reams of internal documents and sensitive material in their bins.

The local NF organiser during the 1980s lived in Cheadle and through doing his bins we were able to follow very closely, and in intricate detail, the acrimonious split that was tearing the NF apart during those years. Some of the material we came across even enabled us to twist the knife on a couple of occasions, and help things along a bit.

Another bin we did was that of a certain far-right activist based in Ashton-under-Lyne, east Manchester. This character had been in the NF since the early Seventies and was heavily into Orange Order politics despite the fact that he was also a Catholic. The quality and quantity of sensitive information that this guy threw away was amazing. There was never any attempt to rip up and destroy documents and letters, and we picked up a lot of stuff that proved very useful to anti-fascists in Manchester.

We stopped doing his bins after we spotted a couple of blokes in dark clothing emerging from his alleyway one night carrying full black bin-liners. We didn't recognise them as fascists or anti-fascists, and I was convinced that they were either Special Branch or their MI5 cohorts. We had begun to notice that there had been a lot more gossipy stuff in the bins about certain left-wing activists allegedly being police informers, and I was convinced that they were planting stuff to cause splits in the left. I didn't like what we were getting into here, and I certainly didn't want to be a part of some spymaster's sneaky little games, so I drove off and left them to it. We had other fish frying in the pan in any case.

In the Belly of The Beast

During the late Eighties I was working at a community centre in Openshaw, a run-down area of east Manchester with more than its share of social problems. Part of my work was in the youth club, and although it was hard work at times I really enjoyed it. In particular there were two lads, Greg and Phil, who I took a liking to because throughout the time I was there, I never once heard them make a racist comment. Phil was into hip-hop, especially Run DMC, and I think that being racist flew in the face of the music he loved.

I talked to Phil and Greg a lot, and during one of our chats Phil mentioned that he had seen a programme a couple of nights before about a guy going undercover in the far-right in Germany. I had seen the programme myself and commented on the bravery of the guy, and the fact that he had done them an enormous amount of damage, possibly saving lives. Phil nodded in agreement and commented that it would be a great buzz to go under cover. Both lads knew that I was involved in anti-racism but not the extent of my involvement, and I had never mentioned *Searchlight* to them.

On my way home that night I thought a lot about what Phil had said, and I could not get the notion out of my head that Phil and Greg would be ideal BNP recruitment material. Both were young, neither had a left-wing history, and shaven-headed Phil was a bit of a hard-case. Perfect. I knew I couldn't do it though. It was ethically wrong. As a youth worker I had a responsibility to them, and couldn't deliberately put them into a potentially dangerous situation. All the same it was a difficult notion to put to the back of my mind.

The city council had plans to close the community centre down, selling off the land to a property developer, and I was re-deployed to another area. I was sad to be leaving a job that I really enjoyed and a couple of months later I went back to see some of the lads for a chat. They told me that Phil was in Strangeways after being arrested for joy-riding, and after giving it a bit of thought I wrote to him and arranged a visit.

Although not happy about being locked up, he seemed upbeat, and looked a lot fitter. We chatted for a while and then I mentioned that I was involved with *Searchlight* and asked him if he was still keen on the idea of going undercover. He was well up for it, and so for security reasons I stopped writing and visiting. Following his release a few months later we met up in Oldham with Mike L. We assured Phil that we were the only ones involved in the operation, and that word of his identity would not go beyond the three people in the room. *Searchlight*, who would lend a hand with any finances, would be aware of the fact that we had someone inside but would not know who he was. We also kept Greg in the dark, although I'm sure that he was aware something was afoot. On his release, Phil was sent to a probation hostel near Altrincham. Although not good news for Phil, it meant that at least we didn't need to set up a new contact address for him.

The different NF groups had more or less faded into obscurity by this time, and it was the British National Party (BNP) that was now the pre-eminent fascist group in the UK.

The BNP had grown in strength throughout the late Eighties due to an increased level of street activity based around their "Rights for Whites" campaign. What this boiled down to was marching into white, working-class areas and telling people that the blacks and the Asians were taking their homes and their jobs and that the Government and local councils were encouraging this process. It was crude but effective.

I think individual fascists tend to be quite pragmatic when it comes to supporting far-right groups and will basically jump on any passing bandwagon that still has four wheels firmly attached to the chassis. Therefore any group that has a modicum of success immediately attracts dis-illusioned individuals and activists to its cause, regardless of what particular brand of right-wing politics are being espoused.

The Manchester and Salford BNP branch operated out of a PO Box, but we decided to write to the national address in Welling, London. It was quite a few weeks before a letter arrived from the Manchester and Salford branch saying that someone would call around for a chat. Phil replied to the local box saying that as he lived in a probation hostel it might be a bit risky if they found out he was involved with the BNP and that he would rather meet away from the hostel. He received a letter a few days later inviting him to the next BNP branch meeting. Yes! I thought, we're in. A dangerous and exciting journey was about to begin in which ultimately we would unmask the Hitler worshippers, cemetery desecrators and race haters that infested Manchester BNP.

As a security measure, the BNP asked Phil to meet somebody outside the Brunswick pub, on London Road, at 7 p.m. on Sunday evening. If everything checked out okay, he would then be taken to the meeting. The following Sunday me and Mike L parked up just in sight of the Brunswick and watched as a guy in his mid-twenties met Phil outside the pub. They shook hands, chatted for a while, and then went inside. About twenty minutes later they emerged, walked around the corner and disappeared from view. I was not absolutely sure where they were going, but I had an inkling it was Mother Macs on Back Piccadilly. Although the landlord was Irish, I was aware that on Saturday afternoons Loyalist/ Orange Order types drank in there, augmented by a sprinkling of BNP supporters.

About an hour and a half later, Phil walked past us towards Oxford Road station as planned. The plan was that he should walk up to the station via the long flight of steps next to the Salisbury pub and then get into the back of our van which would be waiting in the station car-park at the top. He got in with a big grin on his face and began animatedly relaying what had happened at the meeting. "Hang on Phil," I said. "Let's take you for a curry, I need to write some of this stuff down." We headed for Rusholme and took a seat in the corner of a restaurant.

As we tucked into our papadoms, Phil recounted the evening's events, starting off with meeting the guy outside the Brunswick, who he said was called Austin and who came from Blackburn. He then gave me a brief overview of the meeting, including details of how many people attended, where they were from, what were the main topics of conversation, and planned activities. We then went over each aspect more closely, with me asking questions, trying to fill in the gaps from Phil's first recollection.

Phil was pretty good in all aspects and had even picked up a couple of names and phone numbers. He said that the organiser was a British Rail guard called Alan Payne who was a hardline racist, referring constantly to black people as niggers and coons. He said that there was also an elderly man present called Gordon who gave him a copy of *Holocaust News*, a paper whose sole purpose was to deny that six million Jewish people had been slaughtered by the Nazis in the concentration camps.

Phil reckoned that the Austin bloke was a bit odd, with a squeaky, almost camp voice. He was wearing a Ku Klux Klan T-shirt under his jacket and his pockets were stuffed full with stickers. There was a middle-aged couple who didn't say a word all evening, and a number of lads of similar age to him who were possibly new members. There was also a lad called Mark who seemed to be the main one pushing for more activity. He made appeal after appeal for people to stop watching *Coronation Street* and get off their backsides and leaflet their areas, sell more copies of their paper, *British Nationalist*, and generally be more active.

We already knew of some of the people that Phil mentioned, but this Mark character pricked our interest. We had suspected for some time that the BNP was running a two-tier operation, with a semi-respectable public face on show for elections and the like, but with a clandestine operation carrying out covert activities under the cover of this public front. This tier comprised of activists drawn from inside and outside the branch, with people brought into Manchester to lend a hand when necessary. The more we heard about this Mark bloke, the more we suspected that he was the man we needed to watch.

At the next meeting, Phil started befriending this Mark Jones character and it became clear during their chats that he was a hardline Jew-baiter. Within minutes of meeting Phil he was trying to persuade him to assist in collecting names and addresses of leading Jews in the city. He also asked him to go to libraries and check out voters' lists and to monitor the Jewish press for clues.

We were doing Alan Payne's bins at the same time as Phil was infiltrating the BNP, and putting together the information obtained through both these sources we started to realise that a campaign against Manchester's Jewish community was about to be launched by the BNP. It came as no surprise to learn then that Manchester BNP members were given leaflets and stickers to take into Jewish areas on the very same July weekend that the main Jewish cemetery in Manchester was attacked and seventy-two graves desecrated. Here was the proof that the BNP's two-tier approach was functioning along the lines we had suspected.

Through Phil we managed to get enough evidence to start naming names, and leaked various details to the press. The revelations about the BNP's anti-Jewish activities caused quite a stir, and the party started to internally combust as they went searching for the source of the leaks. Fortunately they were way off the mark and some other poor sod copped the aggro. Nevertheless it was time for Phil to pull out. He had caused the BNP considerable damage, with some members being forced to leave town only one step ahead of the law; others left because they felt things were getting out of hand, while some of the younger members were put off by all the nazi stuff.

Phil felt he had gone as far as he could go. The buzz was wearing off and being around these nutters had affected him, especially as he could see other young people being corrupted by the BNP. He felt guilty that he was in some way setting these kids up and so it was agreed that he should pull out. Through a contact we found Phil a flat, and also helped him with some money to buy furniture and other stuff. Phil was a tough little customer and was not worried about the BNP seeking revenge, but we were only a phone call away if he needed a hand. I personally don't think that the BNP will ever come after him, because even to this day they deny that they were ever infiltrated. Shortly after his adventures, Phil met a woman and moved in with her. I haven't seen him for several years, but respect to you mate, you were a diamond.

Wigan

I nearly came seriously unstuck in Wigan once, when in a moment of madness I decided to photograph and videotape an NF meeting in the town. We knew that the Front were making a big push in the Wigan/Bolton area and that they were hoping to recapture some of the ground they had recently lost to the BNP, so it came as no surprise when we learned that they were planning to hold a major rally somewhere in the town. Local contacts in Wigan turned up trumps with the date and time of the meeting, although they couldn't find out its exact location.

I drove up separately from the main anti-fascist contingent, having decided that I would concentrate in the main on surveillance. Although I was well known and therefore likely to be recognised by some of the old Manchester NF, most of them had dropped out by now or had joined the BNP, and I felt that I would probably get away without being recognised by any of the out-of-towners. The plan was to float about with my professional-looking camera and rigged-up press card and try and get as many pictures of the Fronters as possible.

About 150 anti-fascists swarmed into Wigan, taking over two pubs in the town centre close to the main railway station. Unconfirmed reports were circulating that the NF were planning to hold their meeting in a hotel on the outskirts of town, but having been thwarted by rumours in the past, usually set in motion by police agents, the anti-fascists decided to sit tight in the town centre. The police were out in force as well, and it was felt that there would be more room to manoeuvre in the middle of town rather than being confined to the outskirts.

Around midday, a number of dodgy-looking characters were spotted loitering about the train station, but just as they were about to be checked out, vanloads of riot police arrived on the scene. The NF were in town. As news spread of their arrival, anti-fascists converged on the station but were prevented from getting too close by the riot cops and dog-handlers. The police arrested a number of anti-fascists as the NF looked on nervously.

With my video camera in hand I was able to walk unhindered through the police cordon and right up to the NF supporters. I asked a young lad who the organiser was, and he pointed out a small, weedy-looking lad who was probably in his early twenties. He obviously fancied himself as a hardcase because he was strutting about behind the lines of police like a cockerel in a chicken coop. I walked up to him, wondering if this was Dave Sudworth, the Wigan NF organiser and football hooligan who had been giving it loads of verbal in the local press over the last few weeks. I introduced myself by saying that I was working on behalf of Channel 4 and was interested in doing a documentary on the NF.

"So fucking what?" he fired back instantly.

"I don't think that kind of reply is particularly good for the image of your party," I replied. "Especially considering that you're the local organiser."

He looked at me for a second, and appeared to be debating what course of action to take. "Okay," he said finally, "but I want to see your ID."

"Of course," I replied, producing my mock-up press pass.

This appeared to do the trick, and he visibly relaxed. "We're waiting for party chairman Ian Anderson to arrive," he told me. "His train should be in shortly. We're planning a peaceful indoor rally at a secret location, but if this rabble give us any trouble" – he waved at the anti-fascist protesters – "we're prepared to defend ourselves."

I then asked Sudworth to do a formal interview, which would give me the opportunity to pan around with the video camera. He agreed, and I was just setting up the camera to do the interview when Ian Anderson appeared. Flanked by two minders, he walked up to Sudworth and introduced himself. Sudworth brown-nosed for a few minutes while Anderson surveyed the scene.

The anti-fascists were still penned in behind lines of police as groups of Fronters continued to arrive at the station in cars and minibuses. A handful of NF-supporting football hooligans ventured too close to the anti-fascists and were chased off after a brief scuffle, but by and large the police had things under control. A senior police officer came over to speak to Anderson and Sudworth, and it was obvious that a deal had been struck to enable the NF to hold their rally without the anti-fascists being allowed to register their protest. The police appeared to be quite happy to act as an escort service for the race-haters and Jew-baiters of the NF while at the same time keeping the anti-fascists penned in like animals.

I spoke to Anderson, using the same blag about working for Channel 4. He seemed pleased that there was some media interest in the event and asked me if I wanted to come to the meeting which was in fact going to be held at a hotel on the outskirts of town. I thought about it for a few seconds and agreed to travel up to the venue with the NF leader in a minibus that had just arrived. As there was not enough transport for all the NF at the station, the police offered to ferry the remaining Fronters over to the meeting in their vans. This did not go down too well with the anti-fascists, who could only watch in frustration as the NF were taxied to their meeting. As we drove away from the town centre I began to regret my decision to travel with the NF and started thinking that Anderson was leading me into a trap. I wanted to get out of the minibus but knew that I was stuck with the NF until we got to the meeting at least.

We arrived at the venue, which was a very posh hotel adjacent to the M6 motorway. I jumped out and walked slowly behind Anderson, camera in hand, wondering if I should carry on or turn back. Something told me that there was something seriously wrong, especially when Anderson began talking to a couple of guys who then looked over in my direction. What was I thinking about coming out here on my own?

I was seriously wavering now but Anderson came over to

say that he had just asked a couple of people whether they were happy to have the press inside the meeting. They said they were okay with it but that any photos would have to be of the front table only. I couldn't really back out now and followed Anderson into the meeting room. As I entered, I felt as if all eyes were on me, and then I saw the unmistakable face of Eddie Whicker staring at me. Now Eddie was one of the NF's genuine hardmen. I had come across him once or twice down in London and he was a game lad. I was certain that he would recognise me, as I had also been to his court case in Stockport following his nicking for carrying an axe at an NF rally in 1985. That clinched it for me. I was off.

I backed out of the room with Anderson staring at me curiously, turned on my heels, and walked quickly out of the building. I crossed a garden and went into another wing of the hotel where there was a reception desk. Looking behind me, I saw that four or five Fronters had left the meeting and were making their way across the gardens towards me. I mumbled to the receptionist about being a journalist who was about to be murdered or something and legged it past her up a couple of flights of stairs and onto a landing.

I walked along a corridor trying doors as I went, hoping against hope that one would open. Then by a miracle I found an unlocked one and dived in. I could hear a commotion outside as the Fronters were banging on doors trying to find me, but I had another problem on my hands now, because there was already someone in the room, or to be more precise, there was someone in the bathroom. This was looking bad, so without any other real options, I went over to the window with a view to making good my escape by jumping out.

It was about a fifteen-foot drop, easy enough under normal circumstances but tricky with an expensive camera in my hands. I made the jump, landing on a patch of soft grass, rolled over and got to my feet. Pretty impressive, I thought, and the camera was in one piece as well. I legged it across a car park at the rear of the hotel, and headed towards a housing estate I could see across the other side of a field. Looking behind me I could see that some of the Fronters had come outside, but I had at least 100 yards on them. I wasn't sure if they were following me with any great vigour but I had to assume that they were.

I jumped a small fence and ended up in a small *Brookside*-style estate. A car with an elderly couple was just pulling out of a drive and I beckoned the driver to stop with my press card. He wound his window down and I quickly explained my predicament. "Get in," he said, and I jumped gratefully into the back seat. They were heading into town and on the journey I explained in more detail what had happened. They seemed to enjoy this little bit of excitement in their lives, and the old guy added that he was an ex-miner who had no time for the NF. When we got to the town centre I could see that there was a large police presence and I learned later that the anti-fascists had been penned in all day with absolutely no chance of getting at the NF.

I went back to Wigan a couple of weeks later and left a big bouquet of flowers outside the house of the elderly couple who had given me a lift. The Wigan episode still gives me the shivers but I learned a valuable lesson that day which was to stand me in good stead for when the fascists began to plot their next move on the North-West.

I was moving more and more towards an intelligence-gathering role and away from the physical stuff as new faces emerged to take up the cudgels against the reinvigorated fascist threat. A new wave of street battles was on the horizon as the Eighties drew to a close, and Anti-Fascist Action was in the process of being re-launched to cope with the renewed threat.

Over to you Dave.

DAVE'S STORY

CHAPTER FIVE

The Ghosts of Cable Street

AS A KID growing up on various council estates in the Sixties, I remember being aware of the fact that there was a class system in this country which helped the rich stay rich and the poor stay poor. I also remember thinking what an unfair system it was that didn't give everyone a fair share and an equal chance. That is not to say that I came from a particularly poor family, because as far as I remember there was always food on the table and a wage coming in, but we were not exactly overburdened with life's riches either. We were a traditional working-class, Labour-voting family. Nothing more, nothing less. My grandfather left the Forces after World War Two and worked on the railways until he retired, while my gran worked her whole life in the rag trade. My mum did various secretarial jobs, while my old man has been a print-worker, gravedigger, milkman and postie.

I was born in Taunton, a small market town in Somerset, but we moved about a fair bit and I also spent parts of my childhood in Bristol and Reddish, near Stockport. I was a fairly bright kid I suppose, but I got into a few scrapes at school because my old folks taught me that the best way to deal with bullies was to stand up to them. I remember coming home snivelling one day after being picked on by a gang of older kids, and my old man telling me that I had to go back and sort it out for myself. I was only eight or nine but I went back into school the next day and started on the leader of the gang. I did okay, I think, because he was taken aback that I had attacked him first, and the fight was only broken up when we were dragged apart by the teachers. I never had any more mither from him or his gang after that, and I never forgot the lessons I learned that day either.

My old folks were never particularly political, but I remember a couple of occasions when the TV screen was nearly put through during election broadcasts by the Tories. The Royal Family and God-botherers were not popular either, and I think these little bits of political thinking had an effect on me, eventually sparking my interest in punk rock when it exploded across the airwaves in 1977. I was a sixteen-year-old secondary-school-leaver at the time, and the whole punk ethos of disillusionment and rebellion neatly summed up the way I felt about the world, especially the Clash, whose brand of political sloganeering seemed a little bit more positive and thoughtful than the nihilism of bands like the Sex Pistols. Music with a political message was a revelation to most kids of my age in those days, because as far as we were concerned there seemed to be an unwritten law stating that songwriters could only write about three basic themes: falling in love, unrequited love and being betrayed in love. No wonder punk came along to give them a good kick up the arse.

After leaving school I got a plastering apprenticeship and knuckled down to learn a trade for a few years. I seemed to spend most of my spare cash on going to gigs or buying clothes and records. I would get paid on Friday and be straight into town to buy whatever punk, reggae or new wave records had been released that week, whether I had heard them or not.

This was in the late Seventies, when the National Front were sweeping all before them and the original Anti-Nazi League had been formed to counter the threat. I never had any time for racism, but in those days I was concerned more with enjoying myself than with getting involved in politics. I did go along to a few of the gigs and carnivals organised by Rock Against Racism, including the big bash at Victoria Park in London, but I went for the music rather than the politics, and I ignored the calls to join the struggle against the nazis. I got home from the carnival at about two in the morning and found my grandfather waiting up for me.

"Where've you been until this hour in the morning, son?" he asked, as I quietly closed the front door behind me.

"I've been to a carnival against the National Front in London," I told him.

"You don't want to get yourself mixed up in politics lad," he told me gravely. "It'll ruin your life."

It wasn't until 1984 that I finally disregarded my grandfather's advice, but when I did, I went for it big style. I walked out of a marriage that had gone wrong ("Too Much Too Young", as the Specials put it) and suddenly found that a lot of my old mates had settled down or moved away. Work was also scarce because Maggie Thatcher was in the middle of decimating British industry, and the building trade had pretty much collapsed. A lot of my mates had moved to London in the early Eighties and they all seemed to be having a good time. I had also heard all these stories about plasterers earning huge sums on building sites in the Smoke, and fancied a bit of that for myself. So on the spur of the moment I packed my stuff into the back of an old Ford Escort and moved to London, sleeping on people's floors and in squats for the first couple of months.

By the mid-Eighties, punk had changed almost beyond recognition and had lost its appeal for me. I was into stuff like the Redskins, The Men They Couldn't Hang and the Pogues at the time, but going to any of their London gigs in those days meant you had to watch your back. Some of these bands had been threatened and attacked by nazi boneheads because of their left-wing and anti-racist politics. The Angelic Upstarts and Desmond Dekker had already had their gigs smashed up

– for being socialist in the case of the former and black in the case of the latter. A number of other bands were also being threatened and it started to look as if the nazis were trying to put themselves in a position where they could dictate who could and who couldn't play gigs in London. After a few months of this I started to think that someone should be doing something about it. To my mind they were just like the bullies at school and I felt that someone had to stand up to them. I began looking around for someone who took this threat seriously, and the only people who seemed aware of what was going on and were prepared to do something about it was a small group of left-wing activists called Red Action.

I had noticed these characters hanging around a few of the gigs, a small gang of casuals and a couple of skinheads, tough-looking lads but friendly enough. They were different from your average lefties who seemed to take themselves too seriously. These lads enjoyed a few beers and a laugh, and in addition they looked like they could handle themselves. I started buying their paper, *Red Action*, and read a few articles about them in various fanzines, recounting how they had turned over the NF in Islington, Greenwich, Bury St Edmonds and numerous other places. After a couple of months I took the plunge and joined, and although I didn't know it at the time, the next twelve years of my life would be dominated by the war against the fash.

At the time, Red Action basically consisted of about twenty-five people in London. A few of them had been involved with the original ANL but had been expelled and slandered when the Squads were disbanded. Over the next few years I got to know some of these characters very well, lads like Mickey O'Farrell, Jimmy W, and Gary O'Shea, whose exploits were already approaching legendary status.

Gary O'Shea, sometimes known as "The General" or "Gosh", was the *de facto* leader of Red Action. He was the brains behind much of RA's strategy and politics and was also a very clever and witty character. Between periods on the dole, he earned a living working on the hod as a brickies' labourer. He was a tough Irish immigrant who could look almost donnish in his trendy, wire-rimmed specs. Mickey O'Farrell left Red Action about a year after I joined. He was from the Hatfield area, and also worked on the sites. Despite the fact that he has not been seen on an anti-fascist activity since about 1987, the fash were convinced that he was still giving them hell nearly a decade later.

Jimmy W was another hoddie. He had a broken nose that had never been properly re-set and the loudest, dirtiest laugh you've ever heard. Jimmy was one of those people who never really trusted modern technology. It took him ages to get a telephone installed in his flat, and then another couple of years to get an answering machine. The message on the tape sounded as if he was standing in another room when it was recorded. "He thinks it's going to steal his soul," joked O'Shea. Jimmy was a real character, who when drunk liked to perform a couple of speciality party pieces. The first involved dancing around on the top of a table, arms out-stretched, with a full pint of beer balanced on his head. The second involved standing up in a crowded pub and chanting "If I Die on a Nazi Street" at the top of his voice, fists punching the air as he sang along. This was a variation on an old US marines song from Vietnam but is better known in certain quarters as a football hooligan chant. The words had been changed to suit the anti-fascist cause, and Jimmy had adopted the song as his own. I once saw him try to perform both party pieces simultaneously in a Hull nightclub. The effect was spectacular, and predictably wet.

For a couple of years I was Red Action's publicity officer, and part of the job description should have included a bit about fending off Jimmy's mad ideas for posters. He once tried to convince me to produce a poster that paraphrased the old SWP slogan "Neither Washington Nor Moscow, But

International Socialism". He wanted our posters to read, "Red Action – Neither Washington Nor Moscow, But International Hooliganism". I managed to fob him off with some excuse or other.

These three lads, together with Big Andy, Carl, Hefty, Pete C, Garpo, Big Tony and a number of others were the backbone of Red Action during the late Eighties. They had fought alongside each other for years and had a common trust and purpose that made them a truly formidable outfit. I was stewarding a meeting around the back of King's Cross Station with O'Shea one evening when we suddenly spotted a large group of unsavoury-looking characters approaching the hall in the gathering gloom. For a few heart-stopping seconds we couldn't work out if they were friend or foe, but as they passed under a nearby streetlamp we clocked a few faces. It was the rest of Red Action's mob arriving late for the meeting. We let out a simultaneous sigh of relief. "I don't know what effect they have on the enemy," said O'Shea, paraphrasing the Duke of Wellington, "but they scare the hell out of me."

Red Action recognised that although the fascists had been driven underground, they had never really gone away and still retained the capacity and potential to cause serious problems. Red Action had been formed to counter this threat, and despite the scorn of many on the Left, they had achieved some considerable successes. "Red Action – the abortion that lived," as someone crudely put it.

These lads were tough and streetwise. They had to be. If you added up all the active fascists and anti-fascists in London in those days, then I reckon that we were outnumbered by about twenty to one. If the fash had ever sussed out how few of us there actually were at the time, I think we would have been in big trouble. As it was, we had to plan everything we did to cause maximum damage for minimum risk. We would turn up uninvited in the most unexpected of places, and wreak so much havoc that the fash thought they were dealing with a far bigger enemy than actually existed. I'd had a little bit of experience of this kind of thing from the football terraces in the late Seventies but that was just like kids getting up to a bit of mischief compared to this. This was war, and it was vicious, bloody and dangerous.

The disparity in numbers between fascists and anti-fascists meant that it was inevitable that we would come seriously unstuck one day, and so people like O'Shea and Jimmy started looking around for allies to build up our forces. Anti-Fascist Action (AFA) was the vehicle that Red Action used to build the anti-fascist resistance. At the time it consisted of us, a few anarchists and lefties, and an assortment of liberal groupings like the Newham Monitoring Project, who seemed to be more interested in increasing their media profile and obtaining European and council funding than in fighting fascism. Red Action was the largest single group in AFA, and provided the bulk of the security stewards and active membership, but because we were politically naive in those days we had allowed ourselves to be edged out of any positions of influence within the organisation. The liberals had manoeuvred themselves into positions of authority in AFA, and as a consequence the organisation was dying on its feet, stifled by an ineffective leadership that thought the best way to fight fascism was to appeal for Parliament to do something about the problem.

AFA's founding statement was drawn up on the back of a beermat by Mickey O'Farrell back in 1985. It simply stated that AFA would "oppose fascism both physically and ideologically". Red Action felt that the organisation had drifted too far away from its original aims, and needed to get back to basics. It saw AFA as part of a militant tradition that stretched back to include the volunteers of the International Brigades in the Spanish Civil War, the veterans of Cable Street, as well as the anti-fascist street-fighters of the 43 Group, the V Corps, the 62 Group and the Squads. Everyone involved in these different struggles from the 1930s onwards saw the need to physically challenge the swaggering incursions of fascist gangs, and we were no different. There was an umbilical link between AFA and these groups, and Red Action saw it as imperative that AFA live up to these historical precedents and not remain the ineffective pressure group that it had become for a moment longer.

It was felt that AFA was far too important to be left in the hands of the chancers whose guidance was allowing it to degenerate politically. It needed to be reinvigorated before the decline became terminal, or its good name would be sullied beyond redemption. Plans were put in motion to set the matter right, and over the next couple of years there was a bloodless coup, with the foot-soldiers of Red Action eventually ousting AFA's liberal leadership and replacing them. At a big meeting in 1989, Red Action and a number of left-wing and anarchist groups, notably the Direct Action Movement, came together to re-launch the organisation along militant and confrontational lines. After several years in the doldrums it was heartening to see AFA start to grow once more, as people up and down the country recognised that here at last was an organisation that walked the walk.

What became known as the Stewards' Group really came into its own around this period, although it was never really an official body with recruitment and membership and stuff like that. It was more of an informal thing, with people who felt confident in their abilities on the streets being gradually accepted into the group, while those who were less confident were given other roles within AFA.

All in all, I spent about two years in London with Red Action and AFA. Throughout this period I was an active and willing participant in the violent struggle against fascism. The main activity in those days was the on-going campaign to oust Ian Stuart (the lead singer of Skrewdriver) and his Blood and Honour cohorts from their base around Kings Cross, but there were also set-piece confrontations around the NF's annual Remembrance Sunday marches and the inevitable attacks on Irish solidarity events to deal with (all detailed in later chapters). I learned invaluable lessons during those two years, lessons that would stand me in good stead when I left London and moved back to Manchester in 1987.

Moving back to the North-West was not something I had intended to do, but six months previously I had started seeing a woman called Michele who was living and working in Manchester. We would see each other most weekends with either me travelling up to stay at her flat in Hulme or her coming down to stop with me in London. We had talked about moving in together but I sort of assumed that it would be her that moved in with me rather than the other way around. However, in October of that year I found out that I was being made redundant from my job as a handyman for Westminster City Council, and then a week later I was told that I would have to quit my flat in Camden. After talking it over, we agreed that it made sense that I should move up to Manchester and make a new start.

Manchester was like a creature emerging from a long hibernation in the late Eighties. After decades of inertia and dormancy, the city was beginning to discover what it was like to be alive again. This was the beginning of the Madchester boom, with bands like the Stone Roses and the Happy Mondays emerging onto the scene, as well as clubs like the Hacienda, which were gaining world-wide recognition and notoriety. Manchester was at last realising its potential, and the landscape of the city would never be the same again.

In contrast to the lively cultural scene, the city seemed to be dead politically. There was almost nothing going on, especially at street level, and the fash were almost completely inactive apart from their annual mobilisation to confront the Manchester Martyrs Commemoration every November. Even this, their solitary public appearance, seemed a bit tired and lacklustre, and it looked like they were just going through the motions.

The NF branch in Manchester had been battered into submission in the early Eighties and eventually fell apart, and units in places like Rochdale and Stockport were either inactive or considered too insignificant to bother with. As a consequence of all this inactivity there was also no permanent anti-fascist organisation. The AFA group that had smashed up the NF in Stockport in 1985 had faded into oblivion as the anti-fascists became victims of their own success and succumbed to the twin lures of family life and careers. Only a couple of individuals remained active and even these were semi-retired.

As the Eighties were drawing to a close, however, it became obvious that something was finally stirring in the murky underworld of Manchester fascism. We started picking up signs that the BNP had been busy in the area and had scooped up and re-organised the remnants of the old NF units right under our noses. They were also making big strides nationally and attracting loads of media attention, and it was inconceivable that they wouldn't make some kind of push in Manchester to capitalise on all this publicity.

Sure enough, signs that the BNP were active again locally became all too apparent. Jewish cemeteries were defaced and desecrated with fascist graffiti, anti-immigration stickers and posters started appearing on lamp-posts in the city centre, and rumours started to circulate that the BNP were going to stand a candidate in Gorton in the General Election.

It was clear that something would have to be done to stop the BNP getting a foothold. So over the course of next few months I started getting people together, contacting anyone who might be interested, including some of the old faces from the Squad. After a series of informal meetings it was beginning to look as if we had the makings of an anti-fascist organisation, and so one evening in a pub in the back streets of Ardwick, we re-launched Manchester AFA. It was invitation only, and about twenty-five people turned up.

I knew that we would be lucky to keep half of these once the real business started, so we had to make the most of them while we had them. I drew up a plan of action which involved taking the fight to the fascists in their own backyards, the white working-class communities that have traditionally provided fascist organisations with their recruits. This basically followed AFA national policy of operating from a working-class position which seeks to undermine fascist propaganda by explaining how fascism has nothing positive to offer working-class communities of any colour, race or religion. I made it clear that violent confrontation was inevitable if we followed this course of action, but if we stuck to our guns, it was a battle that we could win. The lefties who turned up were a bit dubious, if not to say a little frightened at the prospect of getting their hands dirty, but with the backing of Gerry, Gary F, Big Dave, Sean E, Toddy, Payman, Carol, Steve and a few others we pushed it through.

Gerry was a Glaswegian exile who had moved south a few years earlier. He was a decorative plasterer by trade, but he gave it up after moving to Manchester, and settled down to a life on the dole. He was an affable character who was serious about his politics and his football (Celtic and United). When he first moved down he was reasonably slim and fit, but inertia and a beer, spliff and curry diet later led him to acquire the nickname Porky. He could also swear for Scotland, and it was rare to have a conversation with him that wasn't peppered with numerous expletives. Gerry was my main oppo for the next 10 years. We were good friends and good comrades, and together we masterminded the fight against the fascists in the North-West.

Gary F was a City supporter from Wythenshawe, and was a bit of an irregular, but a good lad all the same. He was a grafter who earnt a living from selling tickets and snide merchandise outside concerts and sporting events. When work on the building sites dried up one winter I earned a few bob with Gary selling T-shirts outside gigs, and Santa hats at Xmas time. I didn't have a problem selling snide tour T-shirts at a third of their official price, especially when the quality was just as good, but I drew the line at ticket-touting.

Toddy was ex-NF from Gorton, but had been onside for a number of years now. He was a sound bloke with a dry sense of humour and the growliest Mancunian accent you've ever heard. He was a keen United and Celtic supporter who liked a pint and a smoke. He also possessed jowls that would make a Mafia godfather proud.

Big Dave was a big, hard-looking lad of Peruvian descent. He was a bit of a gentle giant really, but he was a staunch anti-fascist who wouldn't compromise his politics for anything. Big Dave persuaded his brother, Wigan Mike, to join AFA a few weeks later by uttering the immortal line, "These guys shoot from the hip." Mike was a more naturally aggressive character than his brother, and despite Dave's corny sales-manship, he liked what he heard about us, and persuaded a couple of his mates to join as well.

If you've read this far you'll know Steve's story. The big-nosed git had been around on the anti-fascist scene for years. He was an affable, easy-going character whose house has been like a drop-in centre for anti-fascists and United supporters alike for years now. At the time he was a teetotaller, and was a handy bloke to have around when you needed a lift home from the pub. I corrupted him a few years later in Dublin with a pint of Guinness and he has never looked back.

One bloke who wasn't at the first meeting was Nads, an Iranian martial arts expert who we nicknamed the "Assassin". He was from East Manchester and was in contact with a small group of Iranian exiles who were also sympathetic to our cause. His main oppo was Payman, another martial artist who was a younger, smaller version of Nads. He naturally enough became known as the "Assassin's Apprentice".

The early meetings were hard work, but as things developed and people settled into their allotted roles, it started to become easier. Steve, for obvious reasons, was given the role of intelligence officer, while I became chief steward. Carol's contribution to AFA over the years cannot be overstated. She was always reliable and took on a lot of the more mundane, organisational work. A couple of the lefties also proved to be reliable and trustworthy in the long run, especially Ben and Mike S. Over the next few months we set about organising this ragbag collection into something resembling a fighting unit, but I knew that we needed more bodies. We leafleted places like Harpurhey, Moston and Gorton, areas that had not seen left-wing political activity in decades. We organised a public meeting in the town hall which attracted a crowd of about 150 people, and slowly, Manchester AFA began to grow.

At that time I had a new job working for a firm based in the Atherton/Leigh area and was trying to combine all this political activity with working fifty hours a week on a building site. I was knackered most of the time, but I knew that we had to act quickly. The fight hadn't even started and we were already on the back foot.

Fortunately, Steve phoned me one evening with some good news. "I've found out where the BNP are holding their next branch meeting," he told me excitedly.

I was curious about how he had come across the information, but didn't press the matter. "Brilliant," I replied. "Where is it?"

"They're using an upstairs room in the Black Lion pub in Salford, and they've got a meeting booked for this Sunday."

There was a temptation when you got hold of a piece of information like this to get a team together and ambush the fash on their way into the meeting. However, we were desperately short of information on the BNP, and I agreed with Steve that we should plant a listening device in the room and try to find out what they had planned. The Black Lion was a big, old-fashioned pub in a run-down, grimy part of town on the border between Salford and Manchester. It was ideal for BNP purposes because it was located fairly centrally but was tucked away in one of those forgotten corners of the city. It was also perfectly situated for what we had planned.

On the Saturday evening before the meeting, I strolled into the pub with Steve and asked the landlady if she could show us around the upstairs room. We told her that we were from a Sunday League football team and that we were looking for somewhere to hold our AGM. I had agreed with Steve beforehand that he should keep the landlady distracted while I looked for somewhere suitable to hide the bug. For some reason Steve went all shy, and the landlady was watching me like a hawk as I walked around the room muttering stuff about electric sockets. In the end I just had to drop the bug in a corner and hope for the best.

"I thought you were going to distract her," I hissed at Steve as we walked out the pub.

"I know," he replied, "but I couldn't think of anything to say to her." This was the only time that I can ever recall the big-nosed git being lost for words.

On the night itself, Steve picked up me and Gerry in his new car, a bright yellow Volkswagen Beetle which he obviously hadn't bought with thoughts of undercover work uppermost in his mind, because it stuck out like a dog's cock. We had to park the car right outside the pub because it was the only place we could get a decent reception due to the bug being fitted with a duff battery.

The area was quiet apart from the odd passing police patrol car, which caused Steve to shrink down instinctively in his seat every time it drove past. His nervousness was infectious, and I unconsciously started doing the same.

"I dinnae know why you're so fuckin' worried," said Gerry from the back seat, his voice thick with sarcasm. "Three big fellas sat outside a pub in a wee yellow car with the engine running. Why on earth would the polis think that was suspicious?"

The bug had not been found and we were able to listen in to the meeting on a small radio with a cassette player recording it for posterity. It was not an impressive showing by Manchester BNP. The entire branch seemed to consist of nothing more threatening than several senile old Mosleyites, some Loyalist fellow-travellers and a variety of odd-bods and spotty students who sat in stiff-legged silence as branch organiser Alan Payne mumbled his way through a rambling two-hour monologue. Aside from a couple of asinine remarks about Prince Charles being "a nigger-loving poof" and a prediction that Saddam Hussein was going to "do over the big noses on Wall Street", it was turgid stuff. It was only when Ken Henderson from Rochdale was introduced as a guest speaker that the relieved audience came to life.

Henderson was a feather in the cap for the BNP. He was an ex-Tory who obviously believed it was better to be a big fish in a small pond than vice-versa. He was well groomed and well spoken, and clearly destined for greater things. He was the north-west BNP organiser, and he had been sent to the Manchester meeting to whip up support for his forthcoming 1992 General Election campaign in Rochdale. He was not impressed with what he saw in Manchester either; that much was clear even through the hiss and static of our somewhat less than state-of-the-art monitoring equipment. Nevertheless he did his best to whip the assembled masses into something akin to a frenzy. Amongst other things he boasted that the national leadership of the BNP had identified Rochdale and the north-west as the area of greatest potential outside London. He bragged that the BNP in Rochdale had "between thirty and forty members" and could double this with the support of other branches in the area. He went on to claim that they were bigger and better organised than the NF branch of the Seventies, and finished his speech to loud, braying cheers, by boasting that "the BNP are going to kick some black ass in Rochdale."

I turned to the other two lads and said, "That sounds like fighting talk to me." Poor old Ken didn't know what he was letting himself in for.

CHAPTER SIX

The North-West Frontier

How the BNP's Lancashire Election Campaign Was Run Off The Rails, 1992–1994

Rochdale. Round 1. The Crystal Chandelier.
(Saturday, 15 February 1992)

Now at last we knew what we were up against. The BNP were not going to make a move on Gorton, which was sensible because it was our turf and they would have been butchered, but they were making a big push in Rochdale.

Rochdale was one of those old mill towns that had never really recovered from the collapse of its textile industry. Situated on the outskirts of Manchester, it was not an unattractive place at first glance, but it did contain several large estates where unemployment was high, wages were low and social amenities few and far between. This mixture of poverty and boredom, combined with the presence of a small Asian community, meant that there was often an undercurrent of racial tension in the town. Inter-racial gang skirmishing was not unusual and I have spoken to people in the town who actually viewed it as a normal part of growing up.

This cocktail of social problems was always likely to prove irresistible for any racist group in the area, and the NF had maintained a continuous presence in the town since the Sixties. Even our predecessors in the Squad had found them a difficult nut to crack, and the NF had only given up the ghost in

Rochdale when the majority of their membership had defected to the BNP in the late Eighties.

One vital piece of information we picked up that evening outside the Black Lion was that the BNP were planning to hold a pre-election rally in Rochdale the following weekend to kick-start their campaign. It was going to be a national event, which meant that we could expect fascists from all over the North and Midlands to attend. John Tyndall and all the BNP bigwigs from London were coming up, along with plenty of security. I was determined that we were going to stop them, but because we were operating with what was basically a new and inexperienced team, I was feeling a bit shady about the whole thing.

I was also a bit nervous because everyone was relying on me now. When I had been out on anti-fascist stuff before, I'd been with the London lads who had done all the planning and shared all the responsibility. I had basically been nothing more than a foot-soldier, a grunt, who was happy to follow the lead of others. Success or failure now rested almost entirely on my shoulders, and I was not sure I liked the feeling.

With less than a week to get our act together we began to spread the word, making sure we got sufficient numbers out for the day. We also passed the information over to the Anti-Nazi League, which had recently been re-launched after 11 years in hibernation. I was curious about which particular version of the ANL we could expect to find ourselves working alongside in the months ahead. Would it be the ANL of street-fighters and physical confrontation, or would it be the ANL of church leaders, soap stars and passive demonstrations?

The ANL of the Seventies started out with a reservoir of working-class lads and lasses who had been drawn into the struggle against the nazis after being involved in other SWP activities like the Right to Work campaign and the Rank and File union groups. These people had been recruited from the factory benches, the building sites and the dole offices, and were tough, no-nonsense characters more than capable of taking the fight to the fascists. It was from these elements that the original Squads had been formed, and it was one of the strengths of the SWP in those days that it could draw in such people.

In the intervening decade, however, the SWP had closed down all these campaigns and seemed to be increasingly orienting themselves towards students and the middle classes. They were devoting less and less time to straightforward class-based politics and were increasingly campaigning on trendy liberal issues like the Campaign for Nuclear Disarmament, student grants and gay rights campaigns such as Clause 28. They were more interested now in clambering on board whatever liberal bandwagon came rattling past their window rather than doing the consistent, principled hard graft that was necessary to build and maintain links with the shop floor, the building site and the council estate.

The SWP now had much more influence in white-collar unions such as NALGO and the NUT than they did in blue-collar unions, and a lot of their activities reflected this. You can speculate on what caused this shift in policy, whether it was the traumatic experiences they had suffered when the last influx of working-class activists had nearly upset the apple cart, or whether it was the huge expansion in student numbers that had caught their attention, but either way, they were now a more white-collar, middle-class and student-friendly organisation than at any time in their history. They had chosen the easy life, the path of least resistance, and they had in the process become caricatures of themselves. Given these developments, we had an inkling of what to expect from the ANL Mark II, but it would be unfair to judge an organisation still in its infancy.

In the wake of the ANL re-launch, a plethora of bright, shiny-new anti-racist/anti-fascist organisations also threw their hats into the ring, each of them calling for unity while simultaneously pouring scorn on the credentials of the others. The whole thing was becoming a circus, but I made sure the information was passed onto each of these various groups anyway and hoped something positive would come out of it. Steve had also found out that the BNP were supposed to be holding their meeting in a pub called the Brunswick near Rochdale town centre, and I decided that the best chance we had of stopping them was to get there early and occupy their pub, hoping to catch them by surprise as they wandered in.

On the day itself we took about fifty up to Rochdale. There were a few faces I knew I could rely on in the crowd – Gerry, Gary F, Payman, Big Dave, and a couple of other lads – but we had a lot of first-timers, including a small group of Jewish students who had tagged along, and we had no idea of their calibre if it went off. We plotted up in the Brunswick, a small, scruffy pub near the town centre. Steve had contacted the other AFA branches from around the north and the place was full of anti-fascists from Newcastle, York, Leeds and Doncaster, bringing our numbers up to about 100. Proof that we were in the right place came when someone went to put some music on the jukebox and found two full LPs of Skrewdriver material on it (Skrewdriver were the leading lights of Blood and Honour, the neo-nazi skinhead music organisation). The thought crossed my mind that at least we would have something to do for later if no fash turned up.

Steve introduced me to Tracey from Newcastle and Paul from Leeds, two of the main organisers of AFA's Northern Network at the time.

"Any news on the BNP?" Paul asked me.

"Well they're meant to be meeting in this pub," I told him. "We've got scouts out looking for them, but it looks like they're lying low at the moment."

"The Doncaster people are trying to track them down as well," said Tracey, "and a couple of skinheads from York are having a nosy around. You better tell your lads to keep an eye open for them. We don't want them getting a kicking by mistake."

Outside the Brunswick, however, Gerry chanced upon a couple of local ANL members tipping off BNP members that we were lying in wait for them in the pub. Not only were they warning off the fash, but they were doing it within earshot of a couple of very interested police officers. To this day I don't understand why they did this. Maybe they were scared by the threat of retribution if it came on top for the BNP, or possibly there was some kind of unspoken "you leave us alone and we'll leave you alone" arrangement, just the kind of appeasement that fascism thrives on.

I wandered over to the town hall, where the ANL and the rest of the anti-racist circus were holding their own rally, and after a couple of hours of congratulating themselves on keeping Rochdale a "Nazi-Free Zone" they announced that the day had been a huge victory for anti-racism and that everyone should now go home. There was a scramble for the waiting coaches and within an hour the place was deserted.

We had no intention of leaving the field but it meant we had to rethink our tactics, because thanks to the ANL our cunning plan to ambush the BNP in the Brunswick had been rumbled by both the Dibble and the fash. We had stopped the BNP holding their meeting in the pub but we knew that they were still in the area. We also knew that they would only make their move once they thought there was no opposition about. If previous form was replicated they would swagger into town and start taking out their frustrations on local Asians or stragglers from the rally.

We needed to regain the element of surprise, and after a brief chat with the other AFA stewards we decided to regroup in another pub. I was hoping that the move might enable us to lose any police spotters we had picked up and I was also hoping that the BNP might show their hand once they saw that the Brunswick was deserted.

We split up into small groups and left the pub at intervals, hoping this tactic might throw the Dibble off the scent. Now it has to be admitted that at this time AFA was not the well-oiled fighting machine that it was later to become, and our small group of about a dozen from Manchester got lost and isolated from the rest of the AFA groups. This was in the days before mobile phones were commonplace, and we were basically wandering around hoping to bump into someone we knew. We were stood near a Y-shaped junction about halfway up Drake Street discussing which direction to take when four or five lads from Doncaster AFA came sprinting around the corner as if the Mongol hordes were on their heels.

"What's happening?" I asked a small dark-haired lad.

"Fascists. Fucking loads of 'em," he shouted in a broad Yorkshire accent as he ran past me.

I looked up the hill and saw a big mob of boneheads running down the hill towards us. We were well outnumbered but it was one of those days when I just knew that I wasn't going to run, no matter how many fash there were. I glanced around and saw Gerry standing beside me looking nervous, with Payman, Big Dave, Ben, and a couple of the other lads just slightly behind us. Ben looked a bit queasy, and I sensed rather than saw a couple of the Jewish students sliding away from the back of the group.

"Stand your ground," I shouted, knowing that once panic set in, it was infectious. If we ran now, people were going to get caught and butchered, but if we stood together, we might be able to face them down. The Donny lads saw that we were making a stand and joined us, and the waverers reluctantly shuffled back into line.

The fash were still streaming round the corner in what seemed like endless numbers but the boneheads at the front of their mob started slowing down when they saw that we were not running away, and their charge came to a stuttering halt about ten paces from us. They started giving it all the usual "come on then" gestures and shouts, but I had them sussed by now. I knew they didn't have the bollocks for it. The Donny lads started throwing rocks and stones at them from on top of a small embankment, which added to the general consternation and confusion in their ranks.

I recognised a few faces amongst the fash mob. Jason Wilcox and the Oldham Irregulars were present, as well as Graham Tasker from the East Midlands and his little mob. There were also a couple of familiar-looking bods from Rochdale itself.

"Come on then you bunch of wankers," I shouted at the bones. "This is supposed to be your town."

Some bonehead wearing what looked like twenty-hole Doc Martens threw a half brick in my direction, and as I swayed to avoid it I drew a Lucozade bottle out of my pocket and stepped forwards. Without warning, the whole fash mob suddenly turned and scattered in all directions, with hollering anti-fascists in hot pursuit. I ended up chasing "twenty-holes" down Drake Street, with Gerry close behind me. The bone tried to escape by running into an Asian-owned taxi office, but the elderly owner pushed him back out of the door. A frenzied game of push and shove followed, with the frightened bone desperately trying to get into the office, and the Asian bloke equally determined to keep him out. Finally the door was slammed shut in the frightened bonehead's face. We'd just caught up with him when we were stopped in our tracks by the sudden squeal of brakes as the police arrived on the scene to save his baldy arse.

"What's going on?" one of the cops demanded as he jumped out of his patrol car.

"We've just been attacked by a gang of skinheads, officer," I replied, as I casually brushed past him and walked back up the hill to rejoin the rest of the lads.

I could tell that the Dibble was not entirely convinced by my explanation, but he seemed to decide that it wasn't worth all the mither and paperwork, and let us go on our way. Once the police were satisfied that the situation had calmed down, they simply drove off and left us to our own devices. We immediately set off down Drake Street again, following the main group of bones who had escaped in that direction. Everyone was buzzing now and full of confidence as they relived the excitement of the last few minutes. We had not gone far when we bumped into the rest of the AFA groups, who were heading back into the town centre again. The fleeing bones had been spotted going back into the Brunswick pub by AFA scouts and without further ado we headed off in that direction.

The attack on the Brunswick took the fash by complete surprise. I was about the fifth or sixth in the pub and the scene was already one of complete carnage. Bottles, pint pots, barstools and pool balls filled the air as the whole place erupted into complete mayhem. I saw Gerry battering some bonehead over the head with a bottle as he tried to make good his escape out the back door, and everywhere you looked anti-fascists were brawling with fascists. One of the girls behind the bar started throwing beer bottles at the anti-fascists until someone started throwing them back at her, causing her to duck behind the bar never to be seen again. Meanwhile the shell-shocked fash were climbing out the windows or cowering in corners to avoid the onslaught. To add to the general confusion someone threw a big glass chandelier into the bar from the room upstairs, which exploded on the floor sending shards of glass flying everywhere.

I hit one bone over the head with a Lucozade bottle as he ran for cover, and then threw the shattered remains at another bone who was shielding himself with a barstool. As he raised the stool to protect himself, I ran in and kicked him in the balls. He fell to the ground with an "ugh" and I booted him in the face a couple of times.

Unbeknown to me, there was also fighting in the pool room and apparently the fash who were trapped in there put up stiffer resistance. I believe Paul from Leeds got hit over the head with a pint pot and there was a rum old battle with pool cues and pool balls before the BNP were finally overwhelmed. I was still in the bar kicking the bonehead all over the place when Gerry grabbed my arm. "Time tae go big man," he shouted. "Let's get tae fuck out of here." I looked around and saw that people were withdrawing from the pub. Job finished and mission completed.

The Brunswick during those few minutes of carnage was a dark and dangerous place to be, and it was a relief to be back out in the daylight. On the way out I noticed that someone had taken the time and trouble to smash up the jukebox. Everyone was buzzing as we climbed back onto the coach and on the way home we were bouncing around singing "If I Die" and "We are the Reds". When we got back to Manchester we went on a marathon piss-up to celebrate the day's success. We ended up in the Royce in Hulme, which in those days did a late lock-in.

During the course of the evening I got chatting to one of the lefties who had travelled up to Rochdale with us. I think he had spent most of the day at the ANL rally, selling papers and listening to speeches. He looked distinctly unimpressed by our various tales of heroism and I eventually got pissed off and asked him what his problem was.

"Well it's hardly a major victory against fascism is it?" he complained. "Beating up a few boneheads in a pub."

I thought about this for a second before replying. "So if a mob of tooled-up fash steamed in here now, in our own pub, and kicked the crap out of us, then you wouldn't regard it as a defeat?"

"Well of course I would," he replied.

I shrugged my shoulders. Nothing more needed to be said. All in all, I was pleased with the day's events. We had stopped the BNP having their rally, chased them off the streets and battered them in their own pub. I often think that if we had run away that day on Drake Street we would never have recovered. As it happens we didn't, and we went from strength to strength after that.

Round One to AFA.

Rochdale. Round 2. Kung Fu International.
(Saturday, 4 April 1992)

A few weeks later the BNP tried again. They announced that they were intending to hold another major election rally in Rochdale on April 4.

In the intervening weeks we seemed to spend every spare moment in the town, gathering information, handing out leaflets, meeting local contacts and generally getting the lie of the land. The night before the rally, Gerry and I ended up in Rochdale police station after getting caught spraying *Red Action* and *AFA* graffiti on some walls near the town centre. The local Dibble kept us locked up over the weekend and also raided our homes in the middle of the night, waking up my baby daughter so that they could search her cot. I don't know what they expected to find there apart from a rattle and some teething gel, but whatever it was they must have been disappointed.

I was annoyed with myself. It was a stupid thing to get nicked for, and on the eve of what promised to be another major clash with the BNP as well. I could not escape the feeling that I had let everyone down. Gerry remained fairly upbeat, but as time wore on I started to get more and more frustrated. I'd had four cell-mates over the weekend, people in for serious assaults and car thefts, and they had all been released before me despite the trivial nature of my offence.

"I'm getting really pissed off with this," I shouted.

"Just try and keep calm Dave," Gerry shouted from his cell. "Just get your heid down and try and relax. Dinnae fuckin' let them know they're getting to you."

"Yeah. You're right," I replied, taking a deep breath and forcing myself to remain calm. Words of wisdom from the wee Scotsman. Whatever next?

Fortunately, while we were pacing our cells, AFA numbers had been boosted by the welcome return of some old faces, including a small crew brought along by Nads. The Assassin was a dangerous man. There was none of this fancy-dan jumping about like a praying mantis with Nads, just straight in there, hard and fast. He was most definitely the strong, silent type, a family man who didn't smoke or drink. His only addiction was physical exercise. He was a man of few words but he had a dry, understated sense of humour that could be very funny at times.

A number of new faces also turned up, including Glen Solo and Gary the Axe and his little mob from Bolton. A busload of Scousers also made the trip along the East Lancs Road, boosting numbers still further. Glen Solo was a mixed-race lad from Hulme. He was a big United and Celtic supporter and a staunch Catholic. He was studying at Manchester University when all this was going on, but was hardly what you might call a stereotypical student. He was a handy lad to have about, and proved to be a reliable anti-fascist over the years, although he had some reservations about AFA's working-class politics.

The Scousers were good lads, and along with Manchester and Doncaster AFA formed the backbone of the Stewards' Group in the north over the next few years. Tall Paul was the main man in Liverpool AFA. He was another martial arts nutter, and there's video footage of him at Waterloo Station standing his ground against swarms of boneheads. He dished out as good as he got that day, despite being completely outnumbered.

The Bolton people were crusty/anarchist types. At first we were a little bit distrustful of them because we'd had previous bad experiences with the cider-drinking, glue-sniffing crusty types who would turn up drunk or stoned and piss everyone else off. The Bolts proved themselves to be sound, committed anti-fascists, however, and were good people to have about. Sartorially, AFA was divided into two groups. There was a smaller faction of anarcho/crusty types from places like Bolton and Mansfield who we nicknamed "Smelly AFA" and then there was the larger group of more casually dressed AFA members who the Smellies nicknamed "Aftershave AFA". The exception to both these camps was Wigan Mike, who was a heavy-metal headbanger, but the less said about his dress sense the better.

Mike was a sound lad. He packed a good punch and had plenty of bottle to go with it. You knew that if you stood your ground then Mike would be right there beside you. He had this bizarre theory that there were actually six different types of heavy rock, and if you caught him in the right mood he would bang on for hours about the various sub-strands of his favourite music. He even convinced me to go along to a rock club with him one night, but it all sounded like the same old regurgitated shite to me.

Steve had told me the details of the BNP's intended meeting place about a week beforehand, and I put everyone in the picture at our monthly branch meeting on the Wednesday. I also proposed a plan of action for the day, so that in theory everyone knew what the script was. The plan was basically a revamped version of the first encounter in Rochdale, and was based once again on the simple premise that the early bird gets the worm. The plan was for AFA's main stewards to arrive earlier than the BNP at their intended meeting place, a pub near Rochdale town centre, and simply take it over, ambushing the fascists as they arrived in dribs and drabs. As I sat in my cell I wondered how it was all working out.

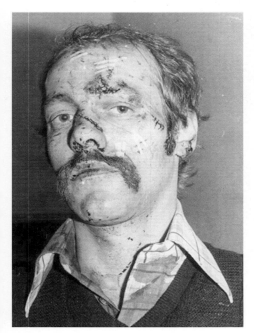

Early Squad member Graeme Atkinson was one of those injured during a combined National Front and Loyalist attack on a National Council for Civil Liberties meeting at UMIST, Manchester in 1975. It proved to be a pivotal moment in spurring anti-fascists to organise and fight back.

Lewisham, South London, in August 1977: Anti-racists make a stand and halt a big National Front march. We had met the guy on the left shortly before it all kicked off.

One of the lads, Mick, launches into the nazis amid the carnage of the "Battle of Lewisham."

The fight spreads to Manchester: These NF supporters in Piccadilly Gardens are about to receive a surprise visit from the Squad.

A robust political discussion ensues between the NF clique (left) and the Squad.

More fighting in Piccadilly Plaza. The National Front drew support from Manchester City fans and held regular paper sales in the city centre in the Seventies until driven out by the Squad.

A fine, upstanding example of the master race: David Sudworth, Wigan NF organiser, circa 1990.

© Morris Carpenter/Insight

The Main Event at Hyde Park, London in 1989: Lots of blood, but very little honour for Britain's nazi boneheads.

BNP supporters gather at the Hare and Hounds in Todmorden, east Lancashire, shortly before a violent visit by Anti-Fascist Action. Circled are John Tyndall (left) and Ken Henderson.

A rare visit to Manchester by a group of BNP members. Seconds after this photo was taken they were legging it down Wilmslow Road. The chubby skinhead in the middle is John Hill of the Oldham Irregulars. On the far right (where else?) is Austin Stonham of Blackburn, writer of oddball letters to anyone who'll ignore him.

Watching us watching them: The police mount surveillance to prevent clashes between AFA and the fash at Burnley, Lancashire, in 1993.

Burnley in 1993, the scene of our impromtu skirmish with the Suicide Squad football hooligan gang.

A sticker produced by Mancester United Anti-facists. Old Trafford has never welcomed racists.

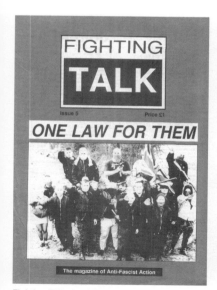

Fighting Talk, the AFA magazine, bearing a picture of some of the "opposition" in typical macho posturing.

An AFA tenth anniversary poster from 1995. The organisation's manifesto was to "oppose fascism both physically and ideologically".

The Bloody Sunday march in January 1995. "All right lads? I'm here to get stuck into the Reds," announced this chap on arrival. Seconds later...

Fascist graffiti in Stretford, Manchester, 1995. Combat 18 were supposed to be the shock troops of the far right but were often bested by Anti-Fascist Action.

According to all reports, the plan went like clockwork. Carloads of BNP were confronted and attacked as they arrived at the pub, while others performed dangerous U-turns in the road to avoid damage to themselves and their cars. A carload of Manchester BNP were ambushed as they arrived on the scene, with Alan Payne being dragged from the car screaming in terror as anti-fascists set about him and the other occupants. They were only saved further pain and humiliation by the arrival of the police. The ANL then turned up in large numbers and began to stage a noisy counter-demonstration with megaphones, placards and blood-curdling speeches. They were annoying in many respects but at least they were in the right place this time, even if they were an hour late.

It soon became clear to AFA stewards that the BNP must have booked an alternative venue for their rally, as nowhere near the expected number of fash had shown up at the original meeting place. Sure enough, AFA scouts reported that they were re-grouping at a pub called the Lord Nelson on the outskirts of town. There was a scramble for cars and minibuses as the AFA contingent raced over to the Lord Nelson. A few fash were stood outside in the pub car-park as the first AFA teams from Doncaster and Bolton arrived, but quickly sprinted inside before any contact was made. Half a dozen AFA lads made an abortive attempt to steam into the boozer, but this time the BNP, with superior numbers, put up stiffer resistance. A fight broke out just inside the pub doorway with the fash using pool cues and bottles to defend themselves. I believe it was during these exchanges that Gary the Axe acquired his nickname (and yes, it was for the reason you're thinking it was).

The result of the initial skirmish was a stand-off, with the AFA lads being reluctant to charge back into the pub until reinforcements arrived and the BNP being too scared to venture outside despite having a pub full of weapons at their disposal. Some bright spark spotted the BNP's transport and the fash were forced to watch in grim silence as their vehicles were wrecked. The rest of the AFA mob arrived just as the police turned up and any further plans to steam the pub were shelved. Then to everyone's surprise, the ANL arrived, and with their help AFA managed to resist police attempts to move the anti-fascists away from the pub for nearly three hours. During this stand-off, the BNP were trapped inside the pub and unable to go to their rally. Eventually the Dibble got things under control again and the master race accepted police advice and were escorted out of town in a convoy of wrecked cars and vans.

This was the only time that the ANL actually attempted to live up to the slogan of "No Platform for Fascists" on the streets of the North-West, and shows what could have been achieved without the weak-kneed leadership of their SWP masters. Gerry and I were eventually released with a police caution several hours after all the commotion had died down. A number of arrests were made at the Lord Nelson and a campaign was launched to help with fines and legal costs for those charged. The BNP were left battered and bruised, and were once again forced to abandon their plans for a rally in Rochdale.

Round 2 to the Anti-Fascists.

Rochdale. Round 3. Smash it Up.
(Saturday, 25 April 1992)

The day of the General Election passed off without incident in Rochdale. A carload of us drove around town all day hoping to bump into BNP canvassers, but they kept a very low profile. I put this down to the fact that they were a bit wary after the last couple of incidents in the town.

The day after the election, I was more interested in finding out the size of the BNP's vote in Rochdale than the size of the

Conservative majority in Parliament. Everyone, including the BNP, knew that they were not going to win the seat, or even come close to the votes of the big three parties, but that was not the point. The point was to attract a lot of publicity, and to use the campaign to build a base of support in the area.

As the results were revealed, I could not decide if it represented a victory or a defeat for the BNP. They got what might be considered a derisory 1.4 per cent of the vote (that's 1.4 per cent of those who actually bothered to vote, not the entire electorate), which was an admittedly tiny percentage, but it meant that 620 people in Rochdale were actually prepared to vote for an openly racist and fascist party. The BNP also did pretty well in East London and fared reasonably well in the East Midlands and Yorkshire seats they contested. These were all areas where they had a strong branch structure. Our immediate concern in Manchester was that some of those 620 voters in Rochdale might be drawn into the BNP's orbit now that they had actually taken the first step and voted for them. I was determined that this would not happen.

Hot on the heels of the General Election that year came the local elections, with the BNP announcing they were standing candidates in the Smallbridge and Kirkholt areas of Rochdale. These were the two estates where they reckoned that the bulk of their votes had come from in the General Election, and also areas where the two candidates, Henderson and David Taylor, had family connections. The two council estates were solidly working class in character, and apart from a couple of beleaguered Asian families, almost exclusively white. They were tough estates where everyone seemed to know everyone else. We knew we would have our work cut out if we were going to make any kind of impact against the BNP here.

The campaign so far had burnt off many of the students and fair-weather anti-fascists who had turned up on February 15, and by this time AFA was virtually the only opposition to the BNP operating in Rochdale. It was rumoured that the

ANL had put in sporadic appearances from time to time, but we never saw much evidence of it. We maintained an on-going level of activity in Rochdale designed to turn the screws on the BNP outfit in the town and keep them under constant pressure. We challenged the BNP claim that Rochdale was their turf by taking over the town centre on a couple of Saturdays, selling copies of the AFA magazine *Fighting Talk* and handing out copies of our own local bulletin, *In The Area*. We also extensively leafleted the Smallbridge and Kirkholt estates, making sure that BNP supporters were aware of our presence. In short, we threw down the gauntlet, hoping that the fash would pick it up, but they never did.

In addition to all this legitimate activity, a small team of "saboteurs" carried out more covert actions to disrupt BNP communications and inconvenience their members and supporters. The saboteurs' activities included cutting phone lines, slashing car tyres and superglueing locks. The Bolton lot were the experts at this kind of thing, and passed on some handy tips culled from the pages of *The Anarchist Cookbook* and similar publications. About halfway through the campaign, Steve picked up a whisper that the BNP were planning a major leafleting session and show of strength on the Kirkholt estate on Saturday, April 25. I decided that AFA should leaflet the same estate at exactly the same time.

It was about this time that I found myself in the position of *de facto* chief steward for AFA's Northern Network activities in the North-West. I don't remember ever actually being elected or appointed to this position at a meeting or conference, it just kind of happened. I had responsibility for anything up to 200 people, and it was a scary thought knowing that one wrong decision on my part could lead to bloody defeat or mass arrests. I tried to put these fears to the back of my mind as I got on with the job in hand.

Gerry was my number two and we made sure that organisation was tight and that everyone knew what they were doing when we arrived on the Kirkholt estate. If memory serves we had about thirty leafleters being accompanied by an equal number of stewards as we wound our way through the area. There was no sign of the BNP, and we were beginning to suspect that the whole thing was going to be a washout, when a car pulled up alongside us. I recognised the occupants as a couple of local lads who we had met earlier in the campaign.

"All right lads?" I said. "What's the score?"

"We've just spotted Taylor driving a minibus full of boneheads away from the estate at high speed," the driver replied.

"Where are they headed?"

"We've got someone following him, and . . . hold on." His reply was cut short when his mobile phone rang. After answering the call, he turned to me and said, "That was one of our lads. He's followed the minibus and another car up to a pub called the Oxford on the outskirts of town. If you've got transport we'll lead you up there."

I was not sure if Taylor was running scared or if he was plotting something, but I felt that we couldn't afford to ignore the info. I got together with Gerry, Tall Paul from Liverpool and Malcolm from Doncaster, and after a quick chat we decided that we should abandon the leafleting session and head up to the pub.

Four minibuses full of anti-fascists screeched to a halt outside the pub and twenty of us immediately charged at the front door. The fash must have posted a lookout outside the front of the pub, because as soon as we arrived the doors were locked and bolted. A few of us tried to kick the door down but it was one of those heavy, old-fashioned oak jobs, and as we didn't have a battering ram handy, the attempt was abandoned.

I heard the sound of breaking glass coming from the rear of the pub and ran around the back to find anti-fascists jumping all over Taylor's minibus and a car parked beside it. The two vehicles were absolutely trashed, but as the anti-fascists started to leave the scene I noticed that somehow, the windscreens of the two vehicles were miraculously undamaged.

"Oi," I shouted. "What about the windscreens?"

"Oh, okay," said Neil, a young lad from Hulme. He picked up two large rocks and threw them through the windscreens. This sparked another wave of attacks on the vehicles which left them even more wrecked. The sound of police sirens filled the air now, and the AFA mob started to scatter in all directions. Everyone knew the score. It was every man for himself. *The Rochdale Observer* reported the following Monday that all the van windows were smashed and four tyres were slashed. Four of the car's windows were smashed and two tyres slashed. The report didn't mention the buckled bonnets, smashed headlights and dented side panels though. While all this was going on, the BNP remained cowering inside the pub.

I had a shady journey back into town, clambering through gardens and hedgerows trying to avoid the police patrols, but I eventually made it back without having my collar felt. The police did try to nick a couple of people for criminal damage, but because they had no real evidence against them, they were forced to let them go. Eventually everyone reported back safe and sound. Taylor later claimed in the paper that he had received a threatening phone call at his home address and had decided to leave the area. I don't know if this is true or not, but if someone did phone him it wasn't us.

A handy lad to have about was Fijian Mike, a local rugby league player who had thrown his lot in with us earlier in the campaign. Aside from being a big brute, he was well respected and knew a lot of people in Rochdale. His dad ran a pub in the town and he had a lot of contacts in the pub trade. I spoke to him a couple of days later.

"All right Dave," he said. "You'll laugh when you hear this."

I looked at him for a second. "Well go on then," I said.

"Well, I went up to the Oxford last Saturday after your lot had paid it a visit, and the landlord told me that the BNP had been absolutely terrified. He said they were cowering in the corner of the pub and that they were pleading with him to keep the doors locked. He reckoned that one of the BNP guys actually crapped his pants in the bar. He said it stank the fucking place out."

Round three to AFA.

Rochdale. Round 4. The Geriatric Unit.
(Saturday, 2 May 1992)

As the weeks rolled by, the BNP's local election campaign and the AFA campaign against it were intensifying. I heard reports that Henderson's car had been wrecked, his phone lines cut and his living room windows smashed. We carried on distributing leaflets on the two estates, and continued to build up local contacts and support. We also contacted the breweries and landlords of all the pubs where the BNP held meetings or drank regularly and succeeded in getting them banned from at least four pubs in Rochdale. BNP canvassers were thin on the ground, and we more or less had free rein in the town.

Meanwhile, Steve and I were continuing to monitor Manchester BNP branch meetings at the Black Lion, and it was clear that they were coming under intense pressure from their Rochdale counterparts because of the suspicion that they had an informer in their ranks. Numbers at their desultory meetings fell even further, until it seemed as if only the old Mosleyites were left. If the regular membership of a particular BNP branch fell below a certain number they became known as a "unit" by the BNP leadership. It was about this time that Manchester BNP picked up the nickname of "The Geriatric Unit" among anti-fascists.

Steve had heard from another source that the BNP were planning to hold another major rally in Rochdale, and we once more prepared to organise opposition. AFA groups from around the north-west were contacted and put on high alert. We booked a coach for the day and filled all the seats. Steve then phoned to tell me that he had heard from *Searchlight* again and that the BNP had cancelled their rally due to all the previous problems they'd had in the town. Apparently they did not want to risk getting any more bad publicity in the run-up to the elections. Steve also told me that he was taking the afternoon off to watch United with his son.

My first feeling was one of relief. After all, who in their right mind would want to spend their Saturday afternoons charging around some moody mill town risking life, limb and liberty, even if it was all for a good cause? Then I realised that we had a coach booked and would lose the deposit if we didn't use it. We also had a shed-load of leaflets that we had to get rid of before election day. The course of action was more or less decided for us. We stood down the other AFA groups in the north and decided on a Manchester-only activity on the Smallbridge estate.

On the day itself, word of the BNP no-show had obviously spread, and the coach was only about two-thirds full. Nevertheless it was not a bad turnout and was more than enough to deal with any local difficulties we might encounter. We made our way to the Smallbridge estate and arranged to meet the coach at the town hall later in the afternoon. I noticed that people were more confident after the run of victories over the BNP, whereas everyone had been very nervous on our first trip to the town. I knew from my time in London that the fash were not as tough as they looked but a lot of the new recruits needed to see it with their own eyes before they would believe it.

The leafleting itself was uneventful, and on the way back into the town centre we stopped off at the Brunswick to check out the situation. The landlord visibly paled as we breezed into the pub.

"Look lads," he pleaded. "I've banned that other lot. They don't come in here any more."

"Well you shouldn't have served them in the first place," said Carol as we checked the place out.

There were no fash about, nor was there any sign that the place was being used by them. The Skrewdriver records had also been taken off the replacement jukebox, and so we decided to give him the benefit of the doubt.

Coming out of the Brunswick, we walked the short distance to the town hall, but as we turned the corner onto the main square, I suddenly found myself stepping on the backs of people's shoes. I looked up to see what was holding everyone up and was confronted by the sight of a large crowd of fascists gathered around the town hall steps. Addressing his followers at the top of the steps was John Tyndall, surrounded by party members holding Union Jacks aloft. We had nearly walked right into the middle of a 150-strong mob of fash holding a rally right on the spot where we were supposed to be waiting for our coach. Fortunately they were so absorbed by the words of Fuhrer Tyndall that they failed to notice us backing quickly around the corner again. There was no sign of the coach, and the BNP rally was between us and the direction from which we expected it to arrive.

"Shit," said someone. "What the fuck do we do now?"

"Stay calm," I said, "and let's put a bit of distance between ourselves and that lot."

"This is bollocks," said Gerry bitterly. "Someone has set us up."

We walked back to a small roundabout about halfway between the Brunswick and the town hall and had a short discussion about what we should do next. At least one of the lads was in favour of steaming into the BNP rally but I argued that there was no point in giving them an easy, morale-boosting victory when up until that point we had had them on the run. Confronting a mob that size meant certain defeat and would set us back months in terms of morale and impetus. In the end, common sense prevailed over bravado and we set about discussing the best plan of escape.

"The best bet," said Carol, "is to lie low somewhere and try to contact the coach company. They could radio the driver and get him to pick us up somewhere else."

"All it needs," suggested Ben, "is for someone to stroll over to the town hall when the coach arrives and ask the driver to come over here and pick the rest of us up."

"Any volunteers?" I asked, as people suddenly took a keen interest in their shoes.

We were still debating what to do when someone spotted the coach. What worked in our favour was that any vehicle coming from the Manchester direction would normally have to drive past the town hall on the opposite side of the road, and then turn around the roundabout to park outside the town hall facing in the direction of Manchester again. We had a few anxious moments waiting to see if the coach swerved towards the town hall before it reached us, but luckily it didn't and we managed to flag it down on the roundabout.

As the coach drove slowly past the BNP rally I was too gutted to even bother giving them any abuse. People were a bit down and crestfallen, and the journey back to Manchester was quiet. It seemed like all our hard work had been for nothing. Back home in Manchester I phoned Steve.

"Fucking hell Steve," I said. "What happened?"

"Why? What's up Dave?" he asked.

"Well you told me last week that the BNP rally in Rochdale was cancelled but we've just been up there this afternoon and nearly walked into a couple of hundred of them having a rally right on the town hall steps. We were lucky we didn't get murdered."

"Shit, Dave," said Steve. "I don't know what's happened.

Something's gone wrong somewhere. I'll get on to *Searchlight* and try to find out what the score is."

A few days later we got an explanation of sorts. Apparently, *Searchlight* had a mole inside the BNP in the Lancaster area and a lot of our information up until that point had come from this source. *Searchlight* claimed that there had been a balls-up in communication with their man, but many muttered darkly that they had let the rally go ahead in order to protect their informant. If this was the case then I suppose it might be argued that it was for the greater good in the long run, but to be honest it didn't feel like it at the time.

We decided to give them the benefit of the doubt, but the incident did put the first small seed of concern in my mind about *Searchlight*, and I was never 100 per cent certain about them after that. We quickly moved on from the incident however, and it was soon forgotten as we concentrated on putting the squeeze on the BNP in the North-West.

The local election results showed a slight decrease in the size of the BNP's vote, with Henderson getting 112 votes and Taylor getting seventy-six. Unbeknown to us at the time, however, was the fact that BNP's active membership in Rochdale had fallen from a high of over thirty in 1991 to less than ten in April 1992. This was due in large part to the pressure exerted by Manchester AFA. The Rochdale BNP branch was also heading for another damaging split between Taylor and Henderson over the latter's conservatism and reliance on the police to deal with the BNP's political enemies. This was to become a recurring problem for them in the north-west over the coming years, as the humiliated street-fighters became more and more frustrated with Henderson's leadership.

Round 4 – Split Decision.

Colne. Round 5. Evidently Chickentown.
(Saturday, 1 May 1993)

Things had gone off the boil in Rochdale for the time being, but like a spot that had been squeezed a bit too early, the infection spread to other parts. BNP units seemed to be springing up all over Lancashire at this time, and it became clear that they had poured significant resources into the Pendle and Burnley areas of the county as there was a big increase in activity and membership in those regions. I suspected that they had deliberately chosen those areas because neither region had a recent tradition of militant opposition to fascism.

Most Mancunians regard Lancashire with the kind of superiority that cultured city-dwelling sophisticates reserve for country bumpkins. They imagine the place is populated by pie-eating Yonners and whippet-owning cousin kissers, but the truth of course is somewhat different. Colne in particular is a pretty little town with loads of second-hand bookshops and cafes. It was also once famous for its socialist football team, the Colne Dynamos. All the more reason then that the BNP shouldn't go unopposed when they put forward a candidate in the town to stand in the local elections.

The BNP's candidate, Shaun Crambie (*aka* Daltry), had labelled Colne as "the last white town in Lancashire" and was clearly intent on making a name for himself in right-wing politics. He was a puny individual who owned the kind of face that made you suspect that the Mancunian prejudice about cousin-kissers might well have some truth to it. This would have been a disadvantage in most political parties, but the BNP leadership was distinctly lacking in the kind of square-jawed Aryan supermen of fascist myth, with party leader John Tyndall bearing more than a passing resemblance to a bulldog with its head stuck out the window of a speeding car.

The BNP once more announced that they were holding a pre-election rally in the area and we began making plans to stop them. A week before the rally we took a couple of teams

up to Colne to leaflet and scout the town. We learned that the
BNP were intending to rally in the Silverman Hall in Nelson,
but as this was only yards away from the main mosque the
feeling was that the police might cancel it.

The day before the event, we learned that the police had
indeed cancelled the Silverman Hall, but that the Midlands
BNP organiser, John Peacock, was travelling to Lancashire to
address a rally somewhere in Pendle. So now we knew it was
definitely going ahead but had no idea where. The general
feeling was that we should show our faces and hope that
something bubbled up on the day itself.

We took a team of ninety up to Colne and settled down in
a big pub near the centre of town to await events. We had a
good crew out that day and it was nearly all security stewards.
We took thirty up from Manchester and there was also a good
show from the Scousers. Wigan, Bolton and Doncaster
brought good numbers and I think even Preston turned up,
which was unusual. We were playing it pretty much by ear,
and we had to accept that there was a fairly good chance that
it would be a non-event, so a lot of the lads were pretty
relaxed. Normally, people stuck to Cokes or fruit juices when
we were out and about but the landlord nearly ran out of lager
that Saturday lunchtime. Scouts were sent out to try to track
down the BNP but failed to find any sign of them.

The ANL were holding a static rally in the town centre,
and Gerry wandered over to see if they'd heard anything. The
ANL claimed that they didn't know anything but Gerry came
back to the pub with some local bloke in tow who I remember
as looking a bit like the folk singer Mike Harding.

"Alright bud?" I asked, as Gerry introduced him to me.
"What've you heard?"

The bloke went through some long-winded explanation of
how he had overheard a conversation between the police and
a council official about the BNP booking the Ball Grove
Recreation Centre at Cottontree for their meeting. He had

passed the information over to the ANL but they hadn't been interested, and then he had noticed Gerry nosing about.

"How do we get to this recreation centre then mate?" I asked him.

"Well if you've got transport, I'll get you there along the back lanes so we'll avoid the police patrols," he offered.

He was as good as his word, and after bolting down our drinks we jumped in our vans and followed him along narrow winding lanes to a country park on the outskirts of Colne. It was at times like these that the presence of the ANL was helpful, because their rallies tended to divert police attention away from us, which meant we could move more freely about the area.

The hall at Ball Grove Park was at the bottom of a steep-sided valley next to a duck pond. We parked along the top of one side of the valley and walked slowly down the slope towards the hall. The BNP were nowhere to be seen, and there were only a few people hanging around outside the hall. We were met by an undercover Dibble who ran up the hill to join us. He clearly assumed we were the BNP, despite the presence of black and Asian lads in our mob, and we certainly were not going to put him in the picture. He was quite happy for us to plot up outside the locked hall and await the arrival of the rest of our "Aryan brothers". The undercover copper was easy to spot because he was wearing one of those silly pink T-shirts that changed colour with your body temperature. The shirt had already turned a darker shade of pink because it was a warm day and he had had run up and down the steep hill once already.

Also waiting at the hall were three or four uniformed Dibble and a couple of unsuspecting fash who some of the lads were itching to batter, but couldn't, because we didn't want to blow our cover. Nevertheless, several cunning plans were hatched during this time. One bonehead had edged warily backwards towards the duck pond and the temptation to push him in was almost too great to resist, but we had to keep the bigger picture in mind.

By now the fash were looking around uneasily at their new-found comrades, clocking the black faces and some of the clothing styles of the anarcho-punky types. The game was nearly up. At that exact moment one of our spotters came running back from the park entrance shouting that the BNP were marching into the park. We moved off towards them with the police happy to escort us towards what they assumed were our racial colleagues.

We crested the brow of low hill just in time to see the BNP come gurning into the park across a small hump-backed bridge. It was a disappointing turnout on their part. There were only forty of them, and far from being pleased to see us, they started backing off across the bridge again, nearly fighting each other in their haste to get away. We sieg-heiled a few times to try to encourage them to come and join us but they were having none of it. The police escorting the BNP didn't have a clue what was going on. I saw Henderson desperately trying to put them in the picture.

"Come on then," I shouted. "Charge." There was a loud roar as we burst into a run, heading straight at the BNP trapped on the bridge, but our timing was slightly awry and the charge was headed off by police horses, dogs and vans.

We were left in charge of the park for the moment, but in the distance I could see the police putting on riot gear and Henderson furiously gesticulating for the officer in charge to clear us away from the hall. Eventually the BNP were escorted into the nearest corner of the park, and under heavy police guard were told to have their rally there. Groups of anti-fascists attempted various charges in an effort to break through police lines but were repulsed. The BNP were subdued and uneasy, and it was probably difficult for them to hear the speeches above the chanting anti-fascists and barking police dogs. PC Pink T-shirt was completely flustered by the turn of events, and his shirt was growing darker by the minute as he raced about trying to restore order.

The fash were well pissed off by this turn of events and a couple of them lost it when we started taunting them with chants of "You dirty fascist bastards" and "You must have come on a pushbike". Ken Henderson stood aloof from it all, watching impassively as the debacle unfolded. He was easy to spot because he was wearing smart black trousers, a shirt and tie, and a horrible, casual-style, brown leather jacket. He looked for all the world like a sales rep, and I later discovered that, funnily enough, that's what he was.

One of the Scousers started pointing back up the hill. "There's four BNP in the car park behind us," he shouted.

"Yeah," said another lad, "I saw them sieg-heiling."

A mob of AFA lads broke away from the main group and charged up the hill towards the car park. I was knackered from all the running around and followed them at a distance. I didn't see much of the fight but apparently the four lads in the car were attacked with bricks and stones as the mob bore down on them. Two of the car's occupants were injured, the other two ran for their lives pursued by anti-fascists who in turn were pursued by the police. From where I stood I could clearly see Ben jumping up and down on the bonnet and it was no surprise when I learned later that he was one of six anti-fascists who were eventually arrested.

The BNP accepted police advice and were escorted out of town again. Meanwhile, PC Pink T-shirt's garment of choice had turned deepest purple, and its exasperated and exhausted owner turned to me and said, "You've done everything you wanted to do, now why don't you just fuck off home."

I looked at him and smiled. "We're not going anywhere until the six lads you've just nicked have been released."

"They won't be getting out until tomorrow morning," he replied.

"Looks like we're here for the night then," I said, as I walked off to join the rest of the AFA group.

I don't know what effect our conversation had on subsequent events at the police station, but the six lads who were arrested eventually got out at about 8 p.m., only a few hours after they had been nicked.

A couple of months later, a few of us went up to Burnley with Ben for his court case. He got a not-guilty as I recall, but from the evidence presented that day it would appear that the four lads battered in the car park were unconnected to the BNP. Several people that I would trust with my life swear that they saw them sieg-heiling; maybe it was meant as a joke or a wind-up, but if that was the case, it backfired badly. They remain the only innocent victims of our actions that I can remember in twelve years of anti-fascist activity.

Shaun Crambie got 162 votes in the election and has never been heard of since. The BNP in Colne were once again out-manoeuvred, out-thought and out-fought by AFA.

Round 5 to AFA.

Burnley. Round 6. Law and Order.
(Saturday, 26 June 1993)

Question: How do you find out where the BNP's secret re-direction point is?

Answer: You phone up the BNP's local election candidate and ask him.

Yes, it's as simple as that. Sometimes it was so easy it took all the fun out of it. Of course you have to pretend to be a racist dickhead, which can be hard, but try imagining yourself with a lobotomy and it gets easier.

Scott O'Sullivan was the blabbermouth. He was standing as a candidate in the Stoops area of Burnley, a working-class estate with a fearsome reputation. A year earlier the Stoops had gained nationwide notoriety when it erupted in a wave of anti-police riots, so obviously O'Sullivan was keen to play down the "law and order" aspects of BNP policy. Unfortunately, due to that one careless moment on the phone, the whole thing blew up in his face.

The BNP had planned a mass leafleting on the Stoops estate and had arranged to meet beforehand in the Hare and Hounds pub in Todmorden. The Hare and Hounds was a big, olde worlde pub about twenty miles from Burnley and was becoming quite a regular venue for BNP activities. Time for a visit.

We parked on a small, secluded estate behind the Hare and Hounds and made our way via a couple of back lanes to the pub. If I had stopped and thought about it for a moment I'd have sent a scout around to do a recce first, because as it was, we were walking blindly around the corner not knowing how many fash were there. There could have been hundreds milling around outside. A small knot of AFA lads had gathered just around the corner from the forecourt waiting for the rest of us to catch up with them. Wigan Mike had risked a quick look around the corner.

"There's a vanload of 'em just pulled up," he whispered, "only about a dozen or so."

"Well let's do it then," I said, as I stepped around the corner.

My heart was thumping as the adrenalin kicked in. There was always an incredible rush of nervous energy in those moments just before it kicked off and this was no exception. As I led the boys around the corner we did our best to appear casual and unconcerned, hoping to get close enough to the fash to have a real pop at them before they sussed us. As we approached them, however, they started to back off warily.

Steve produced a Union Jack from his coat pocket and started waving it around in the hope of confusing them for a moment, but they were having none of it. Not even a chorus of "Rule Britannia" worked. The fash made a dash for the front door of the pub at the exact moment we sprang forward to try to head them off. I managed to land a decent punch on one of them before he got inside, and his mates had to run a gauntlet of punches and kicks as they tried to follow him. Once inside the pub they were again attacked by AFA lads eager to continue the row. The few normal punters inside the pub at that time of day looked on in shock and consternation as a running battle involving barstools and pint pots spoilt their quiet lunchtime drink. The fash were chased out the back of the pub and ran over fences and fields to escape their pursuers. Someone put the pub windows through and the BNP van was also wrecked before we made good our own escape.

We knew that our action would only delay the BNP and not force them to cancel altogether, so we made our way by various routes back to Burnley, eager for a second bite at the cherry. Our plan was to park up somewhere quiet and await the arrival of the full BNP mob. Unfortunately, it soon became clear that it was going to be impossible to get onto the Stoops, due to a huge police presence in the area. Already alerted to the possibility of trouble by the events at Todmorden, they stopped and searched every van in the area. We were pulled over twice, the first time by a couple of Dibble in a patrol car. One of them chatted away to us for a while in a very reasonable and friendly manner while the other slipped in the killer question: "So have you been anywhere near Todmorden today?"

"No officer," I replied, hoping I had remembered the correct route we should have taken from Manchester. "We came through Bacup."

He drummed his fingers on the side of the van for a while. "Okay," he said, before walking off to question the lads in the next van.

The second time we were stopped was by the riot police, who pulled everyone out of the vans for questioning. No arrests were made, but it was made clear to us that we were not going to be given any room to manoeuvre at all that day. I spoke to the other stewards and we decided to pull out of town before the police started getting really moody.

When the BNP did eventually show up, their numbers were dwarfed by the huge police presence on the estate. The Dibble had obviously decided to use the BNP activity and the earlier events at Todmorden as just the excuse they needed to put on their own show of strength in the area. To the local residents of the Stoops it must have seemed like the BNP had invited the police to accompany them onto the estate, and they treated the fash with open contempt from then onwards.

Scott O'Sullivan polled a measly fifty-three votes in the election. A clear thumbs down for the law and order candidate.

Round 6 to AFA.

Burnley. Round 7. The Suicide Squad.
(Saturday, 28 August 1993)

For a short while during this period I had a job in a distribution warehouse, picking building tools for delivery to hardware shops and builders' merchants around the North-West. It was a boring job that I only did to earn a few quid to pay off some debts and put some food on the table, but the funny part of it was that I used to tell all the lads at work what I got up to with AFA. They were really into it, and whenever they knew something was happening at the weekend I would walk into work on the Monday and be met with a barrage of questions. "How did it go?" they'd ask, or, "Did it kick off?" I'm sure they thought I was making it all up.

We were really busy politically at around this time as well, and it seemed like we had only just got one round of local elections out of the way when along came another lot. This time the BNP announced they were standing two candidates in Burnley: Scott O'Sullivan again, and David McNee. They also announced plans for a major march and rally in the town on August 28. The police decided to let the march go ahead, which we thought was a strange decision given that Burnley FC were also playing at home that day.

I had a busy week in the run-up to the Burnley march, because Manchester AFA had organised a tour of the north by a German anti-fascist, and it was my job to accompany him to the various towns and cities where he was due to speak. The highlight of the tour was a bizarre mix-up in Preston where we turned up for a meeting in the town hall only to find that the mayoress had organised a civic reception for us. It was a surreal experience watching all these civic dignitaries fêting a German Communist/Autonome who back in his home town of Gottingen lived in a big shared squat and was therefore in constant conflict with his own local authority. Apart from the Preston farce, the tour went reasonably well, and proved doubly useful. The first benefit was that it kept people abreast of the situation in Germany and helped us forge international links, but it also gave us the opportunity to spread details of our plans for the Burnley march to the rest of the Northern Network whilst maintaining a strict "radio silence".

I had learned a valuable lesson from the last time we were up in Burnley and suggested meeting up in Nelson and catching the train into town, thereby avoiding the police surveillance teams looking out for vans and minibuses full of lads. I knew that it would be impossible to avoid the police spotters once we were in the town itself but at least we would be in the area we needed to be, unlike when the police had kept us off the Stoops estate in June.

The initial phase of the plan worked well, and on the day itself about 150 AFA members disembarked from the rattler at Burnley Central Station with the police nowhere in sight. On a previous visit I had earmarked a pub where I thought we could lie low until the BNP arrived, and with this in mind we swerved the town centre and kept to the back streets, hoping to remain incognito until we reached our destination. The plan came unstuck when a few stragglers at the back of our group were attacked by members of Burnley's football firm, the Suicide Squad. By all accounts it was a brief battle, with the attackers being chased back into their pub before the main body of stewards were even aware that anything had happened.

We were attacked again by a bigger mob charging out of another pub waving Union Jacks and singing "Rule Britannia". A hail of bottles and glasses sailed through the air before we got our act together and chased them back inside again. The police had arrived by this time and were starting to make loads of arrests, and it didn't pass unnoticed that it was mostly our lot being nicked.

Several lines of Robocop riot police now separated us from the Suicide Squad, who were growing in number with every passing moment. This was the main Burnley firm with all their top boys present. There were a few casuals among their mob but in the main they were a right scruffy outfit compared to their peers in the more fashionable towns and cities. I seem to remember that dungarees featured prominently that day. Chants and taunts were exchanged between the two mobs, and a few of the younger Burnley fans were dancing around behind the police lines, giving it the big one. I get really pissed off when I see that. I hate all that play-acting from behind the safety of a police cordon.

The situation had reached a stalemate. Huge numbers of police separated us from the Suicide Squad and it would indeed be suicide to attempt to charge through that lot. We needed another angle of attack, and I noticed a small, unguarded side street which emerged onto a pedestrianised shopping precinct right opposite the pub. We charged up the street and got about twenty yards away from the Suicide Squad, scattering small groups of Burnley supporters in our wake before the police headed off the charge with dogs and horses. The little pricks who had been giving it loads of mouth earlier had fled for their lives, terror etched on their faces, but the main Burnley firm had stood their ground, and once the police had restored order we were back in the stalemate again.

During this second stand-off, the leader of the Burnley firm crossed police lines to have a word *capo y capo*. He was a real monster of a man, and wore a white King Billy T-shirt stretched over his beer-gut. I decided that now was not the time to debate the finer points of Northern Ireland politics with him.

"Your lot had a good go back at us," he said in a broad Lancashire accent. "Fair play."

I nodded, waiting to see what else he had to say for himself.

"We're off to the match now," he continued, "but if you're still in town when it's finished we'll meet up somewhere away from the Old Bill and have it out fair and square. Mob against mob."

"We've got no quarrel with Burnley supporters," I told him evenly. "We're only interested in the BNP."

"Listen," he replied. "We're not having any outsiders wandering around our town mob-handed. I don't care if it's your lot or the BNP, anyone still in town at five o'clock is getting it."

I personally thought we could take them but that was not the reason we were in Burnley. We were here to stop the fash from marching and we had not even set eyes on a single BNP member yet. The situation calmed down after the Suicide Squad departed for Turf Moor and we strolled down to the ANL rally, which had remained static throughout the furore up the road. We hung around there for a while mingling with the crowds while we tried to find out where the BNP were hiding. They had been due in town about half an hour ago.

Alan, one of the Bolton lads, wandered over for a chat. "I've just been speaking to a couple of Burnley fans who were hanging about," he said.

"Oh yeah?" I replied "I hope they were friendlier than that prick in the King Billy T-shirt."

"A bit," he said. "They told me that they'd given some BNP members a kicking in town a couple of weeks ago, not because they were fash but because one of them was wearing a Rochdale shirt."

I rolled my eyes heavenwards. "They really don't like outsiders in this town do they? It's like being in the Village of the Damned or something."

"It's probably 'cos they're all inbred," chirped one of the Wigan lads.

I ignored the chance of an easy putdown and looked at my watch. "Let's give it an hour or so, and if the BNP don't show, we'll get the fuck out of here."

We spent the rest of the afternoon hanging around under the watchful eyes of the riot police, waiting for the BNP to show up. We waited and waited, and when it eventually became obvious that they were not going to appear, we withdrew in good order back to the train station. It felt like a defeat. We had taken a lot of nickings and had not seen a fascist all day – but as events turned out, it proved to be anything but a defeat.

We learned later that just at the moment we were emerging from Burnley Central Station, the police had been preparing to escort the convoy of BNP coaches and cars into town for their march. Then of course, it had kicked off between AFA and the Suicide Squad, and the last thing the police needed was another mob in town. They stopped the convoy and told the BNP that because of the public order situation their march was cancelled.

The BNP's leadership, including Tyndall, Richard Edmunds and Ken Henderson, meekly complied with police instructions and moved out to Bacup where they were allowed to hold a twenty-minute rally. Some BNP members tried to sneak into Burnley but most were rounded up by the police, including four no-marks from the Oldham Irregulars, a group of fash who were apparently connected to the Fine Young Casuals (Oldham's football firm).

Internal feuding followed the BNP capitulation, with punches being thrown by irate fascists bemoaning their leadership's lack of bottle. There had always been friction between the deeply conservative middle/upper-class leadership of the BNP and the more openly nazi, working-class membership who felt that standing in elections was pointless and that winning control of the streets was the real route to power.

One result of the weekend's activity was that David McNee withdrew from the election campaign and urged people not to vote for him. He later complained that "the egoist, media-seeking Tory regional leadership" had "allowed the reds to rule the roost." The repercussions of the day's events rumbled on for some time, with Burnley BNP splitting down the middle and other local branches losing disillusioned members. Incidentally, the few BNP who did make it into town unwisely ventured up to Turf Moor to sell copies of their paper *The British Nationalist*. True to their promise, the Suicide Squad kicked them all over the pavement.

Worse was to follow for the BNP. In the election itself, McNee managed thirty-two votes, while O'Sullivan got the grand total of nine votes, which meant that even some of his proposers didn't vote for him. As the BNP in the North-West continued to implode, we stood back and admired the results of our handiwork. The victory in Burnley had been achieved almost by accident, but it had caused the BNP more problems than anything we had done previously.

Events in London were to cast a shadow over our good humour however, because the following week the BNP managed to get Derek Beackon elected as councillor for the Isle of Dogs. A small success for a party with pretensions to power you might think, but it was the first time a BNP member had ever been elected to a position of authority. This small but significant achievement managed to deflect some of the criticism that was beginning to build against the BNP leadership and their strategy, and enabled them to gloss over the Burnley debacle.

I was gutted. We had dealt the BNP a telling blow in the North-West but all our good work had been undermined by events in London.

Round 7 – Split Decision.

Rochdale. Round 8. Out for the Count.
(Thursday, 5 May 1994)

The BNP were on a high after their local election victory on the Isle of Dogs in September. They were getting saturation media coverage, and as a result of this they were receiving more membership enquiries than they could cope with. In the run up to the next round of local elections in May, Steve heard from one of his sources that the BNP were discussing the possibility of putting up candidates in Tameside, Rochdale, Oldham, Burnley, Blackburn and even Manchester itself. It was obviously going to be a busy few weeks. In the end there must have been a reality check, because the BNP eventually decided to play it safe and announced that they were putting up only three candidates in Rochdale. Henderson was standing in Smallbridge again, Janet Appleyard was standing in Kirkholt and Ian Baker in the Newbold area.

We also heard that the National Front were thinking about standing a candidate in Wigan. There was a small number of

NF supporters in the town who were part of an outfit called the Goon Squad, an aptly named football firm who had attached themselves to Wigan Athletic FC. We had never really taken them seriously in the past; I mean we are talking about Wigan Athletic here. Wigan Mike and a few of his boys had crossed swords with this outfit on a couple of occasions and were distinctly unimpressed by their prowess on the streets. Their leader seemed to be a weedy individual called Dave Sudworth, who although he certainly was not a coward, wasn't a fighter either, an unfortunate combination which left him in possession of a face that would have confused Picasso. His mates were a lot more sensible. They were just cowards. We were in control of the situation in Wigan, but a high-profile election campaign in the town could change all that. We put a lot of work into Wigan, and in the end either the NF were frightened off by our response to their challenge or the rumour had been a red herring all along. Either way, there was no NF candidate in Wigan that year, but there was a new AFA branch.

Meanwhile, in Rochdale there was a real election contest going on, or so we thought. In fact the BNP there were as difficult to find as the NF had been in Wigan. In contrast to previous campaigns, they called no public meetings, rallies or marches, and relied chiefly on a letter writing campaign to the local paper for publicity. In fact, we only spotted the BNP once during the entire campaign, and that was when we turned up to leaflet the Smallbridge estate on the same day as a BNP leafleting team. Our reputation had obviously preceded us, because the first we knew of their presence was when somebody spotted two carloads of fash leaving the estate at high speed, never to return. We went on to distribute thousands of leaflets on the estates in which they were standing without encountering another BNP member.

On the day of the election we toured around a few of the polling stations in Rochdale to see what was happening, but everything was quiet. It was starting to look as if the BNP weren't even going to show on polling day itself. Then, late in the afternoon, we began hearing reports that the ANL had been chased away from a couple of polling stations on the outskirts of town. We did a quick tour to see what was going on, but if anything had happened then there were no visible signs, save for a couple of flustered-looking polling station officials. By this time it was beginning to feel like we were chasing shadows.

Later in the evening we met up with AFA groups from Liverpool, Bolton and Wigan, and settled into a pub near the town hall to await the arrival of the BNP candidates for the count. I had noticed the pub on a previous occasion, and noted that it had a good view of the front of the town hall. We could sit in here all evening if need be and keep a watchful eye on the situation.

At about 9 p.m., the ANL set up a noisy picket outside the town hall. They kept up a constant barrage of noise, waving around their big, round, bright-yellow placards.

"Look at that lot," sneered one of the Scousers. "They look like a bunch of toddlers with huge yellow lollipops." The name stuck and from that moment onwards the ANL became known as "The Lollipop Brigade".

After an hour or so, a rumour started doing the rounds that a couple of minibuses full of tooled-up fash had been spotted in the town. This fitted in with the stories we had heard of the ANL being chased away from the polling stations earlier, and I sent out a couple of spotters to try to track them down. After a fruitless search they returned a couple of hours later with nothing to report.

Now I always believed that it was important to try and track down the source of these rumours so that we could make a decision about what action to take based on the quality of the information received. The other useful effect was that it tended to deter people from talking bollocks and starting all these rumours in the first place. On this occasion the trail went cold, and no-one seemed to know where the original information had come from. Whatever the truth of the matter, we were fairly confident that we could deal with a couple of vanloads of fash, so I decided that the best option was to sit tight and wait to see what developed.

By 11 p.m., we had heard that the three candidates and their agents had been smuggled into the town hall in the back of a police van. Pretty humiliating I should imagine for Janet Appleyard, who was also rumoured to be a member of the Knights of the Ku Klux Klan. Nevertheless it meant that any chance of inflicting a damaging blow on the BNP had been lost. Even the ANL were subdued as they realised they wouldn't have the chance to shout "nazi scum off our streets" at a load of nazis swaggering arrogantly past them.

Time was called in the pub, and after a short discussion with the Scousers we decided that there was probably no point in hanging around any longer. Shortly after closing time we climbed in our vans and started to head off home. We were driving back past the town hall when Big Dave suddenly shouted, "Oi!" and pointed out the window. "Look at that fuckin' lot," said Gerry as a large group of BNP approached the ANL picket. They had emerged from a small tree-lined park by the side of the town hall where they must have been waiting in their minibuses all evening. They had probably spotted us in the pub earlier and waited for us to leave before making their move. As the ANL moved politely aside to allow the fash to gain control of the Town Hall steps, we jumped out of our vans as they screeched to a halt and steamed into the back of them.

The effect of the attack was similar to a large stone being thrown into a small pond, as the terrified fash scattered into the lines of police and ANL, who in turn retreated from the fleeing boneheads. There was a scrum at the entrance to the town hall as half a dozen fash tried to burst through the doors in an attempt to escape. A lone usher struggled valiantly to keep them at bay, and eventually succeeded in shutting the doors on them. Bottles and bricks flew across the forecourt as individual battles broke out all over the place. A small group of Asian lads who had turned up to support the ANL were the only ones to stand their ground as the fash scattered into them, and they were left brawling with a couple of big ugly boneheads.

The momentum of the charge had taken a handful of us up to the top of the steps and into the middle of the remnants of the fash mob. I fronted up a bonehead who had found himself stranded when the town hall doors were slammed shut in his face. He was cornered and panicky, eyes darting wildly this way and that. I hit him full in the face with one of the best punches I have ever thrown, and his nose immediately burst open, spraying blood all over his jacket. I managed to land a couple more blows before I was grabbed by a Dibble who tried to arrest me. I struggled free of his grip and retreated before he had a chance to grab me again.

As the fighting raged on, the police slowly regained the initiative, driving a wedge between the retreating fash and the AFA stewards. When the dust settled it was AFA and the Asian lads who were left in control of the Town Hall steps, and the fash who were cowering behind the lines of police. The fash were put in their vans and eventually escorted out of town. As we sorted out the details of the lads who had been arrested, I noticed that Gerry had got chatting to a couple of the Asian lads. It looked a bit like a world championship grinning competition from where I was standing.

"Who are you lot?" they were asking him excitedly. "That was brilliant. The nazis fucking shit themselves."

"We're AFA," replied Gerry, beaming proudly. "Anti-Fascist Action."

"Respect to AFA," they shouted as they crowded around him, high-fiving and making respect signs.

I had to laugh, especially when I looked across at the downcast faces of the ANL, who were beginning to sheepishly creep back into the square again. They had shown their arses yet again, and this time there was no hiding it.

On the way home a couple of the lads mentioned that they thought that some of the BNP mob had Scottish accents, and Steve confirmed with *Searchlight* that they had been bussed down from Aberdeen to help out with security for the Rochdale candidates. We later found out that this was because the BNP in the North-West could no longer muster enough bodies to ensure the safety of their candidates. The Rochdale branch had been whittled down to its bare bones by AFA's on-going opposition, and although their share of the vote actually increased slightly in the election, this was only to be expected after Beackon's victory in September. Incidentally, Beackon himself lost his Isle of Dogs seat the very same night, although his share of the vote increased.

Not long after the fracas on the town hall steps, Henderson resigned from the BNP, claiming he could no longer cope with the pressure. Rochdale had once been regarded as an area of great potential for the BNP, but in a little over two years, AFA's Stewards' Group had practically turned it into a no-go area for them.

Round 8. AFA wins by a knockout.

CHAPTER SEVEN

London Calling

THERE ALWAYS SEEMED to be something happening in London. If it wasn't a fascist event that had to be stopped, it was one of ours that had to be defended. The capital was the venue for a lot of the fascists' national demonstrations and events and London AFA often called for a national mobilisation to make sure they had enough people out to challenge whatever numbers the fash turned out. This meant that on a pretty regular basis we would head down to London to help out with whatever was planned. We caught the train, we drove down in cars and vans, we hired coaches, and on a couple of occasions we even hitch-hiked. The journey was time-consuming, tedious and expensive, but because people in London were relying on us to make the effort, we knew it had to be done.

Remembrance Sunday 1986–1991

The National Front's annual Remembrance Sunday commemoration was a rare beast. It was one of the few occasions the NF would show its face publicly in central London in the late Eighties. Every year after the official televised procession, the NF were allowed to hold their own small march from Victoria to Whitehall to lay a wreath at the Cenotaph. It was a peculiar spectacle as the assorted weirdoes and thugs spruced themselves up for the day and tried to make themselves look respectable. They had their own marching band and colour party, which rather than inspiring thoughts of plucky British Tommies in the trenches, ironically brought to mind images of goose-stepping nazis.

The NF's colour party came to a sticky end one year in a King's Cross burger bar. The Fronters were ambushed there by a mob of anti-fascists, and as the trapped fash attempted to defend themselves the fight spread into the kitchens and up and down the length of the restaurant. In the middle of the brawl, one anti-fascist picked up a chair to defend himself against a flagstaff-wielding nazi only to be informed by an American tourist that the seat was already taken.

For a couple of years in the mid-Eighties, AFA organised their own march in opposition to the NF's, but it was felt by many, especially those in the Stewards' Group, that this was having no effect on the fascists and hampered our ability to manoeuvre on the day. The last thing that we wanted was to be stewarding an ineffectual march through London while mobs of fascists roamed the streets attacking people at will. It also became a regular occurrence during these years that at some point in the day the Fronters would team up with the Chelsea Headhunters and attempt to attack the Anti-Apartheid picket outside South Africa House on Trafalgar Square. Clearly things would have to change.

In 1986 the AFA's Stewards' Group headed back to Trafalgar Square after the march and was just in time to prevent a full-blooded assault on the picket by the NF/ Headhunters. We were stood outside St Martin-in-the-Fields when the fash approached the picket from across the top of the square. We spotted them at the same time as they spotted us. They were giving it loads of verbal, stuff like "Come on then you Red faggots" and "Kill the Commie scumbags". They were a right mouthy bunch, but you could sense that they were a bit uneasy. They started gesturing for us to come across the road and have a go at them. So we did. We climbed over the railings and walked casually towards them. Lads like

Mickey O'Farrell, Jimmy and Big Kenny, who was a real man-mountain, were at the forefront, and you could see the Headhunters getting windy. All of a sudden they took fright and legged it up towards Leicester Square before a blow had been struck. Stragglers and fash who got separated from the main mob were picked off, including one hapless individual who was invited to hide in a darkened doorway by two shady characters known as One-eye and Del-boy. Hopefully the fash remembered where the doorway was later so that he could pick up his missing teeth. Now there's a valuable lesson in life for you: never step into a darkened Soho doorway with two complete strangers. Maybe they should put it on the national curriculum.

We were ecstatic. We had chased off the notorious Chelsea Headhunters, who were regarded as one of the top hooligan gangs in the country in those days. Now it is probably fair to say that it was not their full match-day firm but it was a significant proportion of them, supplemented by a number of NF as well. O'Shea had a theory about why they had run away so quickly. Mind you, he had a theory about everything.

"It's 'cos they don't really believe in the politics like we do," he surmised. "It's just a game to them, having a row with other football mobs. They thought they were coming here today to have an easy time slapping around a few daft Commies, but they met a determined mob who believed in what they're fighting for and they couldn't handle it." I nodded in agreement as he continued his rant, flecks of spittle forming at the corners of his mouth. "Besides, they're all from places like Reading and Basingstoke these days. We're the ones who come from the inner cities."

Earlier in the day we had been treated to the sight of a bonehead attempting to escape the clutches of an anti-fascist who had hold of his braces. The confused bone couldn't work out why he couldn't escape his attacker despite all his furious efforts. I was reminded of those *Scooby Doo* cartoons where the characters run frantically on the spot for a few seconds before speeding off. After a short time the braces broke and the bone ended up catapulting himself in front of a car.

Another clueless individual was "Alex from Chelmsford", who had previously made the mistake of putting his name and photo all over the cover of a pro-nazi bonehead fanzine of which he was the editor. He was spotted wandering around all on his own by an anti-fascist skinhead called Tim, who hailed him by name and called him over.

"All right Alex?" said Tim, as the hapless victim approached. "Have you ever heard of a group called Red Action?"

"Yeah I have," replied Alex. "Why?"

"'Cos you've just met them," said Tim, booting him in the balls.

We heard a couple of days later that the fash had been briefed earlier in the day by one of their leaders, who had fired them up with a speech declaring that they would wipe the floor with opposition.

"What about Red Action?" asked a voice from the crowd.

"You don't have to worry about them," declared the fash organiser smugly. "They're just a bunch of old men in duffel-coats."

We were lucky with our timing in '87 but we knew we could not be lucky every year, and from that point onwards the Stewards' Group decided that they would operate separately from the march and its organisers. This was basically the start of the Stewards' Group acting as an autonomous organisation. For a year or so afterwards there were actually two groups known as AFA: the liberal, anti-racist march organisers and the militant, anti-fascist Stewards' Group. Within a short while, the liberal wing of AFA had withered on the vine and it was left to the street-fighters to carry the torch.

In 1988 the anti-fascists were in control of the streets of

central London from the early morning onwards. In terms of the main threat from the NF/Headhunters it was virtually a re-run of '87, with the fash again charging across Trafalgar Square to attack the anti-apartheid picket, and again running away from AFA before a blow had been struck. The Headhunters tried again later, approaching Trafalgar Square from a different direction, but the end result was still the same.

In 1989, we changed tactics again and took over the fascists' assembly point at Victoria Station, including Shakers bar, where the fash had traditionally gathered for a pre-march drink. Fronters were attacked as they arrived, including two of the Headhunter's top boys, who breezed into the bar either unaware or arrogantly dismissive of the threat within. I hit one of them with a pint pot and Nads bottled the other one. They ran out the pub squealing to the police for protection.

Meanwhile, the NF march had been delayed for over an hour due to on-going problems caused by the anti-fascist presence. When it did eventually start it was accompanied by a 200-strong counter-demonstration that harried it all along the route of the march. It was mostly just verbal stuff that was being thrown at the marchers, but the occasional heavy object was seen sailing through the air into the middle of the NF group. At one point we started singing, "Two world wars and one world cup" at the marching nazis, a not-so-subtle reference to the fact that Mosley and the BUF had actually supported Germany in World War Two.

I was grabbed around the throat by an ugly-looking Dibble who pushed me up against a set of railings. "We should just let the NF get stuck into you fucking wankers," he sneered.

"Sounds like a good idea to me," I replied.

"They'd fucking murder you," he said with a malicious smile.

I thought about putting him right, but brushed him off and walked away instead, unwilling to get drawn into a debate that would only end up with me spending the night behind bars. I had only taken two steps when I heard a loud thud followed by the sound of breaking glass behind me. I looked back to see that the plod had been felled by a bottle thrown from within the NF ranks. He was lying on the ground, blood pouring from a head wound, and was eventually taken away on a stretcher. The NF looked demoralised and subdued as they finally laid their wreath at the Cenotaph, and for the first time ever they did not have the confidence to attack the anti-apartheid picket later that afternoon.

By 1991, the situation in central London had calmed to such an extent that AFA felt able to organise a 4,000-strong march through Bethnal Green on Remembrance Sunday instead of attempting to confront the dwindling NF activity. The Bethnal Green march was part of an on-going series of activities against the BNP's Rights for Whites campaign in the East End. I travelled down for a few of the activities in the East End, but nowhere near enough to tell the complete story. That particular tale will have to be told by someone else, but an AFA leaflet from 1998 gives a flavour of the campaign and its major events:

> By 1990 the BNP by now the largest far-right party, launched the "Rights for Whites" campaign in East London. AFA rose to the challenge, by ambushing two election meetings in quick succession, and for the first time since the 1970s took over the BNP/NF Brick Lane paper sale. This was followed by an intensive campaign of work in the area. 60,000 leaflets were distributed door-to-door, AFA speakers addressed meetings in schools and with community groups. BNP pubs were targeted, while a 10,000 strong Unity Carnival in the summer of 1991 put anti-fascism back on the national agenda. In November 1991, a 4,000 strong AFA demon-stration against race attacks marched through the BNP

heartland of Bethnal Green unopposed. An event that led directly to the relaunch of the ANL.

Well it could also be argued that it was the success of the AFA march, coupled with the fact that SWP paper sellers were getting battered by BNP hit-squads the length and breadth of the country, which eventually forced the SWP's hand. You start looking a bit ridiculous telling people that the fascists are no threat when they chase you out of town every time you try to sell your papers.

Unfortunately, the first ANL activity in the East End resulted in an embarrassing set-back for the anti-fascist movement as a whole. The ANL leadership had called for outsiders to come into Whitechapel for a mass leafleting session. This resulted in their members and supporters walking into a glaringly obvious ambush, which left several of them very seriously injured. They were the first members of the ANL Mark II to discover that a change of initials provides little protection against fascist aggression.

Apart from a handful of genuine hardmen, we regarded the BNP and those on its political fringes as being pretty much all mouth and trousers. They had nothing that would seriously worry even a half-decent football firm, but they were more than a match for the likes of the ANL. Tony Lecomber was a leading BNP member with a hard reputation but after bumping into AFA on a couple of occasions he soon acquired the nickname "Tarmac" for his regular and close association with the pavement. Other people with reputations, like Phil Edwards, Charlie Sargent, Will Browning, Alan Thompson and Gary Hitchcock, were all close to the BNP during this period, but AFA had confronted and beaten them all on several occasions.

The Whitechapel incident not only dented ANL morale and skulls, but gave the BNP an important psychological boost at a time when AFA had them on the back foot. In the eyes of the watching local population, the BNP's prowess as street-fighters had now been re-established, and the left were relegated once again to the status of hapless victims.

This was only the start of the ANL's madcap adventures, which eventually culminated not only in damage to the reputation of the SWP/ANL, but to the anti-fascist movement as a whole. One particular bugbear that we were confronted with time and again by locals was the SWP/ANL poster bearing the legend "Refugees Welcome Here". The fact that a load of middle-class outsiders were flouncing into communities beset with all the problems associated with extreme poverty, and basically telling local people that they should accept further strain on the precious few resources available, did more damage to anti-racism than any far-right propaganda ever could. "That poster has been the BNP's best-ever recruiting sergeant," remarked O'Shea.

Swastika Eyes 1986–1994

Not that I would ever advocate cruelty to animals, but if you kick a dog up the arse every time it pisses on your carpet then it eventually learns to stop. Nazi boneheads, on the other hand, never seemed to learn. No matter how many times you kicked them, you would still see them wandering around in full skinhead regalia, covered in nazi badges and patches, blissfully unaware of the next battering lying in wait for them just around the corner. Maybe they were victims of their own propaganda; maybe they really believed that they were the invincible Aryan warriors of fascist myth. I reckon this has to be the case, because it seemed to me that they were constantly shocked and surprised to find themselves rolling around in the gutter on the wrong end of a hiding.

Unlike Manchester, London had a big nazi skinhead scene, based around the Blood and Honour organisation. Blood and Honour was run by Ian Stuart Donaldson (*aka* Ian Stuart, lead singer of Skrewdriver). It was not a political organisation as such but promoted nazi skinhead bands like Skrewdriver, No Remorse and Brutal Attack. The music was badly played, unlistenable heavy metal/punk crap and the lyrics were banal racist drivel. Here's a typical example from a No Remorse song called "Bloodsucker":

> Sells his goods at double price
> That's how he makes his bread
> Filthy little Paki
> Won't stop until he's dead
> He's the immigrant with the false grin
> Behind it lies a mind of sin.

Or how about this charming ditty called "We've Got the Guns" from the same band:

> You rape 'cos you're a nigger ape
> We've got the guns so you better run nigger scum
> We're gonna swing you by your neck

Whoever said that the devil had all the best tunes clearly hadn't heard this lot. It was turgid stuff. But whatever the merits of the music, it was a growing and profitable phenomenon for all those involved. Blood and Honour were making thousands and thousands of pounds out of gigs, records, T-shirts, badges and other merchandise. They were also busy extending their network across Europe, the USA and even Australia. In addition to lining their pockets, bands like Skrewdriver played benefit gigs for the likes of the Ku Klux Klan, the BNP and the Ulster Defence Association.

Between 1987 and 1989, London AFA had forced a number of shops openly selling Blood and Honour merchandise and regalia in Carnaby Street to shut down, and had started a campaign to close down a similar operation in Riding House Street near Soho. The campaign used a variety of tactics, including mass pickets outside the shops themselves, publicity to embarrass the local authorities into taking action, as well as ambushes and acts of sabotage and vandalism. The bones had also been kicked out of a number pubs in and around Carnaby Street and Kings Cross and had been forced to tread a lot more warily around certain parts of central London. AFA also threw down a challenge to Blood and Honour by hosting a number of Angelic Upstarts gigs in London which the fash were unable to disrupt. All these successes had created problems for Blood and Honour and caused them to lose face, but it was clear that their gigs were going to have to be seriously disrupted if they were going to be badly hurt. The opportunity presented itself on 27 May 1989.

The Main Event, 27 May 1989

Blood and Honour were infuriated by the success of the AFA campaign against their Carnaby Street outlets. The shops had been their first attempt to go mainstream after years of organising in a semi-clandestine manner. Up until that point, most of their merchandise was being sold by mail order or at gigs, but they obviously expected to make bigger bucks and more political capital by coming out into the open.

In the spring of 1989, London AFA learned that Blood and Honour were intending to hold a major concert somewhere in the centre of London on May 27. This was their response to AFA's campaign against their shops and pubs. For the first time ever, Blood and Honour announced that they were going to hold a publicly advertised gig in London. It was intended to be biggest concert held by the far right anywhere, with seven bands appearing and over 1,200 tickets sold. Thousands of leaflets advertising the gig under the name "The Main Event" were distributed all over Europe and beyond.

Blood and Honour gigs were very difficult to stop or disrupt. Leaflets advertising them would be distributed only to known contacts and supporters, and even then they would not state where the venue was, but merely give details of a re-direction point. The bones would then be taken by coach or moved in large numbers by public transport to the secret venue, which could be many miles away. Alternative venues would also be booked for the night under false names in case anti-fascists found the original venue and got it cancelled.

On a couple of occasions in the past we had got hit-squads together and managed to ambush a few of the bones en route to the gigs, including Ian Stuart himself more than once. We were aware, however, that this tactic was only scratching the surface of the problem and was not causing them much damage. However, now that Blood and Honour had thrown down the gauntlet and come out into the open, it presented the forces of anti-fascism with an opportunity to finally meet them head on.

I seem to recall that for some reason only three of us travelled down from Manchester for this – myself, Nads and Gary F – but for us it would be an unforgettable day. We met up with the London AFA lads in a pub in Kilburn and caught the tube to Marble Arch station, where we were due to meet other AFA supporters at Speakers' Corner in Hyde Park. Everyone was pretty quiet on the tube journey. There were only about 100 of us, and we knew that Blood and Honour could easily attract ten times that number, so I guess we were all a bit apprehensive. To distract myself I got talking to Big Tony, one of the London lads, and he told me that they had found Blood and Honour's original venue at Camden Town Hall and had got it cancelled, but that they were sure to have a back-up venue booked for somewhere else.

Speakers' Corner was also Blood and Honour's re-direction point. London AFA had called for people to meet in the same place as the bones, but an hour earlier. The Stewards' Group arrived even earlier. It was a bright, sunny morning in London, and people were out enjoying a quiet stroll in Hyde Park when we swept out of Marble Arch station into Speakers' Corner, scattering small groups of boneheads in our wake. These were mostly foreign skinheads or out-of-towners who had arrived in London early and had nothing better to do than hang around the re-direction point. A larger group of about twenty older boneheads attempted to make a stand but were overwhelmed by sheer weight of numbers. This was a vicious little battle and serious hand-to-hand fighting took place before the bones were scattered. They ended up either fleeing for their lives or being kicked all over the tarmac by anti-fascists. Tourists looked on in horror as the fighting spread all over Speakers' Corner.

I was buzzing now, full of adrenalin, and Gary F and I paired off against two bones who'd wandered unwittingly into our path. I found myself facing a tough-looking Swedish bonehead (but then it's easy to look tough with a shaved head, big boots and combat gear). After a brief struggle I pulled him towards me and simultaneously hit him full in the face with a can of fizzy pop which sent him flying about six feet across the park into a heap. He struggled to his feet and I hit him again.

An elderly American tourist tried to intervene on the bone's behalf. "I think he's had enough now," he pleaded.

"He's a fucking fascist," I shouted. "It's never enough."

This appeared to do the trick as the American walked casually away from the scene and never even looked back. I hit the bone again, and finally sparked him out. My can of pop was crumpled, but still miraculously intact.

I looked at Gary F who had a big, mad grin on his face as he went on the prowl looking for more victims. Most of the early arrivals had been chased out of the park by now, but there were more arriving all the time. These newcomers were also attacked and chased by gangs of anti-fascists. If all the bones had been able to mob up, things might have been different, but as it was, we had a field day. The bones never got it together, probably because they didn't know each other, and there was no-one to give them any leadership. The one man who could have provided it was Nicky Crane, the top man of Skrewdriver Security. He turned up with a minibus full of bones but soon got on his toes when a flying column of anti-fascists charged out the park to confront him. I was at the front of the charge and I was pretty relieved to see him run away. Crane was one of the few genuine hard men on the bonehead scene, and ironically, given the nazis' extreme homophobia, he was also openly gay. He died a few years later from AIDS, and it was only after his illness had deprived him of his strength and vitality that his Aryan brothers found the courage to openly criticise his sexuality.

Our numbers were being swelled all the time by anti-fascists arriving for the counter-demo, and the police and fash were being run ragged. Police resources were stretched that day because thousands of Muslims were also marching through central London on a big demonstration against Salman Rushdie's book *The Satanic Verses*. For a few short hours we more or less had free rein in Hyde park and the surrounding areas. Fights broke out in the McDonald's on Oxford Street as anti-fascists charged out of Speakers' Corner to attack any boneheads in the vicinity. I remember one bonehead leaning on a set of railings who was appalled when a bloke on a bicycle pedalled up and punched him full in the face.

A coachload of bones attempted to pull up on the road beside Speakers' Corner but was met by a barrage of missiles, including a metal dustbin and a crash barrier. The driver put his foot down and sped away minus a couple of windows but with his passengers still on board. The coach company was called Amber Valley Coaches. Remember that name.

After a few hours it became obvious that the demonstration against Salman Rushdie must have finished, because vanloads of riot police were starting to arrive on the scene. By now it was long past the time when Blood and Honour were due to meet, and there was probably nothing more that could have been done at Speakers' Corner anyway, so the London lads put the word out that we were withdrawing from the area via Marble Arch tube station.

As we walked down the steps towards the station concourse, we bounced into more nazis coming up. I booted one in the face, and turned around just in time to see Nads punch another bonehead on the side of the jaw. The bone's legs just collapsed underneath him.

"Did you see that?" grinned Nads. "He went down like a sack of shit." I wasn't surprised; there was fifteen stone of muscle, twenty years of martial arts training and a knuckle-duster behind that punch. Anyone would have done the same.

More fights broke out on the station concourse as another small group of bones wandered unwittingly into the middle of the anti-fascist mob. This lot were completely overwhelmed and kicked all over the place. Nads put on a training exhibition for us as he helped a large, semi-conscious bonehead stay on his feet purely by the use of viciously delivered uppercuts. The entertainment was curtailed by the arrival of the riot police, and the gravity-defying bonehead was allowed to slump to the ground. We were eventually pushed onto the tube train by the relieved riot cops, who were happy to see the back of us.

We stayed on the tube for only one stop and emerged again at Oxford Circus station, hoping to double back in search of more pickings. The sight that greeted us as we came out of the station completely kiboshed that plan. It was the Amber Valley Coach again, driving slowly down Oxford Street with its cargo of boneheads still on board. The coach was again pelted with missiles and the driver had to jump a red light to escape the bombardment. A few solitary bones wandering lost around Oxford Street were also attacked, and it was during one of these exchanges that I was grabbed by an irate police sergeant.

"I have reason to believe," he told me, "that you have recently been involved in, or are about to be involved in, incidents of serious physical assault."

I knew he had nothing on me, it was the phrase "or are about to be involved in" that told me I was unlikely to be charged with anything. Just to be on the safe side, however, Debbie, a female steward from London AFA, came over and put her arm through mine. "Why are you harassing my boyfriend?" she shouted at the sergeant. "He's done nothing wrong. He's been out shopping with me all afternoon."

The flummoxed Dibble looked at us in bewilderment for a moment. "Just get out of the area and stay out," he said in exasperation.

The advice was good, because the police were all over us by now, and the only way to lose them was to get out of the area altogether. We eventually ended up in a pub near Euston where we settled down for a celebratory drink.

I was knackered. It was a combination of coming down from the adrenalin high and the sheer physical effort of chasing and fighting people all afternoon. However, no sooner had I settled down to enjoy my pint when there was a shout from one of the lads drinking outside. I ran to the window and looked out to see the Amber Valley coach yet again. This time it had pulled up at some traffic lights outside the pub, its occupants oblivious to the excitement their arrival had generated. There was an immediate scramble as we raced outside, picking up bottles and glass ashtrays as we went. The coach came under another hail of missiles before it managed to speed away to safety again. By now the coach was looking in a sorry state, and contained some very pissed-off-looking bones. They must have thought that the whole of London was full of anti-fascist headcases.

Later in the evening, a small group of anti-fascists attacked the Blood and Honour shop in Riding House Street, smashing the front windows and pouring bleach over the stock inside.

This attack was the culmination of many months' work, including pickets, petitions and numerous other protests, all of which eventually forced the shop to close.

We learned the following day that the Main Event had gone ahead in the Red Lion pub in Gravesend, Kent. Seven hundred nazis eventually made it down there but the venue held only 400, meaning that 300 couldn't get in, and a further 500 never even found out where it was. Blood and Honour were in a state of complete disarray for some months after May 27. They lost a £900 deposit on Camden Town Hall and a lot more money was lost refunding the bones who couldn't get in. They also lost a lot of face for failing to confront AFA at Hyde Park, and lost a lot of respect from their comrades abroad who complained about the shambolic organisation of the event.

Following the events of May 27, Ian Stuart left his house in King's Cross and moved to Derbyshire. We heard rumours that the Chelsea Headhunters were trying to muscle in on the Blood and Honour cash cow and were making threatening noises in his direction. There was, however, another reason for his swift departure from London, and that was the activities of a certain ex-Manc by the name of Hefty who harassed and attacked the Blood and Honour leader at every given opportunity.

The area around King's Cross and Euston was bandit country. Lone fascists, small groups of nazis and even whole firms came to grief in the streets around the two stations. Hefty and a few other lads, namely AJ, Carl, Pete G, and Gavin, used to operate around that area and chanced upon Stuart on a number of occasions. They gave him and his followers a few serious hidings at various times, but the event that seemed to give Stuart the real horrors was when he went out early one morning to buy a newspaper and a pint of milk, and was hit across the head by a large Mancunian wielding a Lucozade bottle. Ian Stuart was a coward and a bully. He liked to throw his weight around when the odds were in his favour, but when confronted on any number of occasions by AFA lads he legged it and left his comrades to face the music.

On another occasion, it was the turn of Skrewdriver's drummer, Des Clarke, to take a beating for the band. Clarke wasn't a skinhead, but a rockabilly who spent most of his time hanging around the pubs and clubs in the Camden area. He got his just desserts one Sunday afternoon in the summer of 1988. I was on a pub crawl with some of the London lads after some political event now lost in the mists of time and memory, and towards the end of the afternoon we decided that it was well past time to get some scran. We headed for a restaurant on Camden Parkway, but as soon as we walked in we spotted Clarke and a bonehead already at a table. We sat down pretending we didn't recognise him, but he clocked us all right, and started looking around nervously. He got up to make a phone call and was overheard to whisper the unfortunate words, "Hello Ian," before AJ hit him in the face with a plateful of spaghetti bolognese and Garpo CS-gassed him. I managed to hit his mate a few times before he ran for cover behind the bar. Unfortunately for the bonehead this was a dead-end, and he was trapped. He looked wildly around for a means of escape before suddenly diving headlong through the serving hatch into the kitchens. He got stuck halfway through, and I managed to grab his legs and stab him in the arse a few times with my fork before he scrambled and kicked his way to freedom.

The two fash had left their coats hung over the back of their chairs, and as we left the restaurant I picked them up, hoping they were carrying their address books around with them. No luck there, but there was enough money to buy everyone a round of drinks. We settled down in a bar near Euston Station where we continued the session well into the evening. The London lads were on top form as I recounted the tale of the fash trapped in the serving hatch.

"I wonder what the kitchen staff thought when a screaming bonehead suddenly jumped through the serving hatch," laughed Jimmy.

"They probably thought he was really hungry," joked O'Shea.

It was several years before Blood and Honour were brave enough to organise another publicly advertised gig in London, and when they did it seemed that they had learned few lessons from the Hyde Park debacle.

The Battle of Waterloo, 12 September 1992

In August 1992, posters proclaiming "Skrewdriver Back in London" were spotted in various parts of the country. They were advertising a Blood and Honour concert due to take place in London on September 12. At first we assumed it was a hoax, because Skrewdriver hadn't even attempted to play in London since The Main Event, but as time went by it became obvious that it was anything but a hoax.

The concert was once more touted to be a massive affair, with up to 2,000 nazis expected to attend and several bands playing, including Skrewdriver, Skullhead, No Remorse and a Swedish band called Dirlewanger. There was a rumour flying about that a mainstream music promoter was willing to seriously back Blood and Honour if the gig proved a success and any opposition was muted or destroyed. Once again the gig was at a secret location with a re-direction point, which this time was at Waterloo Station at 5.30 p.m. We heard on the grapevine that both the BNP and the British Movement (BM) had been approached to help with security for the event.

By coincidence, a week before the concert AFA's Unity Carnival was due to take place on Hackney Downs in London. A request was made for stewards to attend from around the country in case the fash tried a pre-emptive strike, but nothing untoward happened and the carnival passed off peacefully.

Maybe the fash were hoping that if they left us alone, we would leave them alone. Fat chance.

The carnival was cold and rain-swept, but at least it gave us the chance to alert an already interested audience to the following weekend's events. In the meantime, London AFA contacted all the various anti-racist and anti-fascist groups with details of what was due to happen at Waterloo, but no-one seemed interested. The ANL suddenly decided that they were holding a march in Thornton Heath, more than fifteen miles away. So it looked like we were on our own, but then we never seriously expected anything else.

Neil Parrish, who had become one of Blood and Honour's main organisers, boasted to the media that he would be available at 4.30 p.m. on the station concourse to give inter-views. A Sky News reporter was worried that he wouldn't be able to find the bones and was told that as they were expecting between 1,000 and 2,000 at the station, "you'll have no trouble finding us". By a strange coincidence, 4.30 p.m. was when London AFA announced that they were also calling a counter-demonstration at the station.

We took about twenty stewards down from Manchester. All the usual suspects were present, including Gerry, Steve, Wigan Mike, Gary the Axe, Solo, Big Dave and the rest. We eventually arrived in the Smoke at 1 p.m. and met up with the London AFA lads in a pub on the Holloway Road. AFA groups from around the country were arriving all the time, swelling numbers to about 200. The atmosphere was tense because everyone knew this was the big one. It really was a case of do or die this time. We had a fair-sized mob out that day, with good numbers from Liverpool, Doncaster and London itself, but it looked tiny in comparison to what I knew we could expect to find at Waterloo.

I tried to push all thoughts of what lay ahead to the back of my mind. I was nervous and tense but did my best to appear laid back and unconcerned. Sometimes it just hits you like that. Sometimes you're really buzzing and up for it, while at others you get a queasy feeling in the pit of your stomach. Either way you have to force yourself to stay cool, especially when you are in a position where other people are relying on you to keep a clear head.

At 3.20 p.m., AFA's Stewards' Group appeared on the station concourse at Waterloo, causing a number of bones to flee for their lives. Three boneheads drinking in the station bar were set upon. The police tried to push their way through the AFA mob crowding at the entrance to the bar in an attempt to arrest those inside, and in doing so missed the guilty parties making good their escape through another exit not ten feet away. We heard rumours afterwards that these first casualties were in fact plainclothes police sent to Waterloo to infiltrate Blood and Honour.

Both Steve and Gerry were involved in early exchanges with the nazis, but Gerry hurt his hand punching someone on the side of the head. He spent the rest of the afternoon complaining about it. "I think I've broken ma fuckin' knuckle," he moaned.

More boneheads were attacked as they entered the station, and the police were forced to cordon off the nazis in the middle of the station concourse. Along with several other AFA stewards I infiltrated the cordon. Once inside I sidled up behind the biggest bonehead I could find and started kicking him surreptitiously in the back of the ankles.

"You're going to die when we get out of here," I whispered into his ear.

He tried to ignore me, but he was shaking like a leaf.

"Did you hear me, you baldy wanker?" I goaded. "When we get out of here I'm going to kill you."

All the colour had drained out of him and for a moment I thought he was going to faint. His misery was brought to an end when the police decided to escort the nazis out of the station to safety, but once outside, and out of view of the

CCTV cameras, they were astonished when their escort suddenly imploded from within as the anti-fascists turned on the boneheads. The bonehead I was goading earlier had shot off like a rabbit, and I only managed to land a couple of glancing blows on the back of his head.

This scenario was re-enacted several times over the next hour and a half as we continued to resist police attempts to force us off the station concourse. While this game of cat and mouse was going on, other groups of anti-fascists were ambushing boneheads coming up the escalators from the tube station.

I was arrested by the Transport Police during one of these scuffles, but for some reason I was never charged with anything, and to my surprise they released me an hour or so later with a warning to leave the immediate area or risk being arrested again. I ignored the warning of course. There was no way I was going to miss this.

The Transport Police at Waterloo Station have a little office at the side of the concourse, and I basically took two steps out of the front door and I was bang in the middle of a full-scale riot again. Boneheads were still being chased and battered everywhere you looked, and the police had completely lost control of the situation.

By 5 p.m., there were nearly 1,000 anti-fascists on the concourse and fights were still breaking out all over the place. Shortly afterwards, the station was shut down at the request of the manager, freeing AFA from the responsibility of holding the concourse any longer and allowing us to surge out into the streets to confront the groups of boneheads mobbing up outside. Neil Parrish was nowhere to be seen.

Everywhere you looked boneheads were being battered and chased. A group of fifty right-wing casuals got themselves trapped under a footbridge, and despite being surrounded by riot police they came under attack from all sides, including an aerial bombardment of broken quarry tiles from the footbridge above. Two London AFA lads, Russell and Gerry, had infiltrated this particular mob in the hope of picking up information on the whereabouts of the gig. The two lads were sieg-heiling with the best of them in an effort to blend in with the fash and secure their confidence. I took careful aim with my quarry tiles in the hope that they didn't end up the victims of "friendly fire", but the area was full of rampaging anti-fascists who weren't in the know, and I bet there were moments when the boys regretted going undercover on that particular day.

Elsewhere, individuals and small groups arriving on foot or by car were picked off as they approached the station. One carload of bones was trapped when the driver made the unfortunate mistake of leaving his window wound down, providing an opportunistic anti-fascist with the chance to reach in and turn his engine off and remove the keys before the vehicle was attacked. The immobile car was nearly turned over.

I saw one panic-stricken bonehead run the entire length of the street with his arms covering his head to protect himself. A sensible enough precaution except for the fact that he couldn't see where he was going and kept running into groups of anti-fascists who gave him the occasional dig as he ran past them. Eventually someone put him out of his misery and tripped him up. I caught him a beauty as he fell, my boot going upwards into his face as he was falling forwards. Within seconds he was unconscious.

Four stations had now been shut in the area due to "rioting", including Charing Cross, making it difficult for anyone to reach Waterloo, although a large mob of bones arrived on foot via the footbridge across the Thames. They soon wished they hadn't as they immediately came under attack. A number of football supporters from various clubs, including Arsenal, QPR, Millwall and Chelsea also found their way to the area and joined one side or the other according to their political beliefs.

The football supporters mostly arrived at Waterloo in ones or twos, or in small groups. Some were attempting to make their way home after the match, while others were attracted to the area by radio reports of the rioting. Millwall and Chelsea arrived mob-handed. Chelsea, as expected, were pretty much on the side of Blood and Honour. The situation with Millwall was less clear-cut. Everyone expected them to be 100 per cent behind the fash but when one of Millwall's main men was approached by Nicky Cooper of the NF pleading for help on Blood and Honour's behalf, he got more than he bargained for. He was apparently sent sprawling by a vicious punch and was told, "We've come to kick their heads in, not go to their fucking stupid gig." However, another well-known face at Millwall, "Tags" or "Taggart", collapsed with a heart attack in the middle of the fascist ranks after coming under an anti-fascist bombardment of bricks and paving slabs.

Skirmishes continued all around Waterloo as the nazis and their police escorts came under concerted attack by large numbers of anti-fascists. The police did not know what to do with their escorts and the fascists themselves did not know where the venue was because Neil Parrish and the rest of the organisers were sat in a pub at Victoria Station. When phone calls were made by the trapped fascists to the organisers demanding that they either be given the venue details or be rescued, they were told that they should try to make their way to Victoria where they would be told the location of the gig.

Fighting had now spread all along the South Bank complex as bewildered theatre-goers ran for cover, evidently unimpressed with the free entertainment we had so thoughtfully provided for them. I suddenly saw a vaguely familiar figure walking towards me, and it took me a second or two to work out if it was friend or foe. It was neither. It was the bloke who plays Phil Mitchell from *EastEnders*. He looked sheepish and worried. "Not so tough in real life are you?" someone sneered as he put his head down and made a beeline for the relative safety of the police lines.

Eventually the police managed to get things under control and escorted the remaining fash to Temple tube station where they were put on a commandeered train out of the area. In the end, less than 400 got into the gig at the Yorkshire Grey pub in Eltham, south-east London. The anti-fascists, meanwhile, were broken up into small groups by the police, cordoned off and escorted on foot across the Thames towards central and north London. I was worried about a couple of people from Manchester who I had not seen all afternoon amid the mayhem, but everyone eventually reported back safe and sound. They were all buzzing, apart from Gerry, who was still complaining about his hand.

We stayed on in London until closing time, winding down with a couple of beers and reliving the events of the previous few hours. After saying goodbye to old and new friends, we climbed into our cars and vans and began the long drive back to Manchester. It had been a long day and I was glad to be heading home to my bed.

The papers the next morning all carried reports of the "Battle of Waterloo" and on the whole the reports were fairly accurate, except for the *Sunday Times,* which attributed the whole thing to the Anti-Nazi League. This might have been because the ANL actually sent out a press release claiming responsibility. On a similar note, I cannot let the occasion pass without mentioning a small lefty sect by the name of Workers' Power, who amid all the carnage and rioting at Waterloo, actually tried to do a paper sale!

On a foggy night in October 1993, Ian Stuart died in a car-crash in Derbyshire. His death opened the door for Combat 18 to muscle in on the Blood and Honour cash cow.

C18 and the Ian Stuart Memorial Gig, 15 January 1994

If anyone could be described as the phantom menace, then Combat 18 (C18) are far more deserving of the title than any collection of characters from Star Wars. When they first appeared on the scene in the early months of 1992, they were accompanied by an massive explosion of hype and hysteria as the media devoted hundreds of column inches and hours of air-time to "this new terrorist threat". All this publicity gave the impression that C18 were a dangerous paramilitary organisation armed with guns and bombs and god-knows what else, whereas the reality was that they were the same old rabble of nazis and right-wing football hooligans that we'd been fighting for years.

C18 were formed when the BNP decided they needed a standing stewards' group to protect their events rather than just relying on whoever turned up on the day. This decision came after London AFA had successfully attacked and disrupted several BNP activities in east London, leaving the BNP's Rights For Whites campaign in the area in tatters. Within months of its formation, however, the group had broken away from the BNP and Combat 18 was born. So in an ironic twist, it appears that the motivation behind the formation of C18, which was basically an attempt to form a right-wing version of AFA, came about directly from the activities of AFA itself.

C18 immediately made a name for themselves by publishing hit-lists of political opponents, attacking soft targets and leaving threatening messages on people's answering machines. The nucleus of the group started out with a hard-core of ex-BNP "hardmen" and other assorted hangers-on but grew to include members of the NF, several Ulster Loyalists, and groups of football hooligans, especially the Chelsea Head-hunters. With the help of the media they built up a myth of invulnerability, but whether they could sustain the myth when they came into contact with AFA was another matter.

The first opportunity to find out came in October 1993 during the ANL-organised Unity Demonstration in South London. AFA scouts located C18 in the Harrow Inn next to Abbey Wood station. They were waiting for the march to disperse in the hope that they could ambush people making their way home. C18 were challenged by AFA but refused to leave the pub until the police arrived. Not an auspicious start.

The next time AFA and C18 crossed swords was on the occasion of the Ian Stuart Memorial gig, which was due to be held in Becontree on 15 January 1994. By this time Blood and Honour was completely under the control of C18, who slandered and attacked the previous organisers and cowed any opposition to their presence within the bonehead scene. C18 slammed the incompetence that led to the defeat at Waterloo and promised a back to basics strategy of secret gigs organised on a word of mouth basis. They promised the boneheads that there would be no more humiliations.

In the event, the day turned into shambles for C18, with London AFA striking the first blow when they rumbled the original venue at Becontree and got it cancelled a few days before the event. AFA knew however that a back-up venue would be booked, and started ringing around trying to get numbers out for the day itself. Manchester AFA got the call-out late in the day and only four of us made the trip down. Gerry and I caught the train and another couple of lads came down later in a van. We met the London lads at a pub near Euston, and about 150 of us caught the tube over to the East End. On arrival at Bow Road we swarmed out of the station and attempted to steam C18's headquarters, the Little Driver pub. About fifty C18 came out to confront AFA but after a moment's hesitation they scattered, possibly unnerved by the zulu chants of the advancing anti-fascist mob; or maybe they were just a bunch of bullying, cowardly scumbags who were not interested in a fight when the odds weren't heavily in their favour.

Someone fired a flare at the retreating fascists but it missed
its target and hit an overhead railway bridge instead, making a
right bloody racket. The charge was eventually halted just
yards from the pub by large numbers of police, who conveni-
ently turned up just in time to rescue the retreating nazis. C18
were still fleeing in all directions, and I saw one leading
member shamelessly climbing uninvited into the back of a
police car. The anti-fascists were eventually rounded up and
put on a non-stop sealed train to Earls Court under police
escort all the way.

Later in the evening we moved out of Earls Court under
cover of darkness, and shook off the police spotters on our
tail. We caught the tube to Waterloo Station where AFA
spotters had reported that C18 were attempting to hold their
gig in a pub called the Wellington. When word reached the
fash of our arrival, C18, backed up by Blood and Honour
boneheads, attempted to charge out of the pub to confront
AFA. They were beaten back by truncheon-wielding riot
police. In the ensuing melee the pub was smashed up and the
landlord cancelled the gig.

Later in the evening, the main AFA mob were hidden away
in a small pub tucked away behind Waterloo Station hoping
to avoid detection by police spotters. I had stepped outside
for a breath of fresh air when I suddenly noticed half a dozen
Blood and Honour boneheads heading unknowingly towards
the very boozer we were drinking in. I strolled casually back
into the pub and raised the alarm, hoping that my demeanour
outside the pub had been nonchalant enough not to have
aroused suspicion.

"Heads up lads," I shouted as soon as I got inside. "Half a
dozen fash heading this way."

The ambush didn't really go according to plan, because as
soon as they stepped into the doorway of the pub the fash
sussed it was moody and only a couple of them got hit. The
rest legged it. We heard on the grapevine a couple of weeks

later that a contingent of German nazis at the gig were so unimpressed by C18's handling of the event that they started brawling with their British "brothers".

The takeover of Blood and Honour was seen as the key to C18's success. In the event it nearly led to their downfall. The huge sums of money generated by the nazi music scene was always going to be a temptation for the greedy little Fuhrers, and sure enough within a very short time allegations surfaced of large sums of money being stolen. This, coupled with Special Branch spies stirring the pot, eventually led to a bout of internal feuding that left one C18 member dead and two leading members, Charlie Sargent and Martin Cross, serving life sentences for murder. It also split the group down the middle, with the Will Browning faction and the Sargent faction at each other's throats.

For all their bluster, C18 actually achieved very little. They claimed the credit for the riot in Dublin in 1995 when England played Ireland but they were not even there. They attempted to build links with Loyalist groups in the north of Ireland but only succeeded in unwittingly introducing M15 and Special Branch spies to the Loyalists. They liked to boast that they were the cutting edge of British fascism but in reality they were more of a danger to themselves and other fascists than they were to their political opponents. In the end they couldn't even build a national organisation. They had strongholds in London and Essex, and to a lesser extent parts of Wales and the Midlands (where they could call upon the services of Aston Villa's football firm), but they had very little in other parts of the country.

Charlie Sargent's brother Steve was fond of adopting pen-names like Albion Wolf when writing articles for C18 magazines like *Thor-Would*, *Wodin*, and *The White Dragon*. Del O'Connor, the Wigan-based C18 member, used to call his little group the White Wolves. Nazi bands associated with C18 included groups with names like Celtic Warrior,

Warhammer and Warlord. Somehow you couldn't escape the feeling that they had played too many games of *Dungeons & Dragons* in their teenage years and just wanted to carry on living the fantasy.

All joking aside, the remnants of C18 have reorganised, and despite their small numbers, they retain the potential to cause serious problems, especially in areas where racial tension already exists. During the summer of 2001, a C18 presence in Oldham caused a serious escalation of racial violence in an area that was already volatile, and provoked several nights of rioting.

CHAPTER EIGHT

On The One Road 1986–1994

Fascism and Loyalism

ANTI-FASCIST ACTION was a single-issue organisation that comprised a number of different groups and individuals who had come together for the sole purpose of opposing fascism. We recognised early on that any attempt to unite these disparate groups around any other issue would inevitably cause splits and disruption.

The question of the war in Ireland was therefore a tricky one for AFA. As with any other issue, activists within AFA held a variety of opinions regarding Irish politics. Some people in the organisation supported the armed struggle of the IRA, others supported the call for a withdrawal of British troops from the province, while many weren't bothered one way or the other, or were vaguely antagonistic towards Irish republicanism.

On the other hand, the links between the far right and Loyalism are many and varied. Leading fascists such as Terry Blackham, Steve Martin and Frank Portinari amongst others have been jailed for their involvement in arms offences linked to Loyalist paramilitaries. Eddy Whicker of the National Front was also implicated in a similar operation. C18 leaders boast of their friendships with leading Loyalist figures such as Johnny "Mad Dog" Adair and Sam "Skelly" McCrory. Both men were pictured on an NF march in 1983 alongside Donald Hodgen, who became a prominent UDA member. Both Adair and McCrory played in a nazi skinhead band called Offensive Weapon in the mid-Eighties and the majority of the thirty-odd nazi skinheads who led the Belfast branch of the National Front went on to form the core of Adair's notorious C Company of the Ulster Freedom Fighters. Blood and Honour bands have long associated themselves with the Loyalist cause and have played numerous benefit gigs for the likes of the UDA. Members of NF, BNP and C18 have all raised funds for imprisoned Loyalist paramilitaries, and fascists from across the spectrum of far-right groups can often be seen on Orange marches.

That there are extensive and reciprocal links between Loyalists and British fascists is undeniable. That these links give weight to the argument that Loyalism is essentially nothing more than a local form of fascism, being based as it is on extreme right-wing supremacist ideas, is open to debate. I would suggest that on this occasion you are judged by the company you choose to keep. My impression of the situation in Northern Ireland is that the treatment of Catholics compares with anything meted out to black people in the Deep South of America. No wonder the far right have such a fetish with Ulster.

Whatever the rights and wrongs of the argument, we had to deal with the facts on the ground, and these were that the Irish community and their marches, meetings and social events often attracted the unwanted attention of a variety of fascist and Loyalist groups, and as anti-fascists we therefore felt we had a duty, and an obligation, to help defend these events.

Bernadette McAliskey Meeting

In November 1988 we were invited by the chief steward of the Troops Out Movement to help out with security for a big public meeting with civil rights activist Bernadette McAliskey in the Conway Hall in Red Lion Square. Word had got around that a joint BNP/UDA mob were planning to attack the meeting and Troops Out's chief steward quickly recognised that they didn't have the numbers or calibre of stewards to deal with the potential threat.

On the night itself a mob of us crept silently through the backstreets of Holborn and appeared suddenly and unexpectedly at the entrance to the hall. The first thing we saw was virtually the entire leadership of the BNP walking brazenly into the meeting. A brawl broke out, and they were attacked with fists, boots and a variety of weapons. Lefty paper sellers scattered in all directions as the BNP were kicked all over the pavement. I saw Nads hit a leading BNP member in the face and as the victim fell over backwards his teeth flew through the air in all directions. It was all over quickly, so quickly in fact that I don't recall that I hit anyone in that first fight. People like Nads were so fast that it sometimes made you feel as if you were wading through treacle.

Nevertheless it was a timely interception and a job well done, I thought, except for the fact that the official TOM stewards and lefty paper sellers went crazy at us, accusing us of stopping people coming into their meeting and wrecking the event. We pointed out that the people we had attacked were fascists intent on wrecking their meeting anyhow, but by now they were too hysterical to listen to reason, and in any case more groups of fascists were approaching the hall. I suppose their plan was to get into the hall in small groups and then once inside they would mob up and cause havoc. If that was the plan then it misfired badly because it simply allowed us to pick them off at our leisure.

Another group came within about ten yards of the hall before they sussed that there was something strange about the large group of shady characters stood nonchalantly outside. They turned tail and fled back the way they had come, pursued by a posse of anti-fascists. By now I had got my act together, and was at the forefront of the pursuing mob. As both groups reached the top of the road, numbers were about even. The bloke I was chasing was a well-known face at Chelsea, and he turned around to have a go. Fair play to him, because I was carrying an iron bar, and I wouldn't have fancied being in his position.

"Come on then cunt," he said, beckoning me forward with his hands. "D'you fucking want it?"

He was backing off and dancing around just out of reach, and I reckoned that he wasn't as keen on having the row as he made out.

"Stop running away and let's just fucking have it," I taunted him.

I had just made up my mind to steam straight into him and get it over with when a mob of fifty fash burst out of a nearby pub and ran straight at us. Fortunately, two police vans screeched around the corner and halted their charge. I quickly hid the iron bar inside my coat and walked back towards the hall. I had gone ten yards when I heard the Chelsea wanker telling the police that I was carrying a weapon. I dodged behind a car and managed to drop the bar into the gutter, but unfortunately it made such a loud clanging noise that I was certain the whole street must have heard it. I was shoved up against a set of railings by a cop. Surely he must have heard the bar hit the ground. It sounded like fucking Big Ben to my ears.

"That bloke just told me you threatened him with an iron bar," he said as he started to search me. "Are you carrying a weapon?"

"No officer," I replied, trying hard not to stare at the iron bar lying in the gutter in full view of anyone half interested in looking for it.

"So what were you doing running up the road then?" he asked as he continued to pat me down.

"I was stewarding a meeting in the hall down the road when that lot attacked it," I said nodding towards the mob of jeering fash and Loyalists.

"Well if I were you I'd get back to the hall and let us deal with them," he said. I politely agreed with him, and scuttled back to the hall sharpish, losing myself in the crowd for a while.

While all this was going on, a lone fascist had somehow managed to sneak into the hall and was looking around desperately for his missing comrades. He was spotted by a female steward and was politely asked to step into one of the smaller side-rooms where he was questioned by four or five large blokes for a while. Over the course of the interview, during which he received no physical harm, both his bladder and his bowels emptied, and he was kicked out of the hall in disgust. I got back just in time to see him being thrown out the back door.

"No. Please don't throw me out," he begged. "Let me stay in the hall."

"What's his problem?" I asked as the door was slammed shut in his face.

"He got it into his head that he was being held prisoner by the IRA," replied O'Shea with a shrug of his shoulders. "He thinks we've got a sniper on the roof waiting to pick him off as he leaves the hall. Stupid prick."

The rest of the meeting passed of successfully, although I did not really get to hear much of it, and afterwards we provided an escort to the nearest tube station for anyone who was concerned for their safety.

A few weeks after the event, it was reported in a number of Loyalist publications that Derek Beackon and Richard Edmonds, two leading BNP members, were among those injured. None of this prevented us from being banned from future Troops Out events, a decision which caused a lot of bad blood over the years.

The Bloody Sunday March

The annual Bloody Sunday Commemoration which was jointly organised by the Troops Out Movement and a number of other groups, took place every January in London. The march to commemorate the shooting dead of fourteen unarmed civilians in Derry by British paratroopers in 1972 always attracted the attention of the far right, and it was a safe bet that there would be some sort of trouble along the route. Despite the ill-feeling that existed between Troops Out and AFA, we maintained a strong presence on the march.

One year, during a particularly gruelling trek through the outer suburbs of north London, four of us were stuck at the back of the march in the pouring rain when someone noticed a bus heading in the direction of the post-march rally. We were wet, we were cold, and we were bloody miserable. The temptation to sit in the warm and dry proved irresistible and we broke ranks and jumped on the bus.

We settled down gratefully in our seats, rubbing the mist from the windows so that we could watch the bus overtaking the straggling lines of sodden marchers. Suddenly someone noticed a group of fash loitering with intent down a side street. They were just geeing themselves up to launch an ambush on the march when we jumped off the bus and bounced right into the middle of them. Blows were exchanged and the surprised fash were chased back down the street before they had the chance to realise that they easily outnumbered us. Further down the street they started getting their heads together and regrouped with the intention of having another pop, but by that time the police had intervened and the two sides were separated.

A couple of years later, following a series of scuffles along the route of the demonstration, Nicky Crane was spotted in the vicinity just as the march was reaching its destination in Kilburn. This was in the days before he outed himself, and he was still actively involved in neo-nazi circles, chiefly as Blood and Honour's head of security. Crane once served twelve months in prison for attacking a black family with a bottle, and was infamous for leading 200 skinheads on a rampage through an Asian area of the East End. Suspecting that he was up to some skulduggery, a group of anti-fascists confronted him, and he was chased out of the area.

Shortly afterwards he was spotted returning to Kilburn in the back of a taxi. This time there was a serious fight and he was knocked unconscious, with one anti-fascist repeatedly slamming the taxi door shut on his head. Three London AFA members were arrested and eventually sentenced to a total of eleven years between them. Big Tony, a twenty-four-year-old hospital porter, got four years, as did Halfbrain, who was also twenty-four and unemployed. Davie P, a twenty-one-year-old Irish building worker with a clean record, got three years. *Red Action* reported on the case in the following terms:

> Nobody, least of all the prisoners, would deny that the case was political – what is equally clear is that the verdict, and particularly, the sentence were political as well. Throughout history, to be effective in fighting the fascists usually means breaking the law, and always means rejecting the power and legitimacy of the forces of law and order. Thus the actions of anti-fascist street-fighters will always be seen as dangerously radical in the eyes of the state, especially when it involves a form of behaviour, i.e. physical violence, which the dominant culture avoids and condemns in everyday life on the part of everyone except itself.

A campaign was launched to ensure all three lads were supported financially, morally and politically throughout their time in prison. It was considered mandatory that all people in prison for AFA activities would receive financial support in any case, and numerous fund-raisers were organised to help in this respect.

Generally speaking, AFA was on top of things in London during this period, but we never had things all our own way. In 1993, C18 managed to call out over 600 assorted fascists, loyalists and right-wing football hooligans in an attempt to smash the march off the streets. About 150 AFA members met in a pub in Notting Hill Gate with the intention of arriving in Kilburn before the march and confronting the fascists. Unfortunately their numbers were too great, and we were forced to sit stewing in the pub for most of the afternoon. Eventually the police arrested 376 of the fascists and cordoned off the rest, allowing the march to go ahead almost two hours later than planned.

AFA forces were split that day, with a number of groups from around the country choosing to attend the march itself, eschewing the increasingly isolationist approach adopted by AFA's London leadership. There was a growing tendency for London AFA to distance itself from activities over which it had no direct control during this period, which I never totally accepted at the time and which I now believe proved damaging to AFA in the long run. I agreed with the argument that AFA should not simply be a security service or police force for the Left, but I felt we should allow ourselves more latitude to judge things on a case by case basis rather than simply boycotting everything and organising independently. After all, a huge morale-boosting victory for the fash in this instance wouldn't have exactly done wonders for our own cause.

I know I wasn't the only person in the pub that afternoon who thought that we should have joined the march once the size and scale of the fascists' turn-out had been identified. Wee Stevie from Glasgow had brought down a group of Celtic Casuals who were none to impressed with the day's events. "This is shite," he muttered. "We've not come all this way just tae sit around in a pub all afternoon."

There were probably another 150 or so assorted anti-fascists on the demonstration that day, including the AFA groups, members of the Republican Bands Alliance, and other anti-fascists. If the police had chosen not to round up the fascists but instead had let them smash the march off the streets, then it would not only have been a bloodbath but an immense propaganda coup for the far right. The 150 of us in Notting Hill Gate, allied with similar numbers on the march, might have been able to force the march through under such circumstances, but divided we were straws in the wind. There were problems between the leaderships of AFA and the Troops Out stretching right back to the Conway Hall incident in 1988, but I failed to see the logic of sitting in a pub in west London while the fash were lording it all over Kilburn a couple of miles across town.

Anti-Internment March
The Anti-Internment march took place every August in London, and was another target for the combined forces of Loyalism and fascism. The march started in Islington and finished in a small park in Archway, and it was almost guaranteed that there would be an attempt to attack it along the route, usually as it neared its destination.

In 1988, the police stood back and allowed the NF to launch a full-scale attack on the front of the march. The attack failed when stewards unconnected to AFA bravely fought off the assault. When it became clear that the attack had failed, the police waded in and arrested thirty of the stewards, to the accompanying cheers and jeers of the Fronters stood across the road.

For the next couple of years the police kept a lid on things, and although there were a number of minor incidents and skirmishes, the fash weren't able to launch a major attack on the march, although they were an ever present threat. The huge police presence in Archway made it impossible to operate without risking large numbers of arrests, so any activity against the fascists had to take place well away from the area.

After the march one year, we headed down to Euston and plotted up in a bar near the station in the hope that the fash might wander through on their way home. Euston was a bit like that in those days: everyone seemed to pass through it. Sure enough, within a short while a mob of thirty fascists and Loyalists were spotted in the area. They were identified as being among the counter-demonstrators, and spotters were sent out to track their movements. We eventually ambushed them in the back streets around Tavistock Square just as they were settling down for a few beers. They scattered on first impact, leaving behind the foolish and the slow to suffer the consequences. The rest were chased back to Euston Station under a hail of pint-pots and beer bottles.

One lone fash got himself trapped in a pub doorway, and a small scrum of AFA lads were giving him a right kicking. I noticed Hefty loitering around the edge of the ruck. He was trying to intervene, but there were too many bodies in the way.

"Leave him alone," he shouted suddenly, pulling people out of the way. "He's had enough."

Everyone stood back, startled by this apparent show of compassion from a man not previously known for his acts of mercy. I have to admit that I was pretty shocked as well, because Hefty was not one for taking prisoners. He had a nasty streak in him when it came to fascists. As the lads moved out of the way, he suddenly produced a bike chain and started whipping the poor fash with it. Hefty had found himself a new toy, and was pissed off because he had not had the opportunity to use it yet.

Later in the pub, Carl mentioned that he thought the fash trapped in the doorway had been Italian.

"What makes you say that?" asked Hefty.

"Because he was shouting, 'Mi, mi, mi,' when you were whipping him with the chain," answered Carl.

"No you dickhead," laughed Hefty. "He was saying, 'My eye, my eye, my eye.'"

The following year saw another large fascist turnout, which was again swamped by the police. There was a big AFA mob on the march that day, but we couldn't get anywhere near the fash, who were pushed back up the road towards Archway Station by the police while we were forced back down the Holloway Road. We plotted up in a pub further down the road towards Highbury, and awaited news on what the fash were up to. A little while later Pete G, a London AFA spotter, burst into the pub with some news. Pete had a pushbike, which was an ideal way for a spotter to move around London quickly without being noticed. For some reason people have a blind spot when it comes to cyclists, and hardly anyone notices a man or woman cycling past them.

"There's a mob of fash, possibly BM from south London, heading this way," he reported.

"How far away?" asked O'Shea.

"About five minutes," he replied. "They've been whacking people leaving the march, and the police are just looking the other way and letting them get on with it. I saw one scumbag stop a woman pushing a pram so that he could spit in her baby's face."

I was really pissed off when I heard this. I think we all were. We had always tried our best to only target active members of fascist gangs, people who had put themselves in the frame and who already knew the risks involved. The fash never made that distinction, and targeted anyone, young or old, who happened to disagree with them and their warped politics. This particular gang of south London pond-life appeared to be even more nasty and virulent than your average fash mob, and we were determined to give them a taste of their own medicine.

A few minutes later the fash sauntered past the pub we were drinking in. We could have confronted them right then and there, but they were across the other side of a busy main road, and would have been long gone before we had a chance to get to grips with them properly. A little more subtlety and cunning was required.

A team of hand-picked lads was despatched in a van to hunt them down. The atmosphere in the van was one of grim determination. I don't think anyone was nervous. I certainly wasn't; I was just intent on inflicting some kind of damage on those fascist scumbags. We cruised around for a short while, tracking their movements, and after a bit we caught up with them just as they were heading down a tube station. We hit them with everything we had: bats, coshes, hammers, even a "Millwall brick" made from a rolled up copy of *The Guardian*. The fash reeled back in shock and horror from the onslaught. A few attempted to fight back, some begged for mercy, while others fled down the tunnel to escape, only to quickly and somewhat comically re-emerge with a tube train hot on their heels.

I confronted one of them as he clambered back onto the platform.

"Leave it out mate," he pleaded. "I've already been done."

He was completely unmarked. "Well you're going to get done again then," I replied.

He retreated a couple of steps. "But you've got an iron bar," he whined.

I shook my head. What did he expect after what they had been doing? Marquis of Queensberry Rules?

Unfortunately, the encounter was interrupted after only a brief scuffle by the tube train pulling into the station, and scores of witnesses disembarking from the carriages. I decided it was too risky to carry on and got out of there before the Old Bill arrived. We felt justice had been done. The fash had been strutting around taking liberties with innocent people leaving the march, but when it came to the real thing they had been found wanting.

While we were busy dishing out rough justice to some of south London's ugliest, the lads who had been left behind in the pub noticed a bonehead in a White Power T-shirt wandering around the area and decided to investigate. The bone was confronted by a small group of AFA lads and fled into a nearby hall, which unfortunately for our hapless chum was the scene of a wedding reception for a black couple. Needless to say, his T-shirt did not go down too well among the mainly black guests, and after the best man and groom had upset the in-laws by jumping all over the bonehead, he was handed back to the anti-fascists waiting outside.

After the march in 1992, a dozen or so AFA lads were drinking in the Enkel Arms on the Seven Sisters Road when they were attacked by a combined mob of C18, NF, Chelsea Headhunters and off-duty squaddies. The odds were about four or five to one in favour of the far right, but the ready availability of weapons in the pub meant that the fash couldn't get close enough to make their superior numbers count, and the battle was conducted at throwing distance without a punch being landed. The only damage sustained was to the pub itself, and even that was minor. In short, the fash had a golden opportunity to finally claim some sort of real victory, but messed it up big time.

CHAPTER NINE

Awaydays 1990–1995

AFA HAD BRANCHES in virtually every major town and city in the country, from Brighton to Fife, from Cardiff to Teesside, and all stops in between. At the 1991 national conference, it was agreed that AFA would operate on a regional basis in order to make the most effective use of our resources. The various regions were the Northern Network, the South, Midlands, Scotland, and so on, with each region comprising between three and a dozen branches according to geography and the number of stewards. Apart from national call-outs when we all went down to London, there would also be regional call-outs to help out a particular branch in your own region, and depending upon circumstances it might also be necessary to travel to another region to help out with whatever problem they were facing.

There cannot have been many places up and down the country we didn't travel to during 10 years of anti-fascist activity. It was not exactly a case of "join AFA and see the world" but maybe we should have used it as a recruiting slogan. A lot of the away trips usually involved supporting some local AFA group unfortunate enough to have a national fascist event land on their doorstep, but sometimes we just turned up to boost the numbers in a local activity we'd heard about. Some of the trips could be a laugh and an excuse to have a few beers in a different town, other trips could be difficult and dangerous.

Blackburn

Blackburn was another of one of those Lancashire mill towns with more than its fair share of racial and social problems. It has a fairly large and well-organised Asian population, and a white, working-class population that has been increasingly disenfranchised from society. Two fascist councillors were elected in the town in 1976, and the BNP were always making themselves busy about the place, trying to revive what they perceived to be a dormant undercurrent of support. In 1989, we were approached by some local anti-racists who had learned that the BNP were planning to hold a rally. We offered our support and travelled up on a couple of occasions to meet local people and discuss tactics.

The BNP were on the rise nationally and were looking for every opportunity to expand into new areas, but they had very little support or public profile in the North-West at that time, and it was always going to be hard for them. In the end their plans for a rally petered out due to lack of local support and the inexperience of their people in Lancashire.

On the day itself, local anti-racists had organised a carnival to protest against the BNP rally, and we took about ten lads up for a mooch around the town. We knew that the fash would be making a nuisance of themselves somewhere in Blackburn and decided to swerve the carnival in the hope of catching a few of them unawares. As we wandered around the town centre, a local bloke pointed out a group of five lads sat on a bench and fingered them as BNP. One of the five had a toddler with him.

We walked up to them and casually asked if they were BNP, pretending that we were out-of-town fash. When they replied that they were, we steamed into them. Nads kicked the biggest bloke clean over the bench, while the rest scattered, apart from the lad with the toddler who was allowed to go on his way unharmed. We chased a couple of them into an amusement arcade, losing one among the fruit machines and video games but capturing the other, who begged me and Gary F for mercy. We released him unharmed. Another small group was chased out of the town centre a little while later, but after that things went quiet for a couple of hours and we decided to go home. As we were getting into our cars we were stopped by the police, and questioned by Blackburn's race liaison officer, who automatically assumed that a gang of working-class lads involved in politics must be right-wingers. This was despite the fact that we had a black lad and a lad of Middle Eastern origin with us. The stereotype of lefties and anti-racists as passive, middle-class students is, it seems, all-pervasive.

Another trip to Blackburn in the summer of 1990 nearly ended in disaster. One Saturday morning, Steve phoned to tell me that *Searchlight* had passed on some information about a Blood and Honour gig being held in Blackburn that very evening.

"What do you expect us to do Steve?" I asked him. "There's no chance of getting enough people out to take on a couple of hundred boneheads at such short notice."

"I know," he replied, "I thought a couple of us should go up there and check it out, maybe try and take some photos."

"Well okay," I agreed reluctantly. It wasn't really how I was intending to spend my Saturday evening, but when duty calls . . .

I was hoping that we could get it all over and done with quick, but unfortunately Steve turned up in yet another of his dodgy motors, and we had to endure a tortuously slow journey to Blackburn. It sounded as if the engine had been stolen off a lawnmower, and as we spluttered our way slowly through the Lancashire countryside, I wondered about the wisdom of this particular trip.

We got into Blackburn at about 6 p.m., and drove around the town centre looking for the club that the fash were supposed to have booked for their gig. There was no sign of anyone, and we were beginning to think that the whole thing had been a wind-up, when we swung around a corner and suddenly found ourselves driving through the middle of a large mob of boneheads.

We couldn't reverse as it would have immediately aroused suspicion, and so we instinctively shrank lower in our seats as the car crawled slowly through the crowd. We were just emerging out the other side when one of the bones suddenly pointed at the car and shouted, "Tilzey." All eyes turned towards us as Steve attempted to accelerate away. For a brief, heart-stopping moment nothing happened; there was no sudden burst of speed, no roar of engines, nothing.

"Put your fucking foot down Steve," I shouted.

"I am," he replied, panic cracking his voice.

The boneheads stared at us in confusion. The original bone who had first spotted us tried again. "It's Tilzey from *Searchlight*," he yelled.

This time there was no confusion, and you could see all the lights being switched on in their little baldy heads. Fortunately the engine kicked into some sort of life and we picked up sufficient speed to outpace the pursuing nazi mob. I leaned out the window to give them the finger as we pootled away, appearing braver than I felt. We got out of Blackburn sharpish after that, well as sharpish as the car would allow, and made our way gratefully home. Just a couple of weeks later, Steve was driving a few of us home from a night out when we heard a loud crunching sound, and the car ground to a halt in the middle of a roundabout, bits of it littering the road behind us.

Blackburn was home to an oddball character called Austin Stonham. He was a BNP member whose fixation with fascist politics verged on the obsessive. He was an ever-present figure at BNP meetings and activities in the North-West, and was a bit like one of those C-list celebrities who turn up at every opening night regardless of how inappropriate the occasion. He used to design and print his own range of stickers and posters which he used to put up everywhere. He once designed a fake "Black Pride" poster that he stuck up in various locations around Moss Side, Whalley Range and Hulme. The posters urged black people to send in their details to a contact address which turned out to belong to the BNP. We spent several nights tearing down his posters and putting up our own, a "Wanted" poster with his name and picture on it. Unsurprisingly, he never ventured into Moss Side again.

He was quite a big lad, but he had curly hair and a babyish face that looked like it would never see the need for a razor blade. He also occasionally wore dungarees which added to the child-like effect. This particular item of menswear must have remained fashionable in the East Lancs area long after they were donated to Oxfam shops everywhere else in the country. Stonham was in the habit of writing letters to AFA and Red Action snooping around for information, but they were so badly disguised they were almost laughable. He once wrote a letter to us claiming to be a representative of the "Church of Britain". One of the more secular branches of organised religion, I should imagine.

He was a minor irritant who used to come into Manchester most weekends and go on long meandering walks around various parts of the city putting up hundreds of fascist stickers on lamp-posts and road signs. He was caught a few times in the city centre by anti-fascists out on the prowl. He was CS gassed on one occasion near Aytoun Street, and on another occasion needed hospital treatment after he was attacked with a Lucozade bottle in a left-wing bookshop in town. He twice had to go running to the police for protection after wandering too close to an AFA activity, and a cunning plan to ambush him had to be aborted when he was pulled over by the police just seconds before the trap was due to be sprung.

Eventually, Steve found out that he worked for a Turkish-owned kebab shop in Blackburn. We paid it a visit one evening to speak to the manager, and the next day he was sacked. We also found out where he lived, and a few weeks later Mr Stonham opened his front door one night to find himself face to face with Mr Stephen Tilzey.

"Hello Austin," said Steve. "I think we need to talk."

Austin looked a little shocked by this turn of events, but nodded.

"Listen," said Steve. "I'm here to do you a favour. You need to think very carefully about what you're doing, because those posters you put up in Moss Side have upset some very heavy people, and you really don't want these characters on your case. I'm talking about real gangsters here, and you and your mates aren't even in the same league as this lot."

After a number of long and entirely reasonable discussions over the following weeks, Stonham realised that the game was up and agreed to quit the BNP.

I don't personally know if all his attention-seeking behaviour was the result of some emotional turmoil or not, but if it helps: "Dave Hann is aware of the existence of Austin Stonham." Feel any better now?

Newcastle, 21 April 1990

Some of the most dangerous situations came when small groups of fascists and anti-fascists chanced upon each other in back-streets, well away from the police. One such situation occurred in Newcastle in 1990. The occasion was a gig by the Angelic Upstarts and Blaggers ITA. Both bands contained AFA members and were near the top of various fascist hit-lists because of their support for militant anti-fascism. Mensi, the lead singer of the Upstarts, was a particular target of the far right. He was a life-long socialist and outspoken anti-racist who had provoked fury among NF members in the late Seventies when he had publicly denounced their attempts to leech around the young kids following his band.

Ever since AFA had faced down Blood and Honour in London during the late Eighties, the Angelic Upstarts had enjoyed a relatively trouble-free time as they toured around the country playing gigs. So when they organised a gig in their home town of Sunderland, no-one anticipated a problem until it came to light that Blood and Honour had coincidentally organised a gig for the same night just a short drive across the Tyne in Newcastle. This was no ordinary gig either; it was a big event featuring local boneheads Skullhead, as well as Skrewdriver and Brutal Attack from London. Of course there were immediate security concerns for the Upstarts gig, and a request was made for stewards in the north to get up to Sunderland and help out with security.

We had a real problem finding any kind of transport in Manchester for this event, and it was only by luck that I chanced on someone who was prepared to lend us his car for the weekend. In the end, after all the uncertainty over transport, only three of us made the journey up to the north-east, me and a couple of lads from Longsight, Sean and Dave Mac.

Sean and Dave were both part of the same extended family that had spawned Hefty. They were second-generation Irish immigrants from one of Longsight's sprawling council estates. Sean was the kind of bloke who used to bring his dirty laundry home to Manchester every month for his mam to wash and iron after he moved down to London, while Dave Mac, sometimes known as Sidebottom after the Timperley-based character with the big, round, papier maché head, was one of the most idle gits I've ever met. They were both really likeable lads, but neither of them ever seemed to have a penny to scratch their arses with, and so it was down to muggins here to cough up for all the petrol, drinks and scran on the journey up to the North-East.

The gig in Sunderland went ahead without incident, with both bands playing storming sets to an enthusiastic audience. Afterwards, while the crew were packing away the equipment, about a dozen of us piled into Mensi's van and headed over to Newcastle for a look around.

We were tooled up with hammers, bats and bottles, and before long we spotted a group of about a dozen boneheads in a chippy near the main railway station. We piled out of the van and the lads steamed straight into the startled bones, creating instant mayhem among the cod, chips and mushy peas.

In the meantime, I had spotted two fash on the opposite side of the street, and shouted for Sean to follow me. I hit the first bone with a rounders bat and he collapsed in a heap in the gutter. Sean went for the second bone, but before he could reach him, the fash pulled out a big hunting knife, about seven or eight inches long. I didn't know it at the time, but Sean apparently had a bit of a phobia about knives, and backed away in a state of near panic.

"Dave," he shouted. "Sort this one out. He's got a blade."

The bone was growling incomprehensible threats in German at me as I squared up to him. I was not particularly keen on knives either, especially when they were being pointed in my direction, but whatever my feelings on the matter, Sean was clearly not up for it, and so it was left to me to deal with *uber*-hunter.

While Sean concentrated on finishing off the first bone, I began fencing with the German nazi, each of us parrying and thrusting trying to find an opening. I don't remember being scared, but I was obviously wary of the fact that this was a knife that could quite easily kill me. It was a blade made for stabbing, not cutting or slashing, and my rounders bat felt a bit pathetic in comparison.

As we continued to stalk each other, I suddenly spotted Dave Mac racing across the road towards us. All he had to do was tap the bone on the shoulder and distract him for a second, but instead of doing that he launched himself at the bone, fists and feet flying through the air. At that exact moment the bone happened to step backwards so that Dave missed him completely and ended up flying between the pair of us in a blur of arms and legs. He landed in a heap on the ground, his loose change falling out of his pockets.

I expected him to get up and help me fight the bonehead, but instead he began crawling around on his hands and knees, trying to find his dropped coins which were rolling all over the pavement. This was turning into a farce. Now I not only had to face a big, angry, knife-wielding bonehead but also had to watch my step in case I tripped over Dave Mac in the dark.

Across the road in the chippy, the battle was still going on when a vanload of police screeched to a halt outside. The main focus of their attention was the participants in the chip shop brawl, but I wasn't going to hang around waiting to get nicked, so I got off sharpish. The bonehead ran after me for a while, calling me a coward in heavily accented English, but his back was to the chippy and I don't think he had seen the police arriving.

I managed to get away from the scene and dump the rounders bat, but I had lost Sean and Dave in the confusion, although I was pretty certain they had not been nicked. Police vans were crawling all over the area by now, and after a quick look around for the two lads, I decided to get off the streets. I wandered into a posh hotel opposite the station and checked in for the night, grateful despite the expense for the sanctuary and the warmth, because Newcastle, even in April, is a cold place to be at night.

After a shower and breakfast the following morning I phoned home and found out that the two lads had been ringing up all night trying to find me. After making good their escape, they had spent the night in a graveyard, and only emerged when a greasy spoon cafe near the station opened at 6 a.m. They were still shivering over their coffees two hours later.

"All right lads?" I asked, as I breezed into the cafe. "What's the score?"

"Where the fuck have you been?" asked Dave Mac looking up from his coffee.

"That posh hotel across the street," I replied.

"We spent the night in a graveyard," he grumbled.

"Yeah," added Sean, "and we've been phoning your Michele all night trying to find you."

"I heard," I said. "I just spoke to her, and she said Sidebottom was crying down the phone, moaning about how cold he was."

"It was bloody bitter out there last night," he complained with a shiver.

"If it's any consolation I was tucked up in a nice warm bed," I replied. "I had a lovely hot shower in the morning, and a really good cooked breakfast."

"Fuck off!" the two of them shouted in unison.

We eventually got out of Newcastle in a taxi, and headed back across the Tyne towards Sunderland. After a panic regarding the whereabouts of the car we had borrowed, we eventually located it in the Gateshead hinterlands, and began the long journey home. All the boys in the chippy brawl were nicked, but were bailed the next day, despite Mensi trying to claim status as a political prisoner. If I remember correctly, everyone received fines and bind-overs at the court case a few months later. I think they were all pretty relieved not to get a jail sentence for that particular escapade.

Scotland the Brave

Glasgow was always a popular destination, with an almost cast-iron guarantee of some kind of confrontation. Edinburgh was good too, but the police seemed to be more on top of things in Auld Reekie, and we always seemed to be on the receiving end of loads of arrests when we travelled up to the Scottish capital.

In Scotland, as elsewhere, Loyalists tended to line up behind the fascist cause, while republicans tended to line up behind the anti-fascist one. It was not an exclusive arrangement by any means, but that's the way it tended to settle in the pot. Therefore you would get an unholy alliance of Loyalists and fascists pitched against anti-fascists, left-wingers and republicans. A notable exception was a young lad who had risen to the position of substitute master in an Orange Lodge and had subsequently been appalled when he received literature in support of right-wing South Africans, the Contras, Unita, etc. He ended up in AFA after a whole series of similar incidents. Sadly he was an all too rare exception.

Football supporters in both cities tended to line up behind the political traditions associated with their clubs. Thus Rangers and Hearts fans tended towards Loyalism and the far right, while Celtic and Hibs went the opposite way. Again this was not all-encompassing, with some Rangers fans seeing the light and joining the anti-fascist cause, while a number of leading Hibbee hooligans in particular have gone over to the dark side.

We had a couple of trips up to Edinburgh in the early Nineties at the invitation of the James Connolly Society. James Connolly was an Edinburgh-born socialist who was one of the leaders of the failed 1916 Easter Rising in Dublin. He was later executed by firing squad for his part in the rebellion against British rule. We were twice asked to help out with security for the annual James Connolly Commemoration in the city. Both times the police banned the march, the second time making loads of arrests when the marchers attempted to defy the ban. Mobs of Loyalists, fascists and off-duty squaddies wandered Edinburgh city centre looking for stragglers and marchers who had been scattered by the police actions, but when the inevitable confrontations occurred it was anti-fascists and republicans who were harried and harassed by the police.

In contrast, we had loads of good trips up to Glasgow.
Whenever we went up there, we stayed with Gerry's parents.
They were a lovely couple who never seemed bothered when
a load of hairy-arsed anti-fascists took over their home for the
weekend. I think Gerry's dad, Bobo, had an inkling of what
was going on but he was pretty sound about it all. He was a
top bloke who could rustle up an excellent cooked breakfast,
and he was also a reliable and unending source of tickets for
the Celts.

One memorable trip took place on 1 December 1991,
when we took a vanload up to help out the newly formed AFA
group in the city. They had picked up some information that
the BNP were holding their annual Scottish rally in the city
and needed some experienced heads to help keep things tight.
We made a weekend out of it and went on the big anti-racist
march through Glasgow the day before and then on to an
AFA social in the evening. We heard during the evening that
elsewhere in the city a woman had been beaten up and kicked
unconscious after she had complained about the behaviour of
a group of sieg-heiling nazis.

It was out of bed early on the Sunday and down to Argyle
Street, where the BNP were meeting in the Gallery Bar. Wee
Stevie had a bundle of paviours' hammers which he handed
around to various people, and we marched the short distance
to the pub where the BNP were gathering. As we got there,
John Tyndall and a couple of his minders were stood
nonchalantly in the doorway. They saw the anti-fascist mob
approaching and scuttled quickly back inside the pub, while
two boneheads who were also in the vicinity panicked and
attempted to escape. They were immediately set upon by the
crowd. Gerry got nicked during these exchanges for bouncing
a Lucozade bottle off some bonehead's skull. While this was
going on I positioned myself just outside the doorway in case
the BNP tried to make a break for it, and sure enough within
minutes two blokes bustled out the door trying to lead a

charge out the pub. For a second I was surprised to find
myself facing Ken Henderson from Rochdale. He was still
casually dressed but minus his obligatory brown leather jacket.
I recovered quickly enough to swing the paviour's hammer
into his mate's face, and that was enough for Ken, who
shouted, "Fucking hell," before leading the retreat back into
the pub.

The police were quickly on the scene and sealed off the
busy street, making a number of arrests, including the two
badly battered bones. Despite the presence of the police, we
chased off a number of small groups of fash arriving for the
meeting, and kept Tyndall and a group of twenty BNP pinned
down in the pub. Small groups of fash were milling about the
area unsure of what to do and where to go. A number of anti-
fascists broke away from the main group outside the pub and
attempted to help them make up their minds.

One group of boneheads dressed in full nazi regalia were
attacked in a narrow alleyway created by a shop hoarding. I
hit one with a hammer and he went down in a heap. Dodger,
one of the Glaswegian lads, started putting the boot into him.
The other lads set about the remaining bones, who scattered
everywhere. While the fighting continued, Christmas shoppers
waited patiently at either end of the alleyway apparently
unworried by the fate befalling the master race. Dodger
apologised to them for the inconvenience anyway. Maybe he
should have got a job working for British Rail. More fash were
cleared out of the area before we returned to the picket
outside the Gallery Bar to learn that Tyndall and his followers
had been smuggled out of the bar via a tunnel that runs under
the pub and emerges the other side of the nearby Central
Station.

After all the excitement had died down we had to go back
to Gerry's parents and tell them their son had been nicked.
They took it quite well under the circumstances. I think they
were half-expecting it. A couple of months later Gerry got a

small fine and therefore missed the chance of a nice holiday in HMP Barlinnie.

East Midlands

For a couple of years in the early Nineties, the various fascist parties had been allowed to grow unchecked in the counties of Nottinghamshire and Derbyshire. The East Midlands region, and especially the area around Mansfield, was fertile ground for them. It was an area dotted with industrial towns and villages, most of which had lost their industries over the previous decades only to find that the ubiquitous heritage centres that had sprung up to replace them were nothing more than piss-takes. The resulting high unemployment, mixed with a degree of resentment towards the traditional parties, was a godsend for the fascists.

Every faction of the fascist movement in Britain was represented in the Mansfield area, from the BNP and NF through to the British Movement, Blood and Honour and the Ku Klux Klan. You had the feeling that they were trying to turn the area into an English version of the Deep South. There were hooded nutters in KKK regalia burning crosses in fields, an increase in assaults on Asian and Jewish people, a Blood and Honour "White Christmas" gig in 1992, and ANL members and anti-racists video-taped, intimidated and then attacked.

The BNP regularly held paper sales in Mansfield town centre, and even launched an anti-pit -closure campaign aimed at miners from the Union of Democratic Mineworkers. Reports filtered back of local miners sporting BNP stickers on their helmets as they went to work. The situation was grim and getting worse at an alarming rate. AFA was struggling to get a foothold in the area and had only limited support, making it difficult for us to operate.

However, it's usually the case that wherever there are fascists, you will also find anti-fascists, and a small group of

locals based around the Mansfield area started getting
themselves organised. They had already noted the Anti-Nazi
League's feeble response to fascist aggression, and allied
themselves to AFA. The Doncaster lads helped them out a
fair bit, going down there to support the various activities
called by the Mansfield crew.

I had a lot of time for the lads from Doncaster AFA,
although the name itself was a bit of a misnomer, because
they seemed to come from all over South Yorkshire area.
Amongst the main faces were Martin from Barnsley, who
unfortunately looked like he shared a hairdresser with Leo
Sayer, Basher from Sheffield, who was an ex-safebreaker, and
Malcolm, who appeared to be the only one who was actually
from Doncaster. He was the main organiser, despite the fact
he was ex-NF.

They were all anarchists and had been involved in political
activity for years. They could pull out reasonable numbers
between them, all good, reliable anti-fascists who knew the
ropes. They couldn't play football to save their lives though.
At the quarterly Northern Network meetings, Manchester
AFA inevitably thrashed them at the post-meeting five-a-side
football matches.

The first big AFA activity in Mansfield was a benefit gig in
the Labour Club. Upon hearing of the planned gig, the
fascists immediately announced that they would never let it
go ahead. The *News of the World* even printed threats by the
fash to "smash the gig". The fash had thrown down the
gauntlet, and it was our duty to respond. Never better than
when faced with a challenge, AFA groups from around the
north provided between 100 and 150 stewards to secure the
building. As we had no idea what kind of numbers we would
be up against, a request was made for stewards to travel up
from London. The request was ignored, and it was from this
date that a rift started to open up between the Northern
Network and London, a rift that, due to London's dismissive

and off-hand attitude to any kind of criticism, never properly healed. It was pointed out that northern stewards were constantly travelling down to London to help out but that the arrangement rarely operated in reverse. There were a couple of honourable exceptions to this rule like Big Tony and Carl, who were frequent visitors to Manchester and the north, but on the whole I think London AFA/Red Action basically viewed many of the branches outside London as being full of useful idiots. They were seen as necessary in the physical fight against the fascists but politically incompetent. They could never quite hide this dismissive attitude, and it eventually got people's backs up.

I raised this issue a couple of times at various meetings in London, pointing out that this high-handed attitude and reluctance to travel outside the capital was creating mistrust and ill-feeling amongst branches in the north. I was fobbed off with unsatisfactory excuses.

About a dozen of us from Manchester travelled down to Mansfield in the Bolt's van, which was a proper hippie/traveller convoy type thing. It leaked petrol fumes into the seating area so that everyone felt sick or high by the time it pootled into Mansfield. It was a good job we didn't have to fight anyone within five minutes of arriving because we were all absolutely wasted.

After the perils of the bus journey from hell, we caught no more than an occasional glimpse of the fash all night, as they did little more than show their faces for the briefest of moments before scuttling off sharpish. Fash scouts in cars had been driving past all evening, and when one drove a little too close to the club his back window was put through and he had to drive through two sets of red lights to escape.

After the gig we made our way back to Manchester, and of course, because the petrol gauge on the van wasn't working, it ran out of petrol somewhere near Glossop at 2 a.m. It was cold and miserable, and to make matters worse I had to get up early the next day to go to a national AFA meeting. Never again.

In the months following the gig, sections of the ANL who were not members of the Socialist Workers' Party jumped ship and joined AFA, mirroring a similar situation in Chesterfield. Bolstered by these successes and an influx of new members, the local AFA group started holding leafleting sessions in Mansfield and outside the pits targeted by the fash. The BNP paper sale in Mansfield finally folded after AFA activity, and for a time the focus moved to Heanor, Nottingham and Leicester and then onto Bloxwich and the West Midlands, and we had to get our road maps out again.

Leeds

I never really enjoyed going to Yorkshire. There was always a slight edge when people found out that you had come across from Manchester anyway, but there was also something about the whole plain-speaking, gruff Yorkshireman mentality that smacked of closed minds and intolerance. I am not talking about everyone here of course, just the minority who would have you believe that it's impossible to be a Yorkshireman if you're Asian, for instance. In addition, the police always seemed to have things pretty well sewn up in Yorkshire, and getting any kind of result was hard work. It must have been all the practice they got during the miners' strike.

We were completely out-manoeuvred by the police when we tried to stop the BNP from holding a rally in Halifax, and ended up miles away from the action. Two trips over to York had also turned into non-events due to police surveillance and fash no-shows. We also had a hard day in Dewsbury in June 1992 when we tried to stop a BNP/ Holocaust Revisionist rally in the town. We were kept well away from the fash, and when a group of frustrated Longsight lads chanced upon the Dewsbury organiser and two of his Leeds minders they launched an assault on the trio and were arrested by plainclothes police and charged with serious offences.

We always found Leeds a difficult city to work in, not least because intelligence services skulduggery was rife in the area and the whole political arena was awash with rumour, speculation and counter-speculation. It was a confusing situation, with trust in short supply as various people were suspected and accused of being police spies and informers. Aside from all this, I also had the impression that some members of the Leeds lot were a bit wary of the local opposition, especially Combat 18, who were starting to strut around the place like they owned it. Leeds had long been regarded as a fascist stronghold in the north, with the Elland Road football ground in particular a fertile recruiting ground for fascist groups. C18 were making a push to be regarded as the pre-eminent nazi group in the city, and they were not going to be shy about who they trampled over to achieve this ambition.

The ANL had been attacked on several occasions in the city centre by nazis armed with machetes and crowbars. Bolstered by a couple of easy victories, C18 had widened their scope, attacking Asian university students, the staff of record shops displaying anti-racist posters, and the leader of the local Trades Council. The homes of AFA members were also attacked, with a crossbow bolt being fired through one front window. This followed an undercover *World In Action* programme which used hidden cameras to identify members of Leeds AFA. C18 did come unstuck when they ambushed two Leeds AFA lads in the city centre one night and ended up having the tables turned on them, leaving one nazi with a hole through his cheek after he was stabbed with a sharpened pencil.

In November 1994, a big AFA mobilisation in Leeds sat in a pub for most of the day while the Leeds AFA spotters merely monitored the movements of the BNP as they made their way to a rally on the outskirts of the city. We took about twenty over from Manchester, including two lads from Droylsden. Pez and Owie were United supporters who were on their first trip with AFA.

Unfortunately, the Leeds lot kept us hanging around for hours while they waited for the perfect moment to attack the BNP, a moment which of course never came. It was the ideal opportunity to finally hit them hard in the city, because Nottingham Forest were playing at Leeds that day and their fans were taking liberties, smashing up pubs and running the police ragged. It was a wasted opportunity. The only contact all day occurred when a BNP scout accidentally walked past the pub that AFA were drinking in. I kicked him in the balls just as he was pulling a blade out of his back pocket.

Back home in Manchester I apologised to the two Droylsden lads for the lack of action.

"What do you mean?" said Pez. "It was brilliant. It's the first time I've ever been able to sit in a pub in Leeds and feel completely safe."

In August 1995 we returned to Leeds. Our numbers were down because of the let-down last time, and only a carload travelled from Manchester. Mike S was the driver. He was a salesman from Prestwich and always had a flash motor handy so we made it across the Pennines in record time. Wigan Mike and his oppo Dave W also made the trip. These two lads were rapidly turning into a deadly duo as far as the fash were concerned. A couple of months earlier they had practically dismantled Blackpool BNP on their own, and a short while after that they bumped into a fledgling C18 outfit in Wigan and tore them apart despite being heavily outnumbered.

I took up the fourth place in the car. It was a bank holiday, and against my better judgement I had been persuaded to go despite feeling poorly. I began to feel worse on the journey across the Pennines, and to add to my misery I was stung on the neck by a bee which immediately made it start swelling. Brilliant.

We met up with the other AFA groups in a pub near the university, and once again the waiting game began. Reports filtered back that a minibus full of BNP from Croydon were parked up by the bus station waiting to be given directions to the meeting, and once again some of the Leeds lot began wavering and prevaricating, urging us to be patient while they continued to monitor their movements. Not this time.

AFA only had a small firm out that day, so we could not afford to wait around until the BNP had mobbed up at their meeting. I also suspected that this was a deliberate ploy, and what Leeds actually wanted was a replay of the previous November. There was no way that we were going to end up twiddling our thumbs in the pub for the rest of the day, so we began pushing for action, and with the backing of the Donny lads we won the argument.

The van carrying the BNP was parked up on a busy street with its side door open. Most of the occupants were still sat inside, reading papers or munching sandwiches, unaware of the approaching danger. We caught them completely by surprise. All the van windows were smashed and the fash were pulled out of the van screaming for mercy. Wigan Mike and Dave W were awesome, a frightening combination of punching power who practically tore the van apart on their own.

I dragged the driver, a big bloat of a skinhead, out of his seat and started hitting him. Then all of a sudden my strength deserted me, and I found myself doing an impression of Superman when Lex Luther unexpectedly produces a snide piece of Kryptonite. Fortunately the Buster Bloodvessel lookalike was no super-villain, and instead of leathering me, he ran off down the road as fast as his podgy legs would carry him.

We took off as well, leaving behind a wrecked van and several members of the master race unconscious on the pavement. We jumped into several waiting cars and got out the area before the Dibble appeared on the scene. We parked up a few miles away and went for a walk in a park until the commotion died down. The police helicopter was out so we sat on a park bench under the cover of a large tree until it flew off elsewhere. Satisfied that we were in the clear we made our way back home.

Even though the victims were from south London, the attack on the fash in their northern stronghold poisoned relations between the BNP and C18 in the city for some time, with the former suspecting the latter of setting them up. Although C18 made some attempts to exact retribution on the anti-fascist movement, the violence never reached the same levels as before.

CHAPTER TEN

The People's Republic of Mancunia

Manchester 1987–1995
WE HAD THINGS pretty much sewn up in Manchester. The city itself was virtually a no-go area for fascists, and had been ever since they were kicked off the streets in the late Seventies. The BNP found that it was impossible to maintain a public profile in the area, while we could hold public meetings, gigs and social events with impunity. The anti-fascist scene in the city was a good one. We drank and socialised pretty much where we wanted, although we tended to use a couple of pubs in Hulme as our locals. The Salutation was a traditional Irish pub which because of its location near the university was beginning to attract a student customer base, while the Gamecock had a reputation as a pub frequented by local gangsters and criminals. It was a rough old place, but the landlord did lock-ins pretty much on demand.

We had two five-a-side football teams who played each other at Ardwick Pitz every week, and even started the process of reforming Red Dynamo to play in the Sunday League. Gerry and another lad called Dave Connolly wanted to call the team Hadjuk Spliff for obvious reasons, but they were over-ruled. A few of us even chanced our arms by attending Nads's karate classes, but his malicious delight in making AFA members train twice as hard as anyone else backfired when we all dropped out within a couple of weeks.

The BNP, meanwhile, were confined to the margins of the city. They could not hold public meetings, marches, or even a regular paper sale, and most of the time they didn't even dare to think about trying. We monitored where they drank and socialised, and if it looked like they were beginning to build a base we came down on them hard.

Longsight 1. Spies Like Us

After reading this far, you might well be under the impression that there was no place for women in AFA, but that would be wrong. Women were involved in all levels of AFA activity, from surveillance and intelligence work right through to the drawing up of political documents and leaflets. All kinds of talents were required to keep AFA functioning. We needed people who could speak confidently on the radio or TV, we needed people who could draw or design posters and stickers, people who could arrange gigs, public meetings, or co-ordinate branch meetings, prison visits and so on.

However, it is probably fair to say that there were very few women involved in the Stewards' Group, but that was because we required people to be honest about whether they felt confident in their own abilities should a physical confrontation occur. In AFA, as in society as a whole, it is the case that fewer women than men are confident of being able to deal with situations involving violence or aggression. Hence the lack of women in the Stewards' Group. We never really had a problem with that. It's not as if we had quotas to fill or anything.

AFA's policy of confrontational politics was set in stone, and while everyone in the organisation was expected to agree with the basic principles of political and physical opposition to fascism, that did not mean that we expected everyone to run around beating up nazi boneheads. Far from it. Recruitment to the Stewards' Group was done on a voluntary basis, with both men and women choosing not to participate if they were uncomfortable with the street-level stuff. Consequently, the Stewards' Group started out having very few women involved in it, and the situation became self-perpetuating, and never really progressed or changed. It was never intended that the Stewards' Group be an exclusive men-only club, but truth be told, there were times when it might well have been mistaken for one.

There were of course exceptions to the rule. In the winter of 1992, an AFA sympathiser was having a quiet drink in a Longsight pub when he spotted a number of BNP members huddled around a corner table. They were deep in whispered conversation with fascist literature scattered all around them. Our man immediately phoned an AFA contact number to report the sighting, and a couple of people drove across town to investigate. Unfortunately, the sighting coincided with several security stewards being out of town, or uncontactable on the night, and the only people readily available at short notice were a female steward called Carol and a skinny, bespectacled lad called Bob, who was an AFA member, but not a member of the Stewards' Group.

Carol liked the odd pint of Guinness, so she didn't need much of an excuse to pop out to a pub. She lived with Gerry in a relationship that made *The Odd Couple* look like a film about two completely sane and normal people. In fact, the dynamics of that particular relationship probably account for her fondness for the black stuff. Bob was a postie from the Abbey Hey area and was a bit of an anarchist. He was stick-thin and not cut out for the physical side of things but he was keen enough.

The two of them walked into the pub pretending to be a loving couple on a night out, and almost immediately clocked the fash. They kept the group under discreet surveillance for a while, trying to listen in on their conversation without appearing too obvious. Under the circumstances, neither of them were under any obligation to do anything, but when two of the BNP members got up from the table and left the pub they were followed out the door by the two lovebirds.

There was a bus-stop by the pub, and the two fash were stood under the shelter, minding their own business, when they were approached by the female steward. Intrigued by the approach the two men looked up and were promptly CS-gassed. The attack was followed up with a swift knee in the groin, leaving one of the men sprawled on the pavement weeping and the other running off down Stockport Road as fast as his legs would carry him.

I heard later that C18 had accused one of the individuals attacked that night of being a mole placed inside the BNP by *Searchlight* magazine. I am not in a position to offer an opinion one way or the other on the matter, except to say that the incident signalled the beginning of a souring of relation-ships between Manchester AFA and *Searchlight*. Manchester AFA's contact address was removed from the back of *Searchlight* magazine and members of Manchester's Stewards' Group were vilified as thugs and bootboys despite the fact that we were hundreds of miles away in Bilbao at the time of the attack.

I have to admit that I was slightly bemused by all this carry-on. I was big enough and ugly enough to handle a bit of name-calling, but it all seemed a bit childish and unnecessary to me. Surely being on the wrong end of a kicking in a Manchester pub at the hands of anti-fascists could only add to the credibility of a *Searchlight* mole if that is indeed what he was. I admit that it might be unpleasant for the person involved, but they surely have to expect this kind of thing to happen from time to time.

The relationship between *Searchlight* and national AFA also worsened considerably over the following years after elements in AFA claimed that *Searchlight* had been working hand in glove with both the police and intelligence services for some considerable time. This was an allegation that had been in circulation since at least the mid-Eighties but it seemed to gain more credibility in the Nineties, and many people wanted AFA to have nothing more to do with them. The fact that *Searchlight* chose this moment to smear some of the anarchist elements associated with AFA certainly did not help.

People were concerned that AFA could be compromised if *Searchlight* was indeed working with the police. They felt that because certain aspects of AFA activity were illegal then it would be dangerous and foolish to remain in close contact with them. Ties between the two organisations were eventually severed at a national level, although local co-operation still existed in some parts of the country.

I had personally lost all trust in *Searchlight* as an organisation, although I respected the bravery and commitment of certain individuals within it. My dilemma was that Steve was a mate. He had put me up when I had nowhere to live when I split up with Michele, and had risked the ire of his own organisation in doing so. He had also put up Gerry and Carol when they were made homeless. Steve still passed on bits and pieces of useful information to Manchester AFA, and I believe he put local interests ahead of his loyalty to *Searchlight*. On a personal level we were still friendly, and I certainly wasn't prepared to cut him out of things completely, although I wanted to try to keep his organisation at arm's length.

Longsight 2. Cracked Actor
A few months after the incident on Stockport Road we received another phone call from Longsight claiming that the area was swarming with nazi skinheads. This was unusual, because Manchester did not really have a skinhead scene, and the few individuals who still dressed in the skinhead style were known to us and sympathetic to anti-fascism. There were a few nazi boneheads in Oldham, but not enough to count as a "swarm". Surmising that there might have been a Blood and Honour gig right under our noses in one of the areas we considered a

stronghold, we got a team together and had a look around. After an hour or so of cruising around the area we spotted nothing untoward and went home mystified.

The next night we had another phone call along similar lines. The caller was known to us, and was trustworthy, but again the skinheads had disappeared without trace by the time we arrived in the area. What was going on? We made all sorts of enquiries trying to find out what the score was, but turned up absolutely nothing. There was not even a whisper of fash activity in the area, which was unusual, because we usually picked up something on the grapevine.

Several months later, all was revealed when the first series of *Cracker* was shown on TV. It was the plot where Robert Carlyle shaved off his hair and went on a killing spree in south Manchester. One scene involved the police raiding a derelict building in Longsight, which in the programme was used as a club by a group of right-wing skinheads. It was all pretty unrealistic as far as we were concerned, because the place would have been razed to the ground within five minutes of opening if we'd had any say in the matter.

I often wondered what would have happened if we had actually bumped into these actors-turned-boneheads at the time. The fash come up with all sorts of excuses to avoid a kicking, but "don't hit me I'm an actor" would have been a novelty. So here's a tip for any aspiring actors who might have to play a member of the master race. Always carry your Equity card with you.

Kenny Rogers – The Rise and Fall of South Manchester BNP

Manchester AFA underwent several line-up changes over the years as various people moved on, drifted away, or dropped out. Ben had more or less packed it in, as had Gary F and a few other people, but the biggest loss was Gerry, who took himself off to the hippy trail in India and never came back. I think the combination of heavy marijuana use and anti-fascism eventually did his head in, and he started to get paranoid. I heard a rumour that he was back in Glasgow but he could be anywhere in the world by now. Wherever he is, I wish him well.

New faces had come along to replace those who had dropped out. Andy Dignam, Jon, Mark T, Priest and Dom had all joined AFA at various stages over the intervening years, and brought fresh life to the organisation. It was just what we needed, I thought, a fresh influx of keen, committed anti-fascists to carry us through the battles that lay ahead.

Andy Dignam was from Salford. He was United through and through, and a lifelong socialist. He had an easy-going nature which belied the fact that he'd had a major heart problem since childhood. This eventually caused his untimely death a few years after joining AFA, aged just twenty-nine.

Jon was fair-haired, bookish and bespectacled. He was an ex-Militant full-timer now resident in Kilkenny. He took over a lot of the organisational aspects of AFA when I started to find it a struggle to keep on top of it all, and he seemed to relish doing all the mundane and boring tasks that beset any organisation staffed by volunteers. Jon eventually became the main AFA organiser in Manchester.

Mark T was a tarmac-layer who was originally from the Wiltshire area. He had been living in Whalley Range for a number of years and had married a local woman. I liked Mark. He was the type of person who would share his last Rolo with you. He was as strong as an ox, but had a tendency to start singing Wurzel songs after a few pints. Priest was an ex-SWP member from Bury who, as his nickname implied, had once trained to be a member of the priesthood. Fortunately, he had seen the error of his ways and rebelled. Dom was a self-employed builder from the Boothstown area who began to push a lot of plastering work my way. He was second-generation Irish and was a big United and Celtic supporter.

I was getting my private life sorted out, and eventually found myself a flat in a tower block in Hulme. I was busy decorating the living room one evening when Steve called around to show me a copy of the latest issue of the BNP's paper *British Nationalist*.

"Have you seen this," he asked, handing me the paper.

It was open on the page that listed all the BNP's contact addresses around the country, and I suddenly noticed that they were claiming that they had opened up a new branch in south Manchester, right in our own backyard. The contact address was a PO box in the very same post office as the one used by Manchester AFA.

We got on the case straight away. The thing about a PO box is that you need to give the Post Office an address so that they can send you the card which you present at the desk when you pick up your mail. The address is also needed in case a box is hired by a dodgy company who rip people off through the postal system. Steve phoned up the Post Office, claiming that he was a customer with a complaint against the owner of the PO box, and was eventually given an address in Chorlton. The address turned out to be right next door to Chorlton Irish Centre, which I thought was a bit cheeky.

We went round there, expecting to be confronted by some tooled-up nazi, but instead found a slightly dazed and confused old hippie woman. Steve was pretending to be a journalist working on a story, but the woman was not as daft as she looked and sussed us straight away.

"He's not a journalist," she said, pointing directly at me. "He's got tattoos on his arms."

"Oh, he's my minder," said Steve, thinking on his feet. Yeah, thanks for that mate.

Anyway, after a bit of a chat, we were invited in for a cuppa, and it suddenly dawned on her what had happened. It turned out that her boyfriend's workmate had persuaded them to let him use their address for some personal business. They had no idea what the business was, but just assumed it was something he didn't want his wife to know about.

The hippie woman lost no time telling us the name and address of this "friend", and within a week the campaign against him was in full swing. His car was wrecked on at least three occasions, his living room windows were smashed, and pressure was brought to bear on him at his workplace through a couple of black lads we knew who happened to work with him.

After the story was leaked to a local newspaper, his wife also came under pressure at her place of work, and it was all looking a bit grim for the newest member of the master race. Within a month he had been approached by an anti-fascist and been offered a way out of the mess he had gotten himself into. We arranged to meet him in the Whalley pub in Whalley Range, and six of us sat discreetly in pairs around the pub while we waited for our man to arrive.

I don't know what I expected him to look like but I certainly was not expecting a Kenny Rogers lookalike. The man could have made a fortune in a Country and Western tribute band. The urge to sing "Coward of the County" as he negotiated his surrender terms was almost irresistible.

"Joining the BNP was the biggest mistake I've ever made," he said miserably. "My wife isn't talking to me, I've been ostracised at work, and my neighbour burst out laughing when he saw the state of my car."

"It can all be stopped," replied one of his interrogators, "but in order to satisfy us that you aren't going back to the fash, we need you to tell us everything you know about the BNP in the North-West."

He became evasive for a while after that, and it was clear that he didn't want to answer our questions. At that point, two moody characters approached the table. One of them was

Nads, the other was Dessie, an anti-fascist from the Eighties who was by now a well-known local "face" about town. He glared down at the frightened ex-fash, who nearly fainted under the withering gaze. "There's one thing that not many people know about me," said Dessie, "and that's the fact that I'm anti-fascist to the core. Now tell these lads what they want to know, because I don't want to have to come back here and see you again."

The fash turned white with fear. He was staring into the eyes of one of the most frightening people he was ever likely to meet, and he visibly wilted.

As the two men turned on their heels and left the pub, the fash was still visibly shaken. "Th . . . th . . . that's Dessie N . . . N . . ." he stuttered.

"It's not him you need to worry about," interrupted one of the interrogators. "It's the bloke that's with him that you need to watch out for."

That afternoon in the Whalley was a bit strange, because we were all trying to keep a low profile, but for one reason or another practically every AFA member in South Manchester happened to stroll past the pub. Before we knew it there was a big group of us in the pub trying to stay sober until Kenny had left.

After he had been allowed to leave we settled down for an afternoon session on the beer. I was curious about what had been said, and debriefed the interrogators before we all got too pissed. There was not much we didn't already know, but it had been more a question of asserting the plausibility of his desire to leave the BNP rather than actual information gathering.

The entire lifespan of South Manchester BNP was less than two months. The swiftness with which the branch was closed down sent shock-waves through the BNP, and confirmed Manchester's status as a no-go area for fascists.

Clowns to the Left of Me, Jokers to the Right

Never attempt political activity when you're drunk. That sage advice should be handed down through the generations. Ignore this advice and calamity will surely follow in your footsteps.

I was out for a few beers one Friday night with Mark T when for some unknown reason we ended up in a pub called the Swinging Sporran near UMIST. Now the Sporran was a bit of a bikers' pub. It was the kind of place which smelt of leather and axle grease, in fact just the kind of place you might find Wigan Mike. He wasn't in that night however, and we ended up chatting to the landlord, who told us that there was a comedian booked for an after-hours function in the bar downstairs. It was getting near closing time, and without thinking too much about the kind of entertainment that might be on offer, we jibbed our way into the room and settled down for a few after-hours drinks.

After wall-to-wall heavy metal for half an hour or so, the comedian came on stage to loud applause from the leather-clad crowd. After acknowledging the applause, his first words were, "There were these two Pakis . . ."

"Shut up you racist prick," I shouted at him, while trying my best to ignore the glowering bikers all around me.

"Oh I see there are a couple of Paki-lovers in the room," replied the comedian.

That was enough for me. I slammed my glass down on the bar and charged headlong at the stage, closely followed by Mark.

Someone tripped me up before I got there, and I ended up sprawled all over the floor, but Mark managed to get onto the stage and the comedian fled in terror, running out of the club as fast as his legs would carry him. I picked myself up and turned around to see a sea of hostile faces glaring at me. Fortunately Mark had more presence of mind than me, and grabbed the microphone, launching into a speech about black people's contribution to rock music. He didn't get much further than Phil Lynott and Jimi Hendrix, but it appeared to do the trick, and a couple of younger rockers even yelled out words of encouragement. I dusted myself off and we eventually retired to the bar, where the landlord bought us drinks and apologised. We spent the rest of the evening engaged in a long series of arguments with various bikers about the nature of racism and fascism.

A couple of weeks later we were back in the Sporran having a quiet drink and playing pool, when one of the lads who had been in the pub during the stage invasion came over and started talking to us. He told us that he had been drinking in a pub in Collyhurst when our old friend, the comedian, suddenly walked onto the stage and started giving it the big racist number again. Inspired by our example, the lad attacked the comedian and chased him out the pub, telling him never to come back again with his racist shite.

Another time when we really should have known better was after the Blaggers ITA had played a benefit gig for Manchester AFA in the Roadhouse in town. Apart from one incident which was easily dealt with, the night had passed off peacefully, and the stewards began to relax with a few drinks as the evening drew to a close. For some reason the conversation turned to the subject of a local fascist who was rumoured to be a C18 member. This particular character was implicated in a graffiti campaign against the Asian owners of a grocery shop which had been repeatedly daubed with Nazi and Loyalist slogans. Steve had got hold of an address for this character a couple of days beforehand, and before we had a chance to think about it properly, a load of us were in the Bolt's van as it headed off towards his home address in Stretford.

An attack was launched on the house, and it was bombarded by an assortment of plant pots, garden implements and other missiles, which mostly landed harmlessly on the brickwork and pebbledash. I found a broom and swung it at the living room window, but the head came off in mid-swing and it sailed harmlessly into the neighbours' garden. Eventually a couple of small windows were broken and we all legged it towards the waiting van.

As I ran towards the van my baseball cap blew off and landed underneath a parked car. I was crawling underneath the car to retrieve it when Gary the Axe started puncturing the tyres with a bradawl. Someone else started smashing the windows, and a couple of bags were snatched off the back seat. I emerged from underneath the car to find it wrecked, and the various miscreants climbing on board the van which was slowly drawing away. They were all looking very pleased with themselves until I caught up with them.

"What the hell did you attack that car for?" I shouted.

"I thought it belonged to the fash," claimed Gary.

"Yeah," said someone else. "We saw you crawling underneath it and assumed you were cutting the brake cables or something."

"I was only getting my baseball cap back," I replied, shaking my head in despair, "not planning a multiple-car pile-up."

The two bags, far from containing valuable information on fascist activity, actually contained a pair of sweaty trainers and a tube of athlete's foot remedy. The only real crumb of comfort that could be drawn from the night's events was that at least no-one had got nicked.

Funnily enough, the graffiti and harassment campaign against the Asian family stopped immediately after our visit to the House of the Fascist Scum, and a couple of weeks later the property was put on the market.

The Manchester Martyrs

Lucozade bottles were the anti-fascist weapon of choice in the early Nineties. I don't mean the big bottles which you give to elderly relatives in hospital, but the smaller ones which fitted nicely inside your coat pocket. They had a couple of advantages over your more traditional weapons, the first being that if it still contains some of its sugary contents, then it is not an obvious offensive weapon and reduces the chances of criminal charges being brought against you. The second advantage is that they were ideally suited as both a hitting and throwing weapon. They were so popular amongst AFA members that we joked about approaching Lucozade for sponsorship.

Some AFA members preferred to carry tins of peas or baked beans, while those of a culinary bent went for more exotic fare like tinned fruit or tins of ravioli. Coshes and bats were still used, and CS gas was becoming more common, but knives were never popular. The fash tended to use blades a lot more than us. I think this was because they were shithouses who weren't actually that good on the pavement when it came down to it.

One occasion where anything went was the Manchester Martyrs Commemoration march every November. The annual march in memory of three Irishmen wrongly hanged in 1867 always attracted significant opposition from both the fascists and Loyalists. During the late Eighties and early Nineties, the march usually started in Longsight and wound its way via a circuitous route through south Manchester before ending up back in Longsight. At the assembly point, and all along the route of the march, the fash and the Loyalists would gather to heckle, and if given the opportunity by the police, attack the march. For a few years in the late Eighties we had a working relationship with the march organisers and carried out a more orthodox and defensive stewarding role while the march was in progress. The hours both before and after the commemoration were a different matter however.

In 1988, following a few years of relative calm, a group of AFA stewards dispersed a mob of fash at the assembly point in Longsight and, following information received from Steve, attacked a number of BNP members after the march in the city centre. The fash were on their way to a meeting in

Mother Mac's, an Irish pub near Newton Street, when they were ambushed.

We had been stewarding the march all day, and no-one was tooled-up for obvious reasons, but the lad who drove us into town had all these odd-shaped blocks of wood in his van. They were like skittles, but shorter and squatter. We found it difficult to keep a grip on them, but we thought that they would be better than nothing.

We bounced into the fash as they were approaching the pub, and immediately recognised them as being amongst the mob of counter-demonstrators from the march earlier. I grabbed one by the collar and dragged him to the ground while a couple of lads tried to hit him with these wooden skittle things, but they couldn't keep a grip on them and they flew out off their hands in all directions. For a few moments it was complete chaos until the fash were finally subdued by boots and fists.

The following year, a vanload of AFA members jumped a group of Loyalists still wandering around Rusholme over an hour after the march had passed through the area. The attack was swift and merciless, and the Loyalists were absolutely butchered. Dessie was bouncing some fella off a chain link fence with a series of haymakers, while Sean moved like lightning to catch and batter some Loyalist trying to make good his escape. I don't think I have ever seen Sean move so fast. He was throwing punches like they were going out of fashion.

While we were climbing back into the van to make good our escape, there was a sudden, terrible scream, and we looked back to see that one of the lads, Paddy Logan, had bitten off the earlobe of one of the Loyalists. It was a chilling moment, even for veterans of dozens of brawls and battles. Paddy was actually a top bloke, but I would not have liked to get on the wrong side of him. He was an ex-boxer from Belfast and had spent his whole life fighting to survive. He had a reputation around Manchester that put the fear of god into lads who thought they were pretty tough themselves.

Gerry and I stumbled into some mither with a load of City supporters in the Albert one afternoon, and it was just about to come on top when Paddy walked in by chance and let on to us. The Blues backed off as soon as they realised he knew us, and it was all, "All right Paddy," and, "Can I buy you a drink Paddy?" It was pathetic to watch. Paddy was fatally shot a few years later by gangsters. It was probably the only way to stop him.

Seven of the Loyalists from the Rusholme incident were hospitalised, and we learned later that they were members of the Liverpool branch of the Independent Loyal Orange Lodge, an extreme grouping who broke away from the Orange Order when they were banned from carrying a UVF standard on Orange parades.

The Manchester Martyrs Commemoration had been a target for Liverpool Loyalists for years. Groups of Scouse Loyalists mingling freely with sieg-heiling nazis was a familiar sight along the route, and the two groups often combined and colluded to launch attacks on the marchers. Following the incident in Rusholme, the number of Loyalists travelling along East Lancs Road to protest against the commemoration declined rapidly.

The relationship between the march organisers and AFA was never straightforward, and in 1990 it disintegrated completely. We were informed that our presence on the march was no longer welcome and all ties were cut. We were not unduly bothered. The march was in serious decline anyway, and the amount of in-fighting and bitching only hastened its eventual demise some years later.

In the meantime, we still felt obliged to offer some protection to those marchers who supported the commemoration, but were unconnected to the committee, because the police were unreliable escorts to say the least. Now we were free from the shackles of actually having to steward the march, we could adjust our tactics accordingly. During the next couple of years we ensured that the demonstration passed unmolested through the streets of south Manchester, and scattered groups of counter-demonstrators at the assembly point and along the route of the march. The fash were aware that we could be anywhere now, and were constantly looking over their shoulders in case we suddenly bounced out of a cafe, a pub or a back-entry.

After a couple of years of this, the fash seemed to lose their nerve, and were scared to stick around for long periods. They tended to turn up late, make a token protest, and then disappear before it came on top. The only highlight during these years was watching Wigan NF organiser Dave Sudworth walking into a lamppost. We had a couple of near misses during this period, including one where half a dozen BNP escaped annihilation by seconds in Rusholme, but on the whole it was difficult to get any kind of result.

Eventually, due to apathy, factionalism and bad organisation, the number of marchers attending the commemoration declined to such an extent that in 1994, the committee could no longer justify holding a march, and instead opted to organise a public meeting in Longsight Library. In the week leading up to the meeting, we had a phone call from Glasgow AFA who passed on some intelligence they had picked up about a coachload of Loyalists planning to travel down to Manchester to attack a "meeting". Putting two and two together, it was obvious that it was the Manchester Martyrs meeting they were planning to attack. We had a prior commitment in Leeds on the day but passed on the information to the organisers in the hope that they would take suitable precautions to safeguard those attending. They dismissed the information out of hand, and basically accused us of scaremongering.

Of course the Martyrs Committee took no security precautions, and their meeting was invaded by a mob of local fascists and Glasgow Loyalists, and only the presence of the police prevented the meeting from being completely wrecked. As it was, those who attended were threatened, abused and intimidated, and the meeting was curtailed. Clearly shaken by the experience, the organisers abandoned the meeting and were escorted out of the building by the police. The irony of so-called anti-imperialists having to be protected by the police was lost on no-one except maybe the organisers themselves.

Although we could perhaps be forgiven a certain *schadenfreude* at the Martyrs' expense, no-one in Manchester AFA really took any great pleasure in the humiliation at Longsight Library. It is true that we had risked injury and imprisonment on their behalf over recent years and received nothing in return except sneers and derision, but the defeat was too close to home to be easily dismissed. The fash were cock-a-hoop over finally getting a result in Manchester, and we knew we had to act quickly to rectify the situation. Luckily the Bloody Sunday Commemoration was in Manchester the following January, and we began making plans to put the fash back in their place.

Bloody Sunday Commemoration, 28 January 1995

This was the first Bloody Sunday Commemoration outside London for many years, and in the build-up to the march there was a lot of media attention, especially as Martin McGuinness (allegedly the Chief of Staff of the IRA) was due to speak. Because of the high media profile of the event, and after the Martyrs disaster in November, we suspected that the fash might turn out big numbers, and therefore requested a national mobilisation of AFA branches to deal with the expected threat. Previous Bloody Sunday marches in London had all been national call-outs, and we didn't really think that there would be a problem. What we didn't take into account was London's reaction to the request. They kicked up a right fuss over the call-out, seemingly unaware of the contradictions with previous mobilisations for this event. London was the dominant force in AFA, and had become increasingly authoritarian and dictatorial over the past couple of years. It seemed to me that they were attempting to control all aspects of AFA policy and practice, and there was a suggestion that they thought Manchester were getting above themselves in calling for a national mobilisation without their authorisation. I also suspected that the bad relationship between London AFA and the Troops Out formed at least a small part of their reluctance to mobilise.

In the event we were surprised to see about a dozen London AFA stewards turn up on the day, bringing the total numbers up to about 110. We plotted up in the Anson's Well pub near the march assembly point in Platt Fields, and secured the area. Policing was light due to the fact that, unusually, both United and City were playing at home in the FA Cup that day. United were playing Wrexham, City were playing Villa.

I had walked the route of the march with Jon H and Priest earlier in the week. "This is going to be tricky," I said. "The march is heading down Wilmslow Road only a couple of hours before City play Villa. If it's running late for any reason then it could get really moody."

"Yeah," agreed Jon H, "and Villa's C18 firm are likely to be out in force as well."

We had worked out an arrangement with the march organisers whereby we would put one team of stewards at the front of the march, and another at the back. We had begun to move into position when the London lot suddenly marched off back down Wilmslow Road taking another dozen or so stewards with them. Apparently they didn't want to steward the march, and were going off to hunt for fash in Rusholme. We carried on with our original plan.

I was in the group at the back of the march as it moved off and headed down Wilmslow Road towards the city centre.

We had gone no more than a few hundred yards when a Scouse steward at the front of the march came running back to have a word. "There's a group of fash outside the Clarence pub. They're trying to wind up City fans to attack the march," he said breathlessly.

"Right," I shouted to my group of stewards. "Let's move."

As we approached the Clarence, I saw a mob of forty assorted fash and Blues taunting and abusing the marchers, and I wondered briefly how the London posse could have overlooked them. From the look of things we had arrived in the nick of time. Tempers had reached boiling point and an assault on the march looked inevitable.

The AFA groups from the front and back of the march converged on the Clarence at roughly the same time, catching the fash in a classic pincer movement. By the time they realised the danger it was too late, and they were trapped. One of the faces I recognised was our old friend David Taylor from Rochdale. He looked like a startled rabbit caught in a car's headlights.

There was a big scrum in the pub doorway as the fash all tried to run into the pub at the same time, and I managed to drag one out and throw him on the ground for a couple of stewards to lay into. I kicked another one up the arse, and he shouted, "Oi!" in such a startled tone of voice that I was momentarily taken aback and he escaped. The rest of the fash were caught like rats in a trap as AFA hit them from all sides, and I saw a couple of Scousers kicking the bloke I had thrown onto the ground all over the pavement. A dozen or so fash eventually managed to escape into the pub but were chased out the back by anti-fascists. One unfortunate individual leapt over a fence into someone's back garden and was savaged by a pitbull.

While all this was going on, a republican flute band had stopped outside the pub and provided musical accompaniment to the brawl. We expected the police to intervene, and instinctively pulled back, half-expecting to have our collars felt. Unfortunately for the fash, the Old Bill were too thin on the ground to do much more than look on helplessly, and a second wave of anti-fascists steamed into the pub looking for victims. The City fans kept well out of the way, and wanted no more to do with their fleeting allies.

I started to get the feeling that we were pushing our luck. "Pull back," I shouted, "leave it now," and we moved away from the scene just as police reinforcements started arriving. We headed into town, and plotted up in the Winchester pub near Oxford Road train station, which was on the route of the march. We had two plain-clothes Dibble in tow by the time we got there, and when we had a quiet moment we politely informed them that they had been sussed and they left the pub looking a bit sheepish.

We moved into Albert Square ahead of the march and finally found the London lot, who had bumped into the demoralised remnants of our earlier encounter on Oxford Road and chased them off again. Clown of the Day award went to one hapless individual with a St George's flag who sidled up to a group of stewards and introduced himself with the immortal words, "All right lads. I'm here to get stuck into the Reds." He was immediately dropped on his arse by an AFA member and a group of Celtic Casuals finished the job.

Three AFA stewards were arrested but later released with cautions. Later on in the evening, the landlord of the Clarence claimed on the radio that £2,000 worth of damage had been done to his pub. The Clarence was nominally an Irish pub, and even put on Irish music sessions in the lounge on weekdays, but the vault was occasionally frequented by Loyalist types, and it had been long suspected that the landlord had sympathies in that direction.

Apprentice Boys March, Bolton, 13 April 1996

Sometime in early April 1996, Steve phoned me with the news that the Loyalists were planning to march in Bolton later that month. In fact it was the English Amalgamated Committee of the Apprentice Boys of Londonderry who were marching, but as they were linked with the UVF, I took his point. I told him that we were naturally interested, but took the attitude that it wasn't really any of our business. After a brief discussion we decided it might be worthwhile sending a small team over to monitor the march and see if they could spot any familiar faces from the BNP or NF, but other than that we probably wouldn't bother our arses with it.

A week later we picked up rumours that C18 were doing security for the march, and all of a sudden it started to look more interesting. We began sniffing around for more information, but for some reason people were staying really tight-lipped on this one. We got a few of the Bolton AFA people on the case, but they failed to find anything of note. We tried phoning around local journalists, and even a couple of councillors, but they hadn't heard anything, or if they had then they weren't telling us.

Sometimes the direct approach is best, and after searching around our files for a few names from the past, we came across a certain Mark Dooley from Bolton, who among other things had a conviction for spitting on and intimidating a four-year-old Asian girl and whose home when raided by the police was found to contain fascist literature and stickers. On the off chance that he might know something, Jon phoned up Mr Dooley, pretending to be a journalist from the *Bolton Evening News*. We were hoping that with his past he might have heard something that he was willing to share with the papers.

His wife answered the phone. "He's not in," she said. "Is it about the march?"

"Err, yeah," replied Jon. "I'm doing a piece on it for the paper, and I was wondering if he knew what time it started."

"Of course he does," she answered. "He's the main organiser. I've got the details here if you want them."

We were barely able to contain ourselves as the poor woman picked up some kind of bulletin and read it out over the phone to Jon. It contained everything we needed, including the name of the pub booked for the meeting and buffet, and the assembly point and starting time for the march.

Our first step was to make sure that the meeting room and buffet were cancelled. The manager of the pub hosting the event was informed of the real identities behind the mystery booking and was warned about what he could expect if the event went ahead. Horrified at the prospect of being associated with nazi race-haters and Loyalist paramilitaries he immediately cancelled. Having been gifted all the information we needed, it was now a matter of making sure we got enough people out on the day itself to ensure that we wouldn't come off second best if it came on top. C18 had a reputation in the media as a serious outfit, but we knew that their so-called notoriety was built on hype and press hysteria, and counted for nothing on the streets.

On the day itself, a group of around 100 AFA members met up in a small pub near Burnden Park on the outskirts of Bolton and made plans to attack the assembly point of the march. The march was due to start from outside the pub that the Loyalists had originally booked for their meeting. It was a biggish boozer on a crossroads at the edge of the town centre.

I talked to Gary the Axe about the best route to the pub. "We can't go through the town centre Dave," he said, "it's covered with CCTV." He produced an *A to Z* with all the cameras marked on it in biro. At least they've done their homework, I thought. "What about trying this way round the back," I suggested, tracing a circular route to the pub. Gary looked at it for a second. "Yeah, that should be okay," he nodded.

Shortly afterwards, the AFA mob emerged from a small car park and charged up a steep hill in an attempt to confront the large numbers of fascists and Loyalists gathering at the assembly point. The police were initially taken by surprise but recovered swiftly enough to prevent a clash. Police dogs and horses were brought in to chase the anti-fascists back down the street, and in the ensuing chaos the police mistakenly pushed three members of Oldham C18 into the middle of the anti-fascist group. They were immediately set upon. I kicked one of them up the arse, and as he turned around instinctively, I punched him in the face, sending him sprawling backwards across the pavement. The other two ended up getting kicked all over the tarmac. C18 members from London, the Midlands and the North watched in red-faced fury as their Oldham comrades were battered in front of their eyes, but they refused to make any attempt to break through police lines and rescue their fallen friends.

With the police now aware of our presence, any further attack on the march was going to be impossible without risking large numbers of arrests, and we retired from the scene in good order. There was nothing to be gained by going back to the scene and giving it the big one behind lines of police. That was not our style. We left that kind of thing to the poseurs in C18.

Because of the swiftness of the police intervention at the assembly point, we had not succeeded in our aim of chasing C18 out of town, but the confrontation did succeed in persuading Greater Manchester Police to cancel the march because they could not guarantee public order. We were happy enough with the result. It wasn't by any means a clear-cut victory, but it had been a humiliating day for both the Apprentice Boys and C18, and all achieved without any nickings.

The day after the events in Bolton, I typed out and faxed a press release explaining why we had felt it necessary to confront those gathering for the march. I detailed the extensive links between Loyalists and fascists, and spelt out clearly to the Apprentice Boys that their march, buffet and meeting room had all been cancelled due to their fraternisation with C18. Re-emphasising the point, I concluded with the phrase, "If you lie down with dogs, then you wake up with fleas." I didn't know it at the time but it was more or less my last meaningful act as an anti-fascist.

Shot By Both Sides
Since the summer of 1993, Manchester AFA had been busy developing a number of projects designed to promote anti-fascist politics in areas outside the normal sphere of political activity. One of these projects was "Freedom of Movement", a collaboration between three AFA lads, Guy, Tim and Roy, and some of the major movers on the club scene such as Justin Robertson, Carl Cox and the like. The idea was to promote anti-fascism amongst club-goers, something which we regarded as a natural progression of the club scene's inherent cultural diversity.

It was not my cup of tea. I was into stuff like Dick Gaughan and Christy Moore at the time, but despite few of us really understanding what the club scene was about, we gave them the green light to go ahead with it anyway. It was an unqualified success, with numerous benefit gigs being organised, and a CD of remixes being released. Manchester AFA's financial problems eased after the money started rolling in from the benefit gigs, and we were able to go ahead with a number of plans that we'd had to put on the back-burner due to lack of cash.

One thing we had wanted to do for some time was to start up an anti-fascist football fanzine in response to the reports we had been receiving of BNP paper sales at various football grounds around the North-West. Now we had the money it was an ambition that could be realised. We called a number of meetings with various interested parties and *Red Attitude*, a Manchester United anti-fascist fanzine, was born. The reason we chose United was because practically everyone who turned up for the first couple of meetings was a United supporter. There had never really been a fascist problem at Old Trafford, and we were aware of the fact that other clubs had bigger problems with fascists and racists, but we couldn't exactly go around pretending to be City or Oldham supporters in order to flog a few fanzines. We decided to make a virtue out of necessity and concentrate our efforts where we were strongest, hoping that supporters at other clubs would follow our lead.

It was ironic that United became associated with anti-fascism while City gained a reputation as a far-right stomping ground, despite the fact that Maine Road was bang in the middle of Moss Side. I put it down to the fact that United's association with Catholicism made it the club of choice for wave after wave of Irish immigrants. Their experiences of racism meant that subsequent generations had a natural empathy with anti-fascism. Even today, if you check out the surnames of Manchester-born United fans you'll find that a large proportion of them still carry at least one reminder of their Irish heritage. All this is not intended to denigrate the efforts of the many City fans who have offered sterling support to the anti-fascist cause over the years.

Red Attitude proved to be a huge success, regularly selling out of its print run, and causing a stir far beyond its circulation. The high point for the fanzine came when Eric Cantona leapt into the stands at Crystal Palace to confront Matthew Simmons, a spectator who was racially abusing him. The spectator had fascist connections and had a history of racist behaviour. Along with the majority of United's hardcore support we leapt to Eric's defence, but the fact that we were an anti-fascist fanzine put us in a unique position. A statement released to the press proved too inviting for them to ignore. It read:

We fully endorse the actions of Eric Cantona at Selhurst Park on January 25th 1995. We feel they were entirely understandable given the racist and foul-mouthed abuse he was forced to endure from the alleged victim.

Supporters of Red Attitude would need no such provocation to attack this racist thug. We believe that racism should not be given the slightest chance to grow in football grounds.

The fanzine also began to make in-roads into the culture of casual racism that pervades a lot of football grounds, and we found far more friends than enemies among United's huge support. The fact that the majority of the fanzine sellers and contributors were match-going Reds helped, as did the backing from well-known United supporters like Boylie and his crew. We produced T-shirts, posters, stickers and badges which all sold by the bucket-load, and a group called Manchester United Anti-Fascists was set up in the hope of encouraging more people to get involved in the campaign.

Boylie and his mates didn't exactly need any encouragement. In one incident at an away match against QPR they attacked a fascist bonehead on a tube train. They also chased a prick called Jason Ankers out of a pub after he appeared on TV giving it the big 'un in a United hat after the riot by England fans in Dublin. A carload of them also cruised past the home of Matthew Simmons when United next played in south London. Apparently there was a short discussion about smashing the front windows, but it looked a bit iffy and they left it, which was probably just as well because it was revealed the next day in the papers that the area was crawling with CID.

We were doing good consistent work at Old Trafford, which was in stark contrast to the debacle unfolding at Chelsea. London AFA had encouraged members of the Chelsea Independent Supporters Association (CISA) to publicise

"Chelsea Anti-Fascist" stickers in its fanzine, but when the inevitable reprisals occurred and CISA were attacked by members of C18 and the Chelsea Headhunters, London AFA were nowhere to be seen. CISA were left on their own, and were eventually hounded out of Stamford Bridge altogether, probably ruing the day they ever came into contact with AFA. London AFA had no base at Chelsea and no business encouraging Chelsea supporters to put their arses on the line unless they were prepared to give them consistent back-up.

Despite this balls-up in London, we considered ourselves to be in the ascendancy by the summer of 1995, especially in the North-West. The BNP had declared in April 1994 that there would be "no more marches, meetings, punch-ups". We had won this phase of the battle. The BNP had retreated from the streets, and now it was our turn to set the agenda.

I was determined that we would not repeat the mistakes of the last generation of anti-fascists, many of whom had succumbed to the lures of inactivity when the fascist threat subsided. I thought that in Manchester at least, we were in a good position, with both *Red Attitude* and Freedom of Movement doing very nicely, and a number of other projects in the pipeline. What I did not know at the time however was that AFA was about to face its most serious challenge, a challenge that would eventually result in the collapse of virtually the entire organisation. The blow was an implosion really, administered not by the fascists, the police, or by any of our other numerous enemies, but by elements within AFA itself.

London AFA, which was completely dominated by Red Action, had put forward a set of proposals designed to push AFA in a more political direction. They argued that now the BNP had retreated from the streets, the continuation of the physical battle against the fascists was pointless, and would only lead AFA up a cul-de-sac. They argued that AFA had to start putting forward positive solutions to the problems faced by people in working-class communities rather than just telling people why they should not vote for the BNP.

To my mind, the actual politics being proposed seemed to make sense, but I had two big concerns. I voiced one of these openly at a number of meetings called by Red Action/London AFA to push forward their proposals. The other I left unspoken.

My first concern involved the fact that AFA groups were for the first time being asked to accept a political programme based on the political philosophy of one particular organisation within it. AFA was composed of a variety of different political groups and individuals united around the principle of "physical and ideological opposition to fascism" and very little else. I feared that superimposing a particular set of political ideals on the organisation would lead to splits and the eventual break-up, or neutering, of AFA. Time was to prove that these concerns were correct.

I could not understand why AFA groups were being forced to decide one way or the other on this issue. If Red Action wanted to build a grassroots, community-based organisation then good luck to them, I didn't see why AFA should be expected to become that organisation, which was basically the hidden agenda behind the Red Action/London AFA proposals. They wanted AFA to dismantle itself and adopt the political programme of this new organisation. It could never work, and I couldn't understand why no-one else could see it. Surely, the ideal role for AFA groups in this situation would be to offer protection and support to this fledgling organisation in areas where it is campaigning directly against the fascists?

My other concern, the unspoken one, was that the people who seemed to be keenest on pushing through these proposals simply weren't up for the physical challenge any more. I didn't have a problem with that, everyone comes to the end of their street-fighting career eventually, and some of these people had been fighting the fascists for twenty years or more. I had nothing but admiration and respect for the bravery and commitment they had shown over the years, but what worried me was that they now seemed to be attempting to change the direction of the most successful anti-fascist organisation in the country to suit their own personal circumstances. What they should have done was either retired from the scene with their honour intact and a chestful of metaphorical medals, or taken the anti-fascist equivalent of a desk job.

Aside from these objections, it seemed to me that both *Red Attitude* and Freedom of Movement were making headway in their own particular areas, and I was reluctant to drop either campaign in favour of Red Action/London's initiative. The work required to get London's project off the ground would inevitably have meant that both Manchester projects would suffer as a result. I suppose I really needed to be convinced that what would be gained was worth abandoning everything we had fought for in the past. I think there will always be a need for an anti-fascist organisation capable of physically challenging the fascists, and Red Action/London's proposals seemed to be moving AFA completely away from that role.

My lack of enthusiasm for this pet project was obviously noted by leading members of Red Action in London, and before long I began to notice that everything I did became the focus for criticism. My replies to these criticisms were picked to pieces, and I began to get bogged down in a series of pointless and petty arguments. Internal politics was never my thing, and I was never very good at it, nor indeed was I particularly interested in it.

I was only a supporting member of Red Action at this stage, having allowed my full membership to lapse a few months beforehand. Following these internal disputes I resigned my membership completely in the hope that it would curtail the internal wrangling, and allow me to concentrate on AFA stuff. AFA was the only worthwhile accomplishment of

RA in any case, so it was not as though I would be missing anything.

My resignation seemed to prompt a whole new whispering campaign against me, which eventually culminated in a series of vicious smears and slanders being used to try and force me to resign from AFA as well. A two-year-old court case in which I was falsely accused of robbery was dredged up and used against me, despite the fact that I was innocent of the charge and found not guilty in court. They also seized on the fact that I was still friendly with Steve, and invented a whole series of completely bizarre and off-the-wall theories to smear us both. The fact that I had started seeing a woman called Louise, who was a member of the Troops Out Movement, also provided them with further ammunition to try and discredit me.

People in London AFA seemed to be working on the basis that if enough mud is thrown then some of it will stick. Ironically, many of the mud-slingers were the very same people who had themselves been subjected to an almost identical campaign when the SWP disbanded the Squads. They had obviously learned their lessons well. I was struck by the fact that things seemed to have come around full circle in the last fifteen years.

By turns I was both confused and angry about the spiral of accusations flying in my direction. On the one hand I felt betrayed by people I trusted implicitly, people who had taught me everything I knew about politics, while on the other hand I was pissed off because I knew that I had done nothing wrong. I was innocent of every accusation levelled against me. I had made mistakes at various times, but they were honest ones made with the best of intentions, and who doesn't make a few errors on their journey through life?

I think the fact that these people never made any moves to formally expel me from the organisation spoke volumes. This would have required them to come forward with some kind of proof to back up their accusations, but of course that proof never existed, because all the allegations were false. They settled instead on making life within AFA impossible for me by using smears and lies.

I had to seriously question whether it was worth all the mither of staying on and fighting my corner, or whether I should just throw in the towel and start a new life outside the political arena. Louise had just given birth to our son, and I had the two of them to consider as well as my own feelings. In a meeting with some of the less hostile members of London AFA it was suggested to me that if I stayed on, it would probably end in bloodshed, and that the resultant infighting could wreck AFA. I did not really want to spend the next five years of my life feuding with former friends and comrades, nor did I want to be accused of wrecking an organisation that I had done so much to build, so I took what I thought was the honourable option, and alongside several other leading members of Manchester AFA, I resigned. I never bore a grudge against anyone who stayed on, and in fact I have spoken to a couple of them since and they all say that they didn't believe any of the shit that was being said about me, but that they wanted to carry on fighting the fascists. I do not blame them for that.

What I did not know at the time, although I had an inkling of it, was that AFA would collapse within five years in any case, torn apart by internal ructions caused by Red Action trying to impose their political programme on it. In 2003, aside from a couple of branches who still remain active around the country, AFA no longer exists as a national organisation in anything other than name and reputation.

For a year or so after I resigned, I kept reflecting on my grandfather's warning about not getting involved in politics because it would ruin my life. He was a lovely old fella who only wanted the best for me, but despite everything that happened, I'm still glad that I ignored his advice. The last six months of my involvement in AFA had proven to be a nasty and unpleasant experience. It was soul-destroying being smeared and stabbed in the back by people I had respected and trusted. I could accept it if it had been the fash who were making my life hell, but being turned on by former friends and comrades was unpleasant and out of order. For a while afterwards I was bitter and disillusioned about the whole of the twelve years I had spent in AFA, but as time moved on I was able to reflect on the positive things that had come out of my participation in the anti-fascist struggle.

These days I feel immensely proud of what I helped to achieve during those years. I had helped to make a difference to people's lives, and played no small part in literally transforming reality, hopefully for the better. With limited resources, but with bucketloads of grit and determination, a motley and ragbag assortment of individuals had stopped the onward advance of fascism in its tracks, setting them back at least a decade, and that has got to be something to be proud of.

I had also made many friends who stuck with me through thick and thin. I remain honoured to have known them and remain grateful for their friendship. We had an amazing and unforgettable adventure together, which although it was brought to a premature end, was still worthwhile. I also had three adorable children who otherwise might never have been born had I not got involved in anti-fascism, and of course I met my present partner Louise through political activity, a person I both love and respect.

. . . There'll be Ten Dead Nazis
at my Feet

FOR A NUMBER of reasons, both personal and political, the authors of this book are no longer involved in the physical struggle against the fascists. In a strange way, being one step removed from the fight has allowed us the freedom to write about what we experienced during those years.

The point of writing this book is not to boast about how brave we were, or to brag about how tough we are. We're neither of those things. In fact, I think the book shows the opposite. It shows how ordinary we were. It shows that ordinary people can stand up to the fascists and beat them. The sincerest wish of both authors is that this book provides inspiration and hope to anyone involved in the struggle against fascism.

The fascists never beat us, they never cowed or broke us, and in the end we were only beaten by people who were supposed to be on our own side. Read into that what you will. That experience is far from unique to ourselves, and any student of history could probably point out hundreds of similar examples over the decades. The point is that, despite the way it ended, we would both make exactly the same choices if we were somehow dropped back into the same situation again. We're also far from unique in that respect.

Hundreds of people were involved the activities of the Squads and the Stewards' Group in Manchester over the years, and although only a couple of dozen of the more active members are mentioned in this book, the task would have been impossible without the wider support of those on the periphery. No group could operate in the manner we did without a network of support to back us up, and the contribution of these "unsung heroes" was greatly appreciated.

Both the Squad and the Stewards' Group were overwhelmingly left-wing and working-class in character, although anyone who agreed that fascist gangs had to be physically confronted was welcome. The principle of physical opposition to fascism tended to act as a deterrent to the middle classes anyway, so in fact we never really had to bother much with vicars, teachers and social workers. Despite this crippling limitation on recruitment (yes I'm being sarcastic), people of all races and religions fought alongside each other in the Squads and the Stewards' Group, and lasting friendships were formed as we stood shoulder to shoulder and faced down the fascist threat.

The reason we beat the fascists time and again, and the reason we didn't run when outnumbered, was not that we were harder or tougher than them, but that we believed in the cause we were fighting for. It was this belief that made us stand our ground even when it looked like all was lost. We put ourselves at the sharp end of anti-fascist activity because we believed in what we were doing, not because of the "buzz" or the adrenalin rush. If that had been the case we would simply have become football hooligans. No, there was a reason for all this swashbuckling and derring-do, and that reason was to prevent the fascists in Britain from making the kind of gains that they have in countries like Austria, France and Germany. In that regard we were remarkably successful given our limited resources.

On a local level, the NF in Manchester went from being the largest branch in the country outside London in 1977, to being nothing more than a shadow of its former self in 1981.

They were torn apart by anti-fascist opposition and never recovered their former strength and influence. Similarly, the series of devastating blows dealt to the BNP in and around Rochdale in the early Nineties effectively derailed the BNP bandwagon in Lancashire and Greater Manchester for a decade. This double blow to fascist ambitions had the effect of ensuring that the city of Manchester has remained a fascist-free zone for more than twenty years. This was achieved despite the fact that anti-fascists started on the back foot on both occasions.

These local successes were mirrored on a national level, with anti-fascists up and down the country picking up the cudgels and fighting back against the bully-boy tactics of the far right. In the Seventies the NF were in the ascendancy, but the countrywide opposition they encountered from militant anti-fascists and the subsequent electoral defeat of 1979 disheartened them to such an extent that they turned to in-fighting and terrorism.

In 1994, the BNP were forced to rethink their "march and grow" strategy after AFA ran them off the streets. Party chairman Nick Griffin told his followers that there would be "no more marches, meetings, punch-ups." Similarly, Blood and Honour's attempts to go mainstream in the late Eighties and early Nineties were effectively dismantled after two set-piece showdowns in London. The Main Event in Hyde Park, and the Battle of Waterloo proved that cropped hair, big boots and a paramilitary uniform don't actually make you a stormtrooper. C18 were also shown to be all piss and vinegar after they were run out of town by militant anti-fascists on several occasions. Their myth of invulnerability was punctured and their reputation was damaged almost beyond repair.

Of course, the litmus test for militant anti-fascism is not whether the fascists can be chased off the streets, but whether they can be kept off them. In Manchester, the policy of physical and political opposition has proved successful, and the fascists have not been able to march or hold public events in the city for more than two decades. The various strands of fascism in Manchester are small and isolated, and the level of support they can call upon is pathetic.

There are two reasons for this. The first is eternal vigilance. Once the fascists had been beaten off the streets, anti-fascists in Manchester were never content to sit back and let them start growing again. Every time they made a move we jumped on them from a great height, throwing their plans into disarray and scaring off potential supporters.

The second reason the fascists found it difficult to regain their foothold in the city was that anti-fascists lived and worked in the same communities as them, making it easier to counter their arguments and cut the ground from under them. It is hard for anyone to operate without a sanctuary or stronghold to scuttle back to, somewhere where they can sit back safe and secure. Fascists in Manchester had to watch their backs constantly, because they knew we could jump out at them from anywhere at anytime.

The following piece was written by Toddy, an ex-fascist who learned this lesson the hard way:

> I first became involved with the National Front in early 1976 after they handed out leaflets outside Spurley Hey school in Gorton, Manchester. I suppose that one of the main reasons I joined the NF was that there was an aura of excitement and danger about them. They were always in the news in those days, and wherever they went there seemed to be loads of trouble.
>
> I attended my first meeting at the Mitre Hotel near Victoria Station, where I met up with the likes of Anthony David Jones, the Charles Hawtrey lookalike, and Karl Kukla, who later became known as "Head the Brick" by his Manchester Parks Dept colleagues after he was hit

by a brick thrown by Polish football hooligans during a England v Poland match. Kukla staggered right into the middle of a Polish live TV programme moaning about how he'd been injured by this brick. Jones and Kukla, along with Scotty, one of the top Man City football hooligans, told us they were not just nazis, but super-nazis. I also met Brian Baldwin, the prison officers' union rep at Strangeways and a member of Column 88 and the League of St George.

I went on my first NF march in Walsall, where I met Robert Relf. I also went on a march in Bradford, and attended meetings in Bolton and Blackburn. All these activities were opposed by left-wing groups who we were told were incapable of causing us any problems because they were mostly "middle-class teachers and lesbians".

Little did I realise at the time that these so-called teachers and lesbians would turn out to be working-class black and white lads from Old Trafford, Salford, Stretford and Moss Side who were most definitely up for smashing the NF off the streets, and not just standing on the sidelines shouting slogans. I would later get to know a few of these lads myself when I finally became involved in the fight against fascism, having learned my lesson the hard way.

My first encounter with the "Reds" or "lefties" was in 1976 at the Grand Hotel on Aytoun Street. John Tyndall was speaking at a meeting booked under a bogus name, the "Manchester Sports Club". I arrived at the meeting on my own, and upon entering the hotel was attacked by a mob who were intent on giving a kicking to any dodgy-looking Fronter types they came across. As I was being kicked and punched up and down the stairs the thought crossed my mind that a few of these "teachers" were a bit handy. I was never to make the mistake of arriving at a NF meeting on my own again.

I remember the day in August 1977 when United were

playing Liverpool in the Charity Shield at Wembley. It was the same day that the NF were going to march through Lewisham, and Manchester NF had booked a fifty-seater coach for the march. I was torn between going on the march or going to Wembley. All my mates were going to watch United, and in the end I decided that I'd go on the march for a bit and head off for Wembley later.

On the day itself I was running a bit late, and I was just coming around the corner into Aytoun Street where the coach was waiting, when I suddenly saw a mob of about a dozen or more charging towards the coach. They were armed with bats, sticks and iron bars, and were wearing crash helmets. They started smashing the coach windows, and were trying to get onto the coach to attack the passengers. The NF on the coach stayed where they were and made no attempt to confront the "Reds". I turned on my heels and headed off to Piccadilly Station, finding safety with United fans on the concourse waiting for trains to London. If it kicked off at Wembley, at least I knew I'd be with lads who were up for a rumble.

After the match, I bought a copy of the London Evening Standard and read the full story of how the NF got a right hammering in Lewisham. Later in the pub, I saw all the news reports on TV and realised how lucky I was to have turned up late for the coach that morning. This was just the first of several near misses and close shaves I had over the following years as the anti-fascists turned up the heat on the NF.

I was really into punk music at the time, and was a big fan of the Clash and the Buzzcocks. I went to see the Buzzcocks at the Anti-Nazi League carnival in Alexandra Park in Moss Side, hoping I wouldn't be sussed out for being in the NF. Luckily I wasn't. I spotted a couple of familiar faces in the crowd, punk-loving NF sympathisers who were in the same predicament as me. We couldn't miss a free gig by the Buzzcocks. After all, they were our band, from Manchester.

I also attended the "secret" march in Manchester which the NF organised after their march in Hyde was banned. The NF were ultra-careful not to let any information slip out about the whereabouts of this march, and none of us, apart from the leadership, knew where we were actually going. We were just told to turn up for our coach in the morning, and we were basically driven around the outskirts of Manchester for an hour or so before heading back into Longsight. We were dropped off near Crowcroft Park, and joined the march which was assembling opposite the park, just off Stockport Road. Shit, I thought, this is only down the road from where I live in Gorton. I was wearing a Derby County scarf which I'd nicked off a Derby fan a couple of weeks previously, and I pulled it up over my face hoping I wouldn't be recognised by anyone I knew.

The march headed up Kirkmanshulme Lane towards Belle Vue and the Greyhound Stadium, and we were literally within shouting distance of the street where I lived. People were coming out of their houses to see the NF marching on their streets, and despite the scarf, I was recognised by everyone who saw me. People were shouting, "All right Toddy, what are you doing with the fucking NF?" Then to cap it all I saw my sister at the side of the road pushing her son Dean, my one-year-old nephew, a lovely mixed-race kid who I adored. I was even on the news, and on the special BBC programme about the march a few days later, probably because of the red, white and blue Derby County scarf I was wearing across my face.

Towards the end of the 1970s I became involved with the British Movement. The BM was run by "Wirral Milkman" Michael McLaughlin from an office in Chester. I got involved with them because, along with all my mates, I was heavily into the skinhead scene, and the BM were very popular amongst skins. We were into all the ska and Two-Tone bands like Madness, the Specials and Bad Manners, and we never saw the contradiction in listening to reggae, ska, bluebeat and rocksteady while flirting with the BM. We hung around with authentic Teds and rockabillies from Rochdale and Heywood who were also ex-NF, and the BM appealed to us all, because in our minds it was all about having the crack, going on marches and having a ruck, particularly when it was summer and the football season had finished.

One of the last activities I was involved in with the BM was a march in Paddington in London. About twenty of us had travelled down on the National Express coach using Persil two-for-one vouchers. As we made our way to Hyde Park we were attacked and chased by those who I learned later were Red Action, Anti-Fascist Action and the Socialist Federation.

On the march itself we had all sorts of stuff thrown at us, and it was halted several times as the AFA mob charged at us. We would have been totally hammered if it wasn't for the Special Patrol Group, who told us that they wanted to step back and let us and the reds sort it out amongst ourselves but were under orders to protect us and keep the peace. They made us break up our flag poles and throw away the Celtic Cross flags which Rockabilly Mike from Tottington had patiently made, and then started whacking us with truncheons, even though we were trying to convince them that we were on their side.

A few weeks later I was accosted by two guys on Longsight Market and was given the option of leaving the BM and the nazi scene or facing the consequences. I told them that I had already decided that for myself after the events on the march in London. After a brief chat they invited me for a pint in the Church pub on Stockport Road, and I basically told them that I was more into the punk and ska scene and that I had *latched onto the BM because the Labour Party were offering me nothing.*

I had also been reading Searchlight *magazine for some time, and became interested in what it was saying, after initially only buying it just to see if my picture was in it from any of the marches. I had also started to buy some lefty papers as well, and had begun to think through what I'd been doing and why I'd been doing it.*

I joined the SWP some time later, but fell out with them after I wrote a letter to their paper criticising their support for the Prison Officers' Association who were threatening industrial action at the time. I pointed out that the POA was riddled with racists, and was basically a pro-Tory union. I also wrote about the brutality that working-class lads suffered at the hands of these screws, and wondered how the SWP could justify supporting these people. A few years later, prisoners in Strangeways rioted against the inhumane conditions in the prison, confirming for me that I had been right all along.

I also became friendly with Viraj Mendis, the left-wing Sri Lankan refugee who had taken sanctuary in a church in Hulme. We had a number of chats about my flirtation with fascism and the reasons why I felt the need to show my face, and get involved in militant anti-fascism. Viraj suggested that I read the Red Action paper, and AFA's music magazine Cable Street Beat, *as they seemed to be thinking along the same lines as me.*

I became a supporter of Red Action, and a member of AFA in 1988, eventually becoming friendly with many of the people who had been after my blood only a few years previously. Over the next decade I supported and attended any number of activities against the fascists the North-West. I also helped launch Red Attitude, *the Man United Anti-Fascist fanzine, alongside a number of other time-served United supporters and anti-fascists from the Seventies, as we continued the fight against the fascists at United matches at home and abroad.*

Toddy is far from the only ex-fascist to have been forced to reconsider the wisdom of his ways following an encounter with anti-fascists. Most, of course, simply drop out of the scene and disappear. A few, like Toddy, take the opportunity to reconsider their actions, and throw their weight behind the anti-fascist cause. As much as anything, stories like Toddy's convinced us that our brand of anti-fascism does work, especially when applied by anti-fascists with roots in the local community.

Where militant anti-fascism has proven to be rather less successful has been in places like Burnley where we didn't have any roots, and had only limited contact with the local population. In 1992 we broke the back of the BNP in the town, but ten years later they managed to get several of their members elected onto the local council. All that our actions had accomplished in the long term was to create a political vacuum in the town, and because neither the Labour Party nor far left had the nous, the desire or the capability to fill the void, the far right stepped back in again.

When the BNP ditched the march and grow strategy in favour of grassroots campaigning in 1994, they not only ducked the AFA haymaker heading their way, but also borrowed a trick from their European counterparts, Haider and Le Pen. This new BNP strategy also ensured that they were well placed to take advantage of the "political" space created in working-class areas by New Labour's abandonment of its traditional support.

AFA had parachuted into Burnley in 1992 like a load of extras from the film *A Bridge Too Far*. Although on the day we had been marginally more successful than the British and American forces on that expedition, the result in the end proved to be remarkably similar. That's not to say that we shouldn't have gone to the town. The BNP had to be stopped from parading through the town centre, and AFA were the only organisation with the determination and the will to do the job. By hook or by crook we accomplished the task that we set ourselves that day, but what should have happened afterwards is that the Left should have capitalised on the breathing space our actions had created for them.

What the events in Burnley point to is the drift of the entire Left away from working-class people towards the middle classes, liberalism and gesture politics. Look at the posters put up by these people to counter fascist propaganda. They consist of nothing more radical than appeals to "be nice to black people" and "don't vote for nazis". This kind of sloganeering really doesn't cut the mustard as far as solutions to problems like poverty, unemployment, immigration and lack of adequate housing go.

Anti-fascism in isolation is also no solution. If we accept that we live in an age where there is no real radical left-wing alternative to the likes of the BNP and the NF, then we also have to be prepared to accept the fact that it is not enough for anti-fascists to kick the far right out of an area and then just leave it in search of the next confrontation. We have to stay behind now, and offer our own positive solutions to racism and intolerance. On the other hand, it's no good building our own little strongholds of support while ignoring the growth of fascism across the other side of town. The two strands are like two sides of the same coin, and cannot be separated.

In a little under two decades, militant anti-fascists in Britain forced the fascists to retreat from the wider political arena twice, once in the late Seventies and again in the early Nineties. We deserve credit for that, but at the same time we have to recognise that pushing them out of the arena is only half the job. We have to offer solutions of our own to the problems faced by working-class communities so that the fascists have no room to grow when they do crawl back out into the daylight again. We also have to accept the fact that until we recognise this, and do something about it, then the fascists will keep coming back.

You have been warned.

THEY SHALL NOT PASS – NO RETREAT